The
Greatest
Hunting
Stories
Ever Told

The
Greatest
Hunting
Stories
Ever Told

EDITED BY
LAMAR UNDERWOOD

THE LYONS PRESS

DEDICATED
WITH DEEP AFFECTION
To the Memory
of Jim Pierce

Whose zest for the outdoor life was only surpassed
by his devotion to magazine publishing's
highest standards of excellence, and a man who
made the words "sportsman" and "gentleman"
his life's code in both words and deeds.

Printed in the United States of America

10 9 8 7 6 5 4 3 2 1

Design by Compset, Inc.

The Library of Congress Cataloging-in-Publication Data is available on file.

Permissions Acknowledgements

Russell Annabel, "Susitna Moose Hunt" from *Hunting and Fishing in Alaska.* Copyright © 1948 by Russell Annabel. Reprinted with the permission of Alfred A. Knopf, a division of Random House, Inc.

Havilah Babcock, "Slim Boggins' Mistake" from *Tales of Quail 'n Such.* Reprinted with the permission of the University of South Carolina Press.

John Barsness, "The Ninety-Seven" from *Western Skies: Bird Hunting in the Rockies and on the Plains.* Copyright © 1994 by John Barsness. Reprinted with the permission of The Lyons Press.

Vance Bourjaily, "In Fields Near Home" from *The Best of Sports Afield,* edited by Jay Cassell (New York: Atlantic Monthly Press, 1996). Reprinted with the permission of the author.

Nash Buckingham, "Bob White, Down't Aberdeen" from *The Best of Field and Stream: 100 Years of Great Writing,* edited by J. I. Merritt with Margaret G. Nichols. Reprinted with the permission of The Lyons Press.

Peter Hathaway Capstick, "The Black Death" from *Death in a Lonely Land.* Copyright © 1990 by Scribner, a division of Simon & Schuster, Inc. Reprinted with the permission of St. Martin's Press, LLC.

Jim Corbett, "The Thak Man-Eater" from *Man Eaters of Kumaon.* Reprinted with the permission of Oxford University Press, New Delhi, India.

Ben East, "Last Shell in the Rifle" from *Bears: A Veteran Outdoorsman's Account of the Most Fascinating and Dangerous Animals in North America.* Copyright © 1977 by Ben East. Reprinted with the permission of Crown Publishers, a division of Random House, Inc.

Charles Elliott, "A Bearded Legend: My Best All-Time Trophy" from *Turkey Hunting With Charlie Elliott* (New York: David McKay Co., 1979). Reprinted with the permission of the author.

William Faulkner, "Race at Morning" from *Big Woods.* Copyright © 1955 by Curtis Publishing Company. Reprinted with the permission of Random House, Inc.

Charles Fergus, "Out on the Land" from *A Rough Shooting Dog.* Copyright © 1991 by Charles Fergus. Reprinted with the permission of The Lyons Press.

Jesse Hill Ford, "To the Open Water" from *Fishes, Birds and Sons of Men* (Boston: Little, Brown and Company, 1967). First published in *The Atlantic Monthly* (1964). Copyright © 1964, 1992 by Jesse Hill Ford. Reprinted with the permission of Harold Ober Associates, Inc.

Ernest Hemingway, "Remembering Shooting-Flying: A Key West Letter" from *Byline: Ernest Hemingway,* edited by William White. Originally published in *Esquire* (February 1935). Copyright 1935 by Ernest Hemingway and renewed © 1963 by Mary Hemingway. Copyright © 1967 by Mary Hemingway. Reprinted with the permission of Scribner, a division of Simon & Schuster, Inc.

Tom Hennessey, "Tracks to Remember" from *Feathers n' Fins* (Clinton, New Jersey: The Amwell Press, 1989). Copyright © 1989 by Tom Hennessey. Reprinted with the permission of the author c/o The Amwell Press.

Gene Hill, "Great Morning" from *Mostly Tailfeathers: Stories About Guns and Dogs and Birds and Other Odds and Ends.* Copyright © 1971 by Gene Hill. Reprinted with the permission of New Win Publishing Inc.

Robert F. Jones, "Are You Lonesome Tonight?" from *Dancers in the Sunset Sky.* Copyright © 1996 by Robert F. Jones. Reprinted with the permission of The Lyons Press.

Tom Kelly, "Forty-Crook Branch" from *Better on a Rising Tide.* Copyright © 1995 by Tom Kelly. Reprinted with the permission of The Lyons Press.

Gordon MacQuarrie, "'Pothole Guys, Friz Out.'" Reprinted with the permission of Willow Creek Press.

John Madson, "Pheasants Beyond Autumn" from *Out Home* (New York: Winchester Press, 1979). Copyright © 1979 by John Madson. Reprinted with the permission of Dycie Madson.

Thomas McGuane, "The Heart of the Game" from *An Outside Chance.* Copyright © 1990 by Thomas McGuane. Reprinted with the permission of Houghton Mifflin Company/Seymour Lawrence. All rights reserved.

Thomas McIntyre, "Spirit of the North" from *Dreaming the Lion* (Traverse City, Mich.: Countersport Press, 1993). Copyright © 1993. Reprinted with the permission of the author.

Patrick O'Brian, "The Dawn Flighting" from *The Rendezvous and Other Stories.* Copyright © 1994, 1974, 1956, 1953, 1950 by Patrick O'Brian. Reprinted with the permission of W. W. Norton & Company, Inc. and HarperCollins Publishers, Ltd.

Jack O'Connor, "Rams in the Snow" from *The Best of Jack O'Connor* (Clinton, New Jersey: Amwell Press, 1977). Copyright © 1977 by Jack O'Connor. Reprinted with the permission of Bradford O'Connor.

George Reiger, "The Wings of Dawn" from *The Wings of Dawn: The Complete Book of North American Waterfowling.* Copyright © 1980 by George Reiger. Reprinted with the permission of The Lyons Press.

Robert C. Ruark, "Mister Howard Was a Real Gent" from *The Old Man and the Boy.* Copyright 1953 by Robert C. Ruark. Reprinted with the permission of Henry Holt and Company LLC.

Ed Zern, "A Mixed Bag of Zern" from *Hunting and Fishing from A to Zern.* Copyright © 1985 by Ed Zern. Reprinted with the permission of The Lyons Press.

Contents

INTRODUCTION	VII	Lamar Underwood
LAST SHELL IN THE RIFLE	1	Ben East
THE DAWN FLIGHTING	8	Patrick O'Brian
THE HEART OF THE GAME	15	Thomas McGuane
IN FIELDS NEAR HOME	26	Vance Bourjaily
RACE AT MORNING	43	William Faulkner
SPIRIT OF THE NORTH	58	Thomas McIntyre
MISTER HOWARD WAS A REAL GENT	65	Robert C. Ruark
SLIM BOGGINS' MISTAKE	82	Havilah Babcock
THE BLACK DEATH	90	Peter Hathaway Capstick
OUT ON THE LAND	95	Charles Fergus
THE NINETY-SEVEN	101	John Barsness
TO THE OPEN WATER	107	Jesse Hill Ford
PHEASANTS BEYOND AUTUMN	115	John Madson
TRACKS TO REMEMBER	123	Tom Hennessey
REMEMBERING SHOOTING-FLYING: A KEY WEST LETTER	126	Ernest Hemingway
A BEARDED LEGEND: MY BEST ALL-TIME TROPHY	132	Charles Elliot
THE WINGS OF DAWN	142	George Reiger
SUSITNA MOOSE HUNT	147	Russell Annabel
GREAT MORNING	160	Gene Hill
DOG UPON THE WATERS	164	John Taintor Foote
THE GAME OF THE HIGH PEAKS: THE WHITE GOAT	172	Theodore Roosevelt
FORTY-CROOK BRANCH	185	Tom Kelly

"POTHOLE GUYS, FRIZ OUT" **192** *Gordon MacQuarrie*

THE FOREST AND THE STEPPE **199** *Ivan Turgenev*

BOB WHITE, DOWN'T ABERDEEN **205** *Nash Buckingham*

RAMS IN THE SNOW **213** *Jack O'Connor*

ARE YOU LONESOME TONIGHT? **220** *Robert F. Jones*

THE THAK MAN-EATER **225** *Jim Corbett*

A MIXED BAG OF ZERN **261** *Ed Zern*

Introduction

WHAT ROBERT RUARK calls "The Horn of the Hunter" sounds early in life for some of us, for others never at all. I do not envy those folks. Like fishing, hunting has been part of my life for so long that imagining a void for these activities seems as unfathomable an idea as trying to come to grips with imagining the size of the universe.

In the first place, I like being outdoors more than indoors. I like being a countryman, to the extent that I can considering my family, job, and other responsibilities, including finances. If I could I would grow, raise, catch, and shoot all of my family's food, taking the lean times with the fat. But that is not possible, because I am very much part of an urbanized world and can find no escape from it.

In one of the finest pieces in this book, "The Heart of the Game," Tom McGuane is reflecting on his attitudes toward his hunting and eloquently hammers home his feelings about hunting to put meat on the table: "I decided that unless I become a vegetarian, I'll get my meat by hunting for it. I feel absolutely unabashed by the arguments of other carnivores who get their meat in plastic, with blue numbers on it. I've seen slaughterhouses, and anyway, as Sitting Bull said, when the buffalo are gone, we will hunt mice, for we are hunters and we want our freedom."

Gathering food is not the only urge that pulls me toward the natural world. In my heart I feel the deep sense that I am part of the same family of life as every wild thing that walks, crawls, swims, or flies. Our homes include fields and marshes, creeks and river bottoms, plains and mountains, bays and oceans, stretching to the ends of the earth. Here I am a watcher—and a student, endlessly observing and learning.

Last evening, when the bare treeline was etched like iron against a January sunset, I watched flocks of robins trying to stay up with flocks of crows that rode the icy wind toward some distant roost. Like the Canada geese before them, more and more robins seem to be staying all winter here in New Jersey where I live. Are they roosting with the crows—or were they simply headed in the same direction by chance? I want some answers. Not because I'm going hunting and need to plot strategy. I'm just watching my neighbors. I want to know what's going on.

The best hunters and anglers I have ever known—and all of the writers—have deep and abiding interest in the natural world. They would not spend five seconds in the company of the so-called "slob hunter" who only wants to blast things, knowing nothing, appreciating nothing, learning nothing. Such "hunters" do not deserve the name. Most of the time, they are violating the law as well as denigrating the activity.

Even further disdain goes out to the sanctimonious pundits who claim they hate hunting because they love nature, yet would not know the difference between a loon and a Canada goose, or a sandhill crane and a great blue heron. I suppose what they think they love is the "idea" of nature, as shown in Bambi-like fantasy movies, and not the real thing itself, which they never bother to see or learn about.

But, we are all hunters here, and it's time to get on with some of the stories that brought us together. The pages ahead will take you hunting for all sorts of game and in places that range from mountain peaks to lowland swamps. The best writers I have ever read will be your guides, and I promise you that their prose will become part of your hunting memories and ignite recollections of your own experiences that make up the hunting scrapbook of your mind.

It has always been my belief that one of the things that makes hunting and fishing so special is that on any given day, things can happen that you will remember for the rest of your days. Very few things in everyday life are like that. Birth, deaths, marriages, graduations, promotions—all those important events that you never forget—come along very infrequently. There is nothing remarkable about most days of our lives, as far as storing memories are concerned. But on any day you step out the door with a rod or gun to put in the truck, something really big can happen. Perhaps the day will someday come when nobody you know will care to hear what that *something* was—a shot well made, a dog's first point or retrieve, the time you turned the big flock of mallards with your calls, the morning you bagged a buck. No matter. You found what you were looking for, and you're keeping it.

—Lamar Underwood

The
Greatest
Hunting
Stories
Ever Told

Last Shell in the Rifle

BY BEN EAST

A T *OUTDOOR LIFE* magazine, the late Ben East's name has always been synonymous with rip-snorting adventures and wilderness tales based on true experiences. When someone who was not an accomplished writer had a good wilderness story to relate, Ben was most often the man assigned to write the piece under the "as told to" or "as told by" sort of byline.

Of course, Ben wrote regular feature articles as well, since he was an active and very experienced outdoorsman who knew the Upper Midwest chapter and verse. Among Ben East's books, his greatest work might arguably be *Bears,* published in 1977 by Outdoor Life and Crown Publishers. A big, physically stunning book illustrated profusely by Tom Beecham, *Bears* is a definitive work on the subject.

"Last Shell in the Rifle," from *Bears,* is one of my all-time favorite Ben East tales. And in this amazing encounter with a polar bear, Ben is not writing someone else's story. *He* is the man down to the "Last Shell in the Rifle."

I have never heard it said better than by Captain Peter Freuchen, the renowned Danish adventurer and explorer who married an Eskimo girl and lived many years in Arctic Greenland.

"No more beautiful animal walks on four feet," he told me once when we were talking about the polar bear.

No matter how long I live, I'm sure I shall never forget the first one I saw outside a zoo. He was standing on a rocky headland, at the top of a cliff that rose vertically from a boulder-littered beach, staring out over a gray and empty reach of sea. A gale was sweeping down from the northwest, savage surf was smoking along the beach, and the sky was black with the clouds of a violent rain squall. Save for the handful of us aboard the schooner, the bear could well have been the only living thing in that wild, storm-swept world.

He was as magnificent an animal as I shall ever lay eyes on. His white pelt was faintly tinged with yellow, and standing motionless at the top of the cliff, he could have been a bear carved out of old ivory. Yet there was about him something wonderfully alive, too, something that proclaimed his rightful place in that desolate, lonely seascape.

It was the summer of 1937. An Ontario man who had hopes of setting himself up in the guiding and outfitting business, taking clients into remote and rarely visited places in the far north, had organized a trip that summer along the east shore of James Bay and into the lower end of Hudson Bay.

He chartered the Venture, a weather-beaten forty-three-foot schooner, auxiliary powered with an old Diesel engine, owned and skippered by Jack Palmquist, then the only free trader competing with the Hudson's Bay Company on James Bay.

Palmquist's crew consisted of a Cree deckhand and a good-humored Eskimo who tended the ancient Diesel as a mother tends a child. Neither spoke English, but the skipper, married to a pretty mission-educated Cree girl, was fluent in her language. The Eskimo also spoke Cree, so there was always a way around the language barrier.

At the trading post and summer camp of the Crees at Eastmain, Palmquist also took aboard a leather-faced Indian pilot to see us through the bleak island-sheltered channels along the coast we would travel. No charts of those waters existed then, and only a Cree who knew them from a lifetime of canoe travel and remembered each island, each headland, each clump of stunted spruce trees could follow the maze of channels and avoid the reefs.

The outfitter had hired three guides and a cook and there were nine clients in the party. I was one of them. We were the first sportsmen to penetrate that wild and roadless country. It was a region that only an occasional roving prospector, the Mounties, missionaries, and the men of the HBC had ever seen. Apart from them it belonged to the Crees and a handful of coastal Eskimos.

Incidentally, the outfitter's plans fell through after one summer, so for many years we were the last as well as the first party of guided sportsmen to travel that coast.

I have roamed the back country of this continent for fifty years, from the Great Smokies and the diamondback-infested flatwoods of Florida to Maine, from the Texas desert to the Aleutian Islands of Alaska, but that treeless and lonely country that I call the land of midnight twilight was the most fascinating place I have ever seen.

The land was untouched, the people primitive, living by the trapline, the fishnet and the gun. We saw steel traps set on low driftwood posts to catch owls for the cooking pots of the Crees; we heard loons called to the gun and shot for the same purpose. At the trading posts we saw summer camps of as many as five hundred nomad Cree trappers, living in roomy wigwams as they had before the whites came.

We fished the virgin pools of whitewater streams where three-pound speckled trout rose to flies, spinners—or even small strips torn from a red bandanna. It was an easy matter for two or three rods to take in a couple of hours all the trout the party could eat at three meals. We had no way to keep fresh meat aboard the Venture, so we lived for many days on a diet of trout and learned to our surprise that it palled rather quickly.

For ten days we camped beyond the sight of trees, carrying our tent poles along and relying on driftwood for our cooking fires. We tramped mossy barrens where ptarmigan were far more plentiful than ruffed grouse back home. When autumn came those treeless barrens would also be alive with geese, beginning their fall flight from summer homes still farther in the north.

Seals followed our schooner, and at night white whales blew close enough to awaken us. The half-wild sled dogs of a dozen Indian and Eskimo camps howled us to sleep time and again. Every minute of the trip was pure adventure.

There was no hunting. The Quebec government was keeping the wildlife, from waterfowl to seals and polar bears, in trust for the Crees and Eskimos, who needed it. But Howard Cooper, a hunting partner of mine from Kalamazoo, Michigan, and I carried collecting permits obtained by two museums back home, authorizing us to take for scientific purposes any birds or animals we chose.

Toward the end of July, the Venture dropped anchor off Long Island. Not the Long Island you have heard about all your life. This one is a rocky sliver of land three or four miles offshore near the southern end of Hudson Bay. We had come now to polar bear country. We left most of the party camped on the island, and Palmquist and his crew took Cooper and myself on a bear hunt.

It was a strange place to look for polar bears. We headed for a small group of treeless islands, not shown on any map we had, lying thirty or forty miles off the coast. We were farther south than the latitude of Juneau, Alaska. Yet the HBC post managers, the Crees and our skipper had all assured us that we would find bears summering on those islands. At the Fort George post a

Cree had even shown us the pelts of three, a female and two cubs, that he had killed only that spring on the adjoining mainland.

We found the island we were looking for but it had no shelter for a boat, and raging seas, driven by a gale screaming down from the ice fields five hundred miles to the north, kept us from going ashore. We found a sheltered harbor on a smaller island half a mile away and landed without difficulty. It was from there that I saw my first polar bear, looking out to sea from his rocky headland.

We watched him for hours through binoculars and spotting scope. In late afternoon the storm subsided and we got a freight canoe ashore on the beach below the cliffs.

Cooper and I and Tommy Lameboy, our old Cree pilot, landed in the canoe. Lameboy had no rifle. Cooper and I were each carrying Model 99 Savages in .300 caliber. At the time I thought them adequate. I would not think so today.

The island was about two miles long and half as wide, rising in vertical cliffs at one end, sloping down to submerged reefs at the other. The top was a rolling expanse of low hills and ravines, all rock and moss, with no vegetation taller than clumps of arctic willow that did not reach to a man's knee. But there were plenty of places for a bear to hide, and ours had disappeared. He had watched our boat as it neared the island, and taken to his heels.

We separated; Cooper and Lameboy headed for the far side of the island, I set out to search the broken sea cliffs. The job was on the hairy side, for there were places where I could round a big rock and meet the bear only three or four steps away. I was moving slowly and carefully when I heard a shot rap out from the direction Cooper had taken, followed almost at once by another. I scrambled to the top of the cliff for a look.

I made out the small figure of my hunting partner, three-quarters of a mile away, but I could see nothing of the bear. While I watched, Howard fired a third shot, and to my astonishment I heard the 180-grain softpoint go whining angrily over my head as a ricochet.

If Cooper was firing toward me the bear must be somewhere between us. And then I saw him, half a mile away, out of rifle range for Howard, running toward me like a big white dog that I had called. I learned later that Cooper had not really had him in range at any time, but had shot in the hope of sending him back my way. He succeeded better than he expected.

I learned something else later. The bear did not know I was there. The face of the cliff behind me was broken by a ravine that ran all the way down to the beach, and there was a well-used bear trail in the bottom of it. That was, in all likelihood, his customary path to the sea and he was coming to use it.

I was aware of mixed feelings. I wanted him to keep coming, for from the time I planned the trip I had wanted more than anything else to take a polar bear. But at the same time, although I had used a rifle for years, starting with a .22 as a boy, I was no crack shot and this bear was the first game I had ever confronted bigger than a whitetail deer. Could I deal with him? Well, I'd soon find out.

I went down on one knee to escape his attention, and watched him come. He dropped out of sight in a shallow dip but when he came up on my side of it he was still on course, traveling at a lumbering, ground-eating run.

I tried my first two shots while he was still too far away for accurate shooting with iron sights. They were clean misses and he paid them no attention.

The next one scored. He braked to a stop, swinging his head from side to side like a big white snake caught by the tail, biting savagely at the top of both shoulders. When it was all over I learned that my 180-grain softpoint had hit him in the back just behind the neck, too high to do any real damage, and had gone through under the heavy layer of fat that padded him, just deep enough to cut muscle and draw blood. I suppose it must have burned like a branding iron.

From his actions I was sure he would go down in a second or two, and in my lack of experience with dangerous game I made a bad blunder. I scrambled to my feet, ready to move closer and put in a finishing shot.

I never got the chance. The instant I stood up he saw me for the first time. He swerved and came for me in a deadly, businesslike charge, head down, running as a cross dog runs to bark at a passing car.

I shot too fast and threw away one more chance to stop him, and as he closed the distance between us to less than thirty yards I felt cold fear of a kind I have never known before or since.

I had started with one shell in the chamber of the Savage and four in the magazine. I had used four. That meant only one was left. There would be no time for reloading and all my confidence that I could kill the bear had evaporated.

Afterward I could not remember firing the fifth shot but my subconscious, if it took over, did a far better job than I had been doing. I heard the whiplash report of the .300 and the bear collapsed as if lightning had struck him. His head dropped between his front legs, he fell and skidded to a stop, rolled almost in a ball. Not so much as a shudder of movement stirred him anywhere.

I sidled away then while I fed five fresh hulls frantically into the rifle. When that was done I began to feel ready for more trouble if it came. I stood and watched for three or four minutes, waiting for some sign of life in the bear.

Then I saw Tommy Lameboy coming across the island at a run, only a hundred yards away. Although unarmed, the old Cree was not running to me. He was running to the bear.

I could not let him arrive until I was sure it was dead. I walked in with the safety off and prodded the big ball of white fur in the neck and ribs. There was no answering quiver, and I stepped back and waited for Tommy.

Together we rolled the bear over enough to pull his head out from beneath his body. The round hole of my last bullet was trickling blood just above the nose, dead center between the eyes. It had mushroomed in the brain and there was hardly a piece of bone bigger than a silver dollar left intact in the skull from the jaws back.

Before we moved the bear I went back and found the five empty cases I had ejected from the rifle. I wanted to know just how close he had been when I killed him. I stepped it off, seventeen paces. Fifty-one feet. I hardly wonder that I had been frightened or that for many nights afterward I dreamed of his final rush, dreamed he was standing over me ready to finish me off. It was a dream that brought me awake in a cold sweat each time.

We hoisted the bear aboard the schooner and took him back to the camp on Long Island unskinned. There Alagkok, our pleasant little Eskimo engineer, offered to take the pelt off.

Alagkok knew no English and of course could not write. But I have never seen hands more deft with a knife.

Three days later, on a somewhat bigger island thirty or forty miles to the south, Cooper made his bear hunt.

The party found anchorage for the Venture in a small harbor and Howard went ashore with Palmquist, Lameboy, and Roy Maguire, one of our guides. Almost at once they found a line of big bear tracks leading up across the sand of the beach, the footprints still wet with water that had dripped from the bear's legs. He had come in from the sea less than an hour before.

Half a mile farther on Cooper spotted a patch of white behind a tangle of driftwood just above the beach. At first he took it for snow, but when Palmquist put a question to Tommy Lameboy the old Cree replied with a firm "Wahb'esco!" the name for polar bear in his language.

The hunters were within a hundred yards of the bear when it heard or winded them and sat up on its haunches. Cooper told me afterward that it was so big it reminded him of a short-legged, burly white horse. He broke its back with his first shot, ran in close and finished it cleanly with a second softpoint in the neck.

Unfortunately, at that time neither Howard nor I was aware of the Boone and Crockett system of measuring and scoring trophies. As a result, the skull of that bear was never measured. But his body measurements, taken with a steel tape before he was skinned, revealed a polar bear of extraordinary size.

He measured 18 inches between the ears, 52 around the neck just behind the head, and 10½ feet from tip of nose to tip of tail. I still believe he would have stood very high on the Boone and Crockett record list.

He was skinned the next morning and the hunters came back to our camp at the mouth of a small river fifty miles south of Cape Jones. Two families of Crees sailed their canoes in behind the Venture, and in return for a sweater, a few pounds of flour, tea, sugar and some canned fruit, the women agreed to flesh the pelt of the big bear.

The scene that evening, lighted by a big driftwood fire behind our camp, is printed indelibly in my memory. Cooper had killed a second bear, to which his collecting permit entitled him, an immature animal that weighed around three hundred pounds, and brought it back to the mainland unskinned. The Cree women took the pelt off before they went to work on the big one, and we gave them a big kettle of the meat.

While they worked by firelight on the bear pelts, their men got two wigwams up and baked bannock for supper. In the dim twilight of that subarctic midnight a grease-rimmed kettle of bear stew was bubbling on the fire and the whole party of Crees was hunched in an eager, grinning circle around it.

The last sound we heard in our sleeping bags that night was the wild and doleful howling of a gaunt, ill-fed Indian sled dog, staked on a babiche leash beside one of the wigwams. His nose was full of the scent of the bear short ribs but such feasts, alas, were not for him, and he sang his hunger song long after silence had settled over the camp.

The rest of the smaller bear Cooper gave to Tommy Lameboy, and when we reached the Fort George trading post, where the old Cree was camped for the summer, we witnessed a strange and ancient Indian ritual. The bear carcass was ferried ashore in one of our freight canoes, and a group of Crees picked the big canoe up bodily with the bear in it, six or eight men on either side. They lifted it to their shoulders and carried it ceremoniously through the camp of some five hundred Indians to Tommy's wigwam. There it was cut up and divided among many families, in keeping with Cree custom when a big animal is killed.

One of the most surprising things about that long-ago bear hunt was the fact that it happened only about a hundred miles farther, as a crow flies, from Sault Ste. Marie in my home state of Michigan than the distance from that same city south to Detroit. The white bear of the North is not always an animal of the arctic ice.

The Dawn Flighting

BY PATRICK O'BRIAN

ATRICK O' BRIAN, WHO passed away in January, 2000, at the age of eighty-five, became an international literary celebrity through his stirring tales of the British Navy in the Napoleonic Wars. Beginning with the novel *Master and Commander,* O'Brian wrote 20 sea-going adventures featuring the characters Jack Aubrey, a British naval officer, and his friend and constant shipmate Stephen Maturin, a physician and naturalist. All bestsellers and available in softcover editions, the Aubrey/Maturin novels, as they are often referred to, overshadow another side of this Anglo-Irish writer: He was a shooter and angler who wrote passionately about both sports back in the 1950s when he was focusing on short stories. Many of O'Brian's finest tales are collected in the book *The Rendezvous and Other Stories,* published in the U.S. by W. W. Norton in 1994. This vivid waterfowling story is from that collection.

The night was old, black, and full of driving cold rain; the moon and the stars had already passed over the sky. But anyhow they had been hidden since midnight by the low, racing, torn cloud and the flying wetness of small rain and sea-foam and the whipped-off top of standing water. Dawn was still far away: from the dark east the mounting wind blew in gusts; it bore more rain flatlings from the sea.

Bent double, with the breath caught from his mouth, a man struggled against the force of the living wind. He walked on the top of a sea-wall that guarded the reclamation of a great marsh. At this point the wall ran straight into the teeth of the wind for a long way; there was no shelter. He had to walk carefully, for the mud had not frozen yet, and it was treacherous going. Behind him his dog, an old black Labrador, picked its way, whining in a little under-tone to itself when the way was very dirty.

A great blast came, halting him in mid-stride; he staggered and stepped back to keep his balance. The dog's paw came under his heel and there was a yelp, but he heard nothing of it for the roaring of the wind. He leaned against it, and it bore him up with a living resilience, suddenly slackening, so that he stumbled again. The false step jerked a grunt out of him.

Thrusting his chin down into the scarf under his high-buttoned collar and shifting the weight of his gun, the man pushed on. All his mind was taken up with his fight; every long, firm step was a victory in little. The hardness of his way and the unceasing clamour at his ears had taken away every other thought. He was hardly aware of the places where the driven wet had pierced through, above his knees, down one side of his neck, and on his shoulder where the strap of his cartridge-bag crossed over. Earlier on he had been irked by the weight of the bag and by the drag of the gun in the crook of his arm, but now he did not heed them at all; the wind was the single, embracing enemy.

At last the sea-wall turned right-handed, running along the south face of the saltings. At the corner he stooped and slid on all fours down the steep side into the lee. At once it seemed to him that some enormous machine had stopped; in the quiet air he breathed freely, and sighed as he squatted in the mud. The Labrador shook itself and thrust its muzzle into his relaxed hand. Ab-sently the man felt for its ears, but the dog was insistent; the custom must be ful-filled. When he had changed the hang of the strap on his aching shoulder the man searched under his macintosh among the scarves and pullovers for an inner pocket; he found half a biscuit and his pipe. The flare of the match in his cupped hands showed his face momentarily, in flashes, as he sucked the flame down; it showed disembodied in the darkness, high cheekbones and jutting nose thrown into distorted prominence. The foul pipe bubbled, but the acrid tobacco was in-stantly satisfying; he drew and inhaled deeply for a few moments.

'Well, that's the first leg,' he said to the dog as he got up. He went on under the lee of the sea-wall, walking heavily in the deep, uneven mud. Fur-ther on there was a place where he had to leave the wall to strike across the marsh for a stretch of open fresh water: there was only one path that led to the mere. At this time of the year the marsh was impassable except by this track, for the land-water had deepened the mud so that a man could sink out of sight in it almost before he knew he was in danger.

Anxiously he counted the time that he had taken walking along the southern wall; if he missed the path he would not get across the marsh for the dawn flighting. He crossed an old, broken sea-wall that joined the other, and he knew that he was near the path. When he climbed to the top of the wall to look for the three posts that would give him his bearings he felt an abatement in the wind: it blew less furiously, but it was colder now—certainly freezing. A flurry of sleet stung his cheek. The wind was veering to the north-north-east. He found the posts and the track; he was glad, for it was easy to miss in the dark, when all that could be seen looked strange, even monstrous.

The dog went before him now, finding out the tortuous way: sometimes a single bending plank led through the deep reed-beds, loud in the wind: treading on the planks stirred the marsh smell. Once there was a rush of wings, and desolate voices fled away piping in the darkness. They were redshanks or some kind of tukes—inedible, and his half-raised gun sank.

Now the wind was at his back; it was blowing itself out in great gusts. A thin film of ice was skimming the top of the puddles, and a more querulous note sang through the reeds. He looked over his shoulder, scanning the eastern sky for the first cold light: there seemed to be a lessening in the darkness, nothing more. He pushed on faster: the way was a little easier now.

Presently large dim shapes came up out of the blind murk before him; they were the trees surrounding the mere. He stopped to take his bearings again, and then he went on cautiously. The ground rose a little; there were brambles and patches of alder, laced through and through with rabbit tracks. Ahead a buck-rabbit thrummed the earth, and three white scuts bobbed away. Very carefully the man came through the undergrowth among the trees: a flick of his thumb and finger brought his dog in to heel. There might well be duck down on the water. Choosing his steps and crouching low in the bushes and then in the reeds, the man slipped down the bank, down the sheltered way, and crept secretly into the butt of cut reeds at the pond's edge.

After a little listening pause he stood slowly up, holding his breath and staring with wide-opened eyes through the shoulder-high reeds. Still a little bent, he peered intently over the water. There were no duck; only a little grebe swam and dived unwitting on the mere. He slowly relaxed, and sat down on the rough, unsteady plank stool in the butt.

He stretched and shook himself, for he was still desperately tired from getting up at two o'clock in the morning, and his eyes prickled. He look to his gun, wiped a clot of mud from its barrels, and propped it carefully in the corner of the butt by his cartridge bag; he was warm now in the shelter of the reeds, and he settled himself comfortably to wait for the dawn flight of the wild duck.

Now that he was in the butt, time seemed to begin again: for the whole of the way out across the marsh it had stopped. He had been trying to race the dawn—quite another thing. By and by he pulled out a packet of bread and cheese, with an apple against thirst, for the marsh water was sulphurous and brackish. He ate bite for bite with the dog, but absently, with his senses on the stretch.

By imperceptible degrees the sky lightened, so that when he looked again he could see halfway across the water. The lake had formerly been a decoy: the hoops for the duck-pipes still showed in the overgrown channels, and a cottage, half-sunk and unroofed, marked where the wild-fowlers had kept their gear.

He was unready, for all his vigilance, when the first duck passed over: one hand was scrabbling in his pouch, the other holding his pipe. With his unlighted pipe in his mouth and his gun in his hands, he listened again: the sound was high above, a sound hard to convey. There was a creaking in it, and a whistling. His ears followed the sound, and the dog stared up into the dim quarter-light. The noise circled round the mere twice, coming lower. Mallard they were, by the sound, and they were coming down. The butt stood on a spit of land with the length of the pond lying out on each side, so that the duck would come in across. He stood with his back to the wind, jiggling his forehand nervously and biting hard on the stem of his pipe. Down, and up again: he caught a glimpse of them, five mallard. They came round lower, the flight-note changed and they braced hard against the wind to land. Up went the gun and his fingers poised delicately round the triggers. The sound of wings rushed closer: he saw the duck, picked the right-hand bird, steadied, and fired, swinging his second barrel into them as they crossed so quickly that the two tongues of flame stabbed the darkness almost at the same moment. There was a splash in front of him, then a threshing in the water. His hands, working of themselves, broke the gun and thrust new cartridges into the smoking breech. He stared up, waiting for the duck to circle overhead, but they swung wide out of range, and he heard them go. The Labrador stood rigid, ears pointing: Fetch, he said, and the dog flung itself into the water. It was back in a minute with the mallard held gently at the shoulder. Stooping, he let the dog put it into his hand, and as he straightened a disturbed sheldrake passed over, gruntling as it flew. It circled the mere twice and came down with a long splash: he had caught a glimpse of the breadth of its wings and had heard its small noise, for the wind was dying now, and he was nearly sure that it was a sheldrake. The bird swam close to the butt, safe in its uneatable rankness, so close that he could see the nob on its beak: he was glad to see it, for it would bring the other duck down.

He lit his pipe, crouching in the bottom of the butt, with his head on one side for the sound of wings. Presently they came, a flight of mallard, and above them, close behind, half a dozen sharp-winged widgeon. The mallard came straight down, sweeping right across in front of the butt with their wings held against the wind and their bodies almost upright; they tore up the water, each making a distinct tearing sound, and settled at the far end of the decoy. At once they changed from things of the wind to earth-bound, quacking ducks, awkward and lumpish in the water. The widgeon, more wary, went round high and fast: they seemed to suspect something, but the duck on the water reassured them, and they dropped down, slipping sideways down through the air on stiff, decurved wings, on the one slant and then on the other, like aeroplanes that have come in too high.

They came straight at the butt, as if to skim over it and land the other side. As he brought his gun up for the difficult shot they saw him and lifted: he fired at once. The first barrel jerked the bird a yard higher and clipped feathers from its wing; the second missed altogether. With a loud and rushing noise, the mallard got up. He stared impassively after the flying widgeon, not allowing himself any emotion, for he was a choleric man, and if he let himself start to kick and swear he might carry on and spoil his whole morning with rage, as he had done before.

Automatically he re-loaded, sniffing the sharp, sweet powder smell: the mallard wheeled back over the pond. He took a chance shot at the lowest and winged it. It came down in a long slope into the brushwood on the other side of the decoy. The dog went after it, but could not reach it, for the bird was in a tall, dense thicket of brambles. The dog came back after a long time and stood bowing in deprecation: the air was quite still now, and the mallard could be heard moving over on the other side. He cast a look round the low bowl of the sky, now almost white, and saw no birds: he walked quickly round the mere, for he hated to leave a wounded bird for any length of time. The brambles ripped through to his flesh, but he got the duck and gripped it by the neck. A strong pull, and the bird jerked convulsively and died.

He looked up: three widgeon were coming over, high and fast, with their pointed wings sounding clear. He flung himself on his back in the rushes. They were right over his head as he raised his gun: the movement was plain, in spite of the rushes, and they lifted high. It was too long a shot, but he fired his choke barrel at the middle bird, making great allowance ahead. The bird seemed to fold, to collapse in the air: it fell like a plummet and hit the ground a yard from his feet so hard that he felt it strike. He stared at the duck with an unconscious grin of pleasure; for it was a wonderfully long shot. He picked it up and smoothed its beautiful ruffled breast with his finger. With a sudden, unforeseen leap, the widgeon came back to life; it almost sprang from his loose hands. He killed it and went back to the butt.

It was a bird worthy of a good shot; a fine drake it was, nearly as big as the mallard in the corner. He smoothed its yellow crest: its blue legs and beak were brighter than any he had seen.

Far away there was the deep boom of a punt-gun. That will get them moving, he said, and the dog moved its tail. A big mixed flight came in: with good fortune he got four barrels into them, killing two mallard and a shoveller. He regretted the shoveller, for by his private rules they were not to be shot. There was something about their coral and prussian blue and white bib and tucker that combined with their disproportionate beaks to make them look too much like agreeable toys. But, firing so quickly, he had not distinguished it.

For half an hour after that, while the first rays of the true dawn showed, the duck flighted in great numbers over the marshes. He shot a brace of teal right and left, a feat that consoled him for many bad misses, and he killed another widgeon and three mallard. But he was not shooting well: the duck were moving very fast, and his tired eyes were strained by the changing light. After seven successive misses—one bird carried away a deadly wound— he felt a wretched frustration welling up. By now the watery sun was showing a faint rim over the sea. All at once he felt very weary; unshaved, dirty and weary, with his eyes hot.

A little time passed and the sun came bodily up. The flighting was over, and he bent to his bag. As he stowed each away he smoothed it with care; he put the exquisitely marked teal on the top and strung the bag up. It was barely a quarter full: he had not done at all well. He knew that on such a good day he should have killed many more. He counted the big pile of empty cartridges against his bag, and he thought of the long walk back. He always had a feeling of reaction after he stopped shooting, when the taut excitement died rather ignominiously away, and now there was a strong vexation of spirit upon him as well as that.

'Oh well,' he said, and slung the bag on his back. He could see far and wide over the marsh now; beyond the sea-wall the masts of the fishing boats showed clearly in the sharp air. It was freezing now for sure. Towards the sea he saw a ragged skein of duck weaving and drifting like a cloud: there was none over the marsh. A curlew cried despairingly over his head; breaking its heart, it was.

The wind had quite died. Stiffly, with a lumbering gait, he went back towards the sea-wall with his dog padding quietly after him.

From far away there came a sound over the marsh on the still, frozen air: he looked round and above, but he could see nothing. The sound grew stronger, a rhythmic beating, strangely musical, and he saw three wild swans.

The light caught them from below and they flashed white against the cold blue. High up in the air, their great singing wings bore the swans from the north: they flew straight and fast with their long necks stretched before them.

The rhythm changed a little, sighing and poignant, and a leaping exaltation took the man's heart as he gazed up at them, up away in the thin air.

The beat changed more, and now they flew striking all together, so that their wings sung in unison as they went over his head. He stood stock still watching them, and long after they had passed down the sky he stood there, with the noise of their wings about his head.

The Heart of the Game

E VERY MATURE AND sensible hunter knows the gamut of emotions that run from sheer exhilaration to downright melancholy. The excitement of the chase and the thrill of succeeding in bagging the game eventually blend into reflections tinged with sadness. A lot of powerful emotional stuff is going on out there.

One of the best writers to ever tackle this difficult subject is Thomas McGuane, whose novels and short stories are literary hallmarks worldwide and whose nonfiction articles on the field sports are some of the finest ever written. "The Heart of the Game" originally appeared in *Sports Illustrated* magazine and was later included in McGuane's superb anthology, *An Outside Chance: Classic & New Essays on Sport,* published in 1990 by Houghton Mifflin/Seymour Lawrence. In 1999 a new collection of McGuane fishing pieces, *The Longest Silence: A Life in Fishing,* was published by Knopf. And in the same year Lyons Press published McGuane's *Some Horses,* a chronicle of horses and the ranching life.

McGuane lives and writes in Montana, and from that home base indulges in his passion for fishing wherever the action is good.

Hunting in your own back yard becomes with time, if you love hunting, less and less expeditionary. This year, when Montana's eager frosts knocked my garden on its butt, the hoe seemed more like the rifle than it ever had before, the vegetables more like game.

My son and I went scouting before the season and saw some antelope in the high plains foothills of the Absaroka Range, wary, hanging on the skyline; a few bands and no great heads. We crept around, looking into basins, and at dusk met a tired cowboy on a tired horse followed by a tired blue-heeler dog. The plains seemed bigger than anything, bigger than the mountains that seemed to sit in the middle of them, bigger than the ocean. The clouds made huge shadows that traveled on the grass slowly through the day.

Hunting season trickles on forever; if you don't go in on a cow with anybody, there is the dark argument of the empty deep-freeze against head-hunting ("You can't eat horns!"). But nevertheless, in my mind, I've laid out the months like playing cards, knowing some decent whitetails could be down in the river bottom and, fairly reliably, the long windy shots at antelope. The big buck mule deer—the ridge-runners—stay up in the scree and rock walls until the snow drives them out; but they stay high long after the elk have quit and broken down the hay corrals on the ranches and farmsteads, which, when you're hunting the rocks from a saddle horse, look pathetic and housebroken with their yellow lights against the coming of winter.

Where I live, the Yellowstone River runs straight north, then takes an eastward turn at Livingston, Montana. This flowing north is supposed to be re-markable; and the river doesn't do it long. It runs mostly over sand and stones once it comes out of the rock slots near the Wyoming line. But all along, there are deviations of one sort or another: canals, backwaters, sloughs; the red wil-lows grow in the sometime-flooded bottom, and at the first elevation, the cot-tonwoods. I hunt here for the white-tailed deer which, in recent years, have moved up these rivers in numbers never seen before.

The first morning, the sun came up hitting around me in arbitrary panels as the light moved through the jagged openings in the Absaroka Range. I was walking very slowly in the edge of the trees, the river invisible a few hundred yards to my right but sending a huge sigh through the willows. It was cold and the sloughs had crowns of ice thick enough to support me. As I crossed one great clear pane, trout raced around under my feet and a ten-foot bubble advanced slowly before my cautious steps. Then passing back into the trees, I found an active game trail, cut cross-lots to pick a better stand, sat in a good vantage place under a cottonwood with the aught-six across my knees. I thought, running my hands up into my sleeves, This is lovely but I'd rather be up in the hills; and I fell asleep.

I woke up a couple of hours later, the coffee and early-morning drill having done not one thing for my alertness. I had drooled on my rifle and it was time for my chores back at the ranch. My chores of late had consisted pri-marily of working on screenplays so that the bank didn't take the ranch. These days the primary ranch skill is making the payment; it comes before irrigation, feeding out, and calving. Some rancher friends find this so discouraging they get up and roll a number or have a slash of tanglefoot before they even think of the glories of the West. This is the New Rugged.

The next day, I reflected upon my lackadaisical hunting and left really too early in the morning. I drove around to Mission Creek in the dark and ended up sitting in the truck up some wash listening to a New Mexico radio station until my patience gave out and I started out cross-country in the dark, just able to make out the nose of the Absaroka Range as it faced across the river to the Crazy Mountains. It seemed maddeningly up and down slick banks, and a couple of times I had game clatter out in front of me in the dark. Then I turned up a long coulee that climbed endlessly south, and started in that direction, knowing the plateau on top should hold some antelope. After half an hour or so, I heard the mad laughing of coyotes, throwing their voices all around the inside of the coulee, trying to panic rabbits and making my hair stand on end despite my affection for them. The stars tracked overhead into the first pale light, and it was nearly dawn before I came up on the bench. I could hear cattle below me and I moved along an edge of thorn trees to break my outline, then sat down at the point to wait for shooting light.

I could see antelope on the skyline before I had that light; and by the time I did, there was a good big buck angling across from me, looking at every-thing. I thought I could see well enough, and I got up into a sitting position and into the sling. I had made my moves quietly, but when I looked through the scope the antelope was two hundred yards out, using up the country in bounds. I tracked with him, let him bounce up into the reticle, and touched off a shot. He was down and still, but I sat watching until I was sure.

Nobody who loves to hunt feels absolutely hunky-dory when the quarry goes down. The remorse spins out almost before anything and the bal-ancing act ends on one declination or another. I decided that unless I become a vegetarian, I'll get my meat by hunting for it. I feel absolutely unabashed by the arguments of other carnivores who get their meat in plastic with blue numbers on it. I've seen slaughterhouses, and anyway, as Sitting Bull said, when the buf-falo are gone, we will hunt mice, for we are hunters and we want our freedom.

The antelope had piled up in the sage, dead before he hit the ground. He was an old enough buck that the tips of his pronged horns were angled in toward each other. I turned him downhill to bleed him out. The bullet had mushroomed in the front of the lungs, so the job was already halfway done. With antelope, proper field dressing is critical because they can end up sour if they've been run or haphazardly hog-dressed. And they sour from their own body heat more than from external heat.

The sun was up and the big buteo hawks were lifting on the thermals. There was enough breeze that the grass began to have directional grain like the prairie, and the rim of the coulee wound up away from me toward the Absaroka. I felt peculiarly solitary, sitting on my heels next to the carcass in the sagebrush and greasewood, my rifle racked open on the ground. I made an incision around the metatarsal glands inside the back legs and carefully removed them and set them well aside; then I cleaned the blade of my hunting knife with handfuls of grass to keep from tainting the meat with those powerful glands. Next I detached the anus and testes from the outer walls and made a shallow puncture below the sternum, spread it with the thumb and forefinger of my left hand, and ran the knife upside down to the bone bridge between the hind legs. Inside, the diaphragm was like the taut lid of a drum and cut away cleanly, so that I could reach clear up to the back of the mouth and detach the windpipe. Once that was done I could draw the whole visceral package out onto the grass and separate out the heart, liver, and tongue before propping the carcass open with two whittled-up sage scantlings.

You could tell how cold the morning was, despite the exertion, just by watching the steam roar from the abdominal cavity. I stuck the knife in the ground and sat back against the slope, looking clear across to Convict Grade and the Crazy Mountains. I was blood from the elbows down and the antelope's eyes had skinned over. I thought, This is goddamned serious and you had better always remember that.

There was a big red enamel pot on the stove; and I ladled the antelope chili into two bowls for my son and me. He said, "It better not be too hot."

"It isn't."

"What's your news?" he asked.

"Grandpa's dead."

"Which grandpa?" he asked. I told him it was Big Grandpa, my father. He kept on eating. "He died last night."

He said, "I know what I want for Christmas."

"What's that?"

"I want Big Grandpa back."

It was 1950-something and I was small, under twelve say, and there were four of us: my father, two of his friends, and me. There was a good belton setter belonging to the one friend, a hearty bird hunter who taught dancing and fist-fought at any provocation. The other man was old and sick and had a green fatal look in his face. My father took me aside and said, "Jack and I are going to the head of this field"—and he pointed up a mile and a half of stalks to where it ended in the flat woods—"and we're going to take the dog and get what he can point. These are running birds. So you and Bill just block the field and you'll have some shooting."

"I'd like to hunt with the dog," I had a 20-gauge Winchester my grandfather had given me, which got hocked and lost years later when another of my family got into the bottle; and I could hit with it and wanted to hunt over the setter. With respect to blocking the field, I could smell a rat.

"You stay with Bill," said my father, "and try to cheer him up."

"What's the matter with Bill?"

"He's had one heart attack after another and he's going to die."

"When?"

"Pretty damn soon."

I blocked the field with Bill. My first thought was, I hope he doesn't die before they drive those birds onto us; but if he does, I'll have all the shooting.

There was a crazy old autumn light on everything, magnified by the yellow silage all over the field. The dog found birds right away and they were shooting. Bill said he was sorry but he didn't feel so good. He had his hunting license safety-pinned to the back of his coat and fiddled with a handful of 12-gauge shells. "I've shot a shitpile of game," said Bill, "but I don't feel so good anymore." He took a knife out of his coat pocket. "I got this in the Marines," he said, "and I carried it for four years in the Pacific. The handle's drilled out and weighted so you can throw it. I want you to have it." I took it and thanked him, looking into his green face, and wondered why he had given it to me. "That's for blocking this field with me," he said. "Your dad and that dance teacher are going to shoot them all. When you're not feeling so good, they put you at the end of the field to block when there isn't shit-all going to fly by you. They'll get them all. They and the dog will."

We had an indestructible tree in the yard we had chopped on, nailed steps to, and initialed; and when I pitched that throwing knife at it, the knife broke in two. I picked it up and thought, *This thing is jinxed.* So I took it out into the crab-apple woods and put it in the can I had buried, along with a Roosevelt dime and an atomic-bomb ring I had sent away for. This was a small collection of things I buried over a period of years. I was sending them to God. All He had to do was open the can, but they were never collected. In any case, I have long known that if I could understand why I wanted to send a broken knife I believed to be jinxed to God, then I would be a long way toward what they call a personal philosophy as opposed to these hand-to-mouth metaphysics of who said what to whom in some cornfield twenty-five years ago.

We were in the bar at Chico Hot Springs near my home in Montana: me, a lout poet who had spent the day floating under the diving board while adolescent girls leapt overhead; and my brother John, who had glued himself to the pipe which poured warm water into the pool and announced over and over in a loud voice that every drop of water had been filtered through his bathing suit.

Now, covered with wrinkles, we were in the bar, talking to Alvin Close, an old government hunter. After half a century of predator control he called it "useless and half-assed."

Alvin Close killed the last major stock-killing wolf in Montana. He hunted the wolf so long he raised a litter of dogs to do it with. He hunted the wolf futilely with a pack that had fought the wolf a dozen times, until one day he gave up and let the dogs run the wolf out the back of a shallow canyon. He heard them yip their way into silence while he leaned up against a tree; and presently the wolf came tiptoeing down the front of the canyon into Alvin's lap. The wolf simply stopped because the game was up. Alvin raised the Winchester and shot it.

"How did you feel about that?" I asked.

"How do you think I felt?"

"I don't know."

"I felt like hell."

Alvin's evening was ruined and he went home. He was seventy-six years old and carried himself like an old-time army officer, setting his glass on the bar behind him without looking.

You stare through the plastic at the red smear of meat in the supermarket. What's this it says here? *Mighty Good? Tastee? Quality, Premium,* and *Government Inspected?* Soon enough, the blood is on your hands. It's inescapable.

Aldo Leopold was a hunter who I am sure abjured freeze-dried vegetables and extrusion burgers. His conscience was clean because his hunting was part of a larger husbandry in which the life of the country was enhanced by his own work. He knew that game populations are not bothered by hunting until they are already precarious and that precarious game populations should not be hunted. Grizzlies should not be hunted, for instance. The enemy of game is clean farming and sinful chemicals; as well as the useless alteration of watersheds by promoter cretins and the insidious dizzards of land development, whose lobbyists teach us the venality of all governments.

A world in which a sacramental portion of food can be taken in an old way—hunting, fishing, farming, and gathering—has as much to do with societal sanity as a day's work for a day's pay.

For a long time, there was no tracking snow. I hunted on horseback for a couple of days in a complicated earthquake fault in the Gallatins. The fault made a maze of narrow canyons with flat floors. The sagebrush grew on woody trunks higher than my head and left sandy paths and game trails where the horse and I could travel.

There were Hungarian partridge that roared out in front of my horse, putting his head suddenly in my lap. And hawks tobogganed on the low air currents, astonished to find me there. One finger canyon ended in a vertical rock wall from which issued a spring of the kind elsewhere associated with the Virgin Mary, hung with ex-votos and the orthopedic supplications of satisfied miracle customers. Here, instead, were nine identical piles of bear shit, neatly adorned with undigested berries.

One canyon planed up and topped out on an endless grassy rise. There were deer there, does and a young buck. A thousand yards away and staring at me with semaphore ears.

They assembled at a stiff trot from the haphazard array of feeding and strung out in a precise line against the far hill in a dogtrot. When I removed my hat, they went into their pogostick gait and that was that.

"What did a deer ever do to you?"

"Nothing."

"I'm serious. What do you have to go and kill them for?"

"I can't explain it talking like this."

"Why should they die for you? Would you die for deer?"

"If it came to that."

My boy and I went up the North Fork to look for grouse. We had my old pointer Molly, and Thomas's .22 pump. We flushed a number of birds climbing through the wild roses; but they roared away at knee level, leaving me little opportunity for my over-and-under, much less an opening for Thomas to ground-sluice one with his .22. We started out at the meteor hole above the last ranch and went all the way to the national forest. Thomas had his cap on the bridge of his nose and wobbled through the trees until we hit cross fences. We went out into the last open pasture before he got winded. So we sat down and looked across the valley at the Gallatin Range, furiously white and serrated, a bleak edge of the world. We sat in the sun and watched the chickadees make their way through the russet brush.

"Are you having a good time?"

"Sure," he said and curled a small hand around the octagonal barrel of the Winchester. I was not sure what I had meant by my question.

The rear quarters of the antelope came from the smoker so dense and finely grained it should have been sliced as prosciutto. We had edgy, crumbling cheddar from British Columbia and everybody kept an eye on the food and tried to pace themselves. The snow whirled in the window light and puffed the smoke down the chimney around the cedar flames. I had a stretch of enumerating things: my family, hayfields, saddle horses, friends, thirty-aught-six, French and Russian novels. I had a baby girl, colts coming, and a new roof on the barn. I finished a big corral made of railroad ties and two-by-sixes. I was within eighteen months of my father's death, my sister's death, and the collapse of my marriage. Still, the washouts were repairing; and when a few things had been set aside, not excluding paranoia, some features were left standing, not excluding lovers, children, friends, and saddle horses. In time, it would be clear as a bell. I did want venison again that winter and couldn't help but feel some old ridge-runner had my number on him.

I didn't want to read and I didn't want to write or acknowledge the phone with its tendrils into the zombie enclaves. I didn't want the New Rugged; I wanted the Old Rugged and a pot to piss in. Otherwise, it's deteriorata, with mice undermining the wiring in my frame house, sparks jumping in the insulation, the dog turning queer, and a horned owl staring at the baby through the nursery window.

It was pitch black in the bedroom and the windows radiated cold across the blankets. The top of my head felt this side of frost and the stars hung like ice crystals over the chimney. I scrambled out of bed and slipped into my long johns, put on a heavy shirt and my wool logger pants with the police suspenders. I carried the boots down to the kitchen so as not to wake the house and turned the percolator on. I put some cheese and chocolate in my coat, and when the coffee was done I filled a chili bowl and quaffed it against the winter.

When I hit the front steps I heard the hard squeaking of new snow under my boots and the wind moved against my face like a machine for refinishing hardwood floors. I backed the truck up to the horse trailer, the lights wheeling against the ghostly trunks of the bare cottonwoods. I connected the trailer and pulled it forward to a flat spot for loading the horse.

I had figured that when I got to the corral I could tell one horse from another by starlight; but the horses were in the shadow of the barn and I went in feeling my way among their shapes trying to find my hunting horse Rocky, and trying to get the front end of the big sorrel who kicks when surprised. Suddenly Rocky was looking in my face and I reached around his neck with the halter. A twelve-hundred-pound bay quarter horse, his withers angled up like a fighting bull, he wondered where we were going but ambled after me on a slack lead rope as we headed out of the darkened corral.

I have an old trailer made by a Texas horse vet years ago. It has none of the amenities of newer trailers. I wish it had a dome light for loading in the dark; but it doesn't. You ought to check and see if the cat's sleeping in it before you load; and I didn't do that either. Instead, I climbed inside the trailer and the horse followed me. I tied the horse down to a D-ring and started back out, when he blew up. The two of us were confined in the small space and he was ripping and bucking between the walls with such noise and violence that I had a brief disassociated moment of suspension from fear. I jumped up on the manger with my arms around my head while the horse shattered the inside of the trailer and rocked it furiously on its axles. Then he blew the steel rings out of the halter and fell over backward in the snow. The cat darted out and was gone. I slipped down off the manger and looked for the horse; he had gotten up and was sidling down past the granary in the star shadows.

I put two blankets on him, saddled him, played with his feet, and calmed him. I loaded him without incident and headed out.

I went through the aspen line at daybreak, still climbing. The horse ascended steadily toward a high basin, creaking the saddle metronomically. It was getting colder as the sun came up, and the rifle scabbard held my left leg far enough from the horse that I was chilling on that side.

We touched the bottom of the basin and I could see the rock wall defined by a black stripe of evergreens on one side and the remains of an avalanche on the other. I thought how utterly desolate this country can look in winter and how one could hardly think of human travel in it at all, not white horsemen nor Indians dragging travois, just aerial raptors with their rending talons and heads like cameras slicing across the geometry of winter.

Then we stepped into a deep hole and the horse went to his chest in the powder, splashing the snow out before him as he floundered toward the other side. I got my feet out of the stirrups in case we went over. Then we were on wind-scoured rock and I hunted some lee for the two of us. I thought of my son's words after our last cold ride: "Dad, you know in 4-H? Well, I want to switch from Horsemanship to Aviation."

The spot was like this: a crest of snow crowned in a sculpted edge high enough to protect us. There was a tough little juniper to picket the horse to, and a good place to sit out of the cold and noise. Over my head, a long, curling plume of snow poured out, unchanging in shape against the pale blue sky. I ate some of the cheese and rewrapped it. I got the rifle down from the scabbard, loosened the cinch, and undid the flank cinch. I put the stirrup over the horn to remind me my saddle was loose, loaded two cartridges into the blind magazine, and slipped one in the chamber. Then I started toward the rock wall, staring at the patterned discolorations: old seeps, lichen, cracks, and the madhouse calligraphy of immemorial weather.

There were a lot of tracks where the snow had crusted out of the wind; all deer except for one well-used bobcat trail winding along the edges of a long rocky slot. I moved as carefully as I could, stretching my eyes as far out in front of my detectable movement as I could. I tried to work into the wind, but it turned erratically in the basin as the temperature of the new day changed.

The buck was studying me as soon as I came out on the open slope: he was a long way away and I stopped motionless to wait for him to feed again. He stared straight at me from five hundred yards. I waited until I could no longer feel my feet nor finally my legs. It was nearly an hour before he suddenly ducked his head and began to feed. Every time he fed I moved a few feet, but he was working away from me and I wasn't getting anywhere. Over the next half-hour he made his way to a little rim and, in the half-hour after that, moved the twenty feet that dropped him over the rim.

I went as fast as I could move quietly. I now had the rim to cover me and the buck should be less than a hundred yards from me when I looked over. It was all browse for a half-mile, wild roses, buck brush, and young quakies where there was any runoff.

When I reached the rim, I took off my hat and set it in the snow with my gloves inside. I wanted to be looking in the right direction when I cleared the rim, rise a half step and be looking straight at the buck, not scanning for the buck with him running sixty, a degree or two out of my periphery. And I didn't want to gum it up with thinking or trajectory guessing. People are always trajectory guessing their way into gut shots and clean misses. So, before I took the last step, all there was to do was lower the rim with my feet, lower the buck into my vision, and isolate the path of the bullet.

As I took that step, I knew he was running. He wasn't in the browse at all, but angling into invisibility at the rock wall, racing straight into the elevation, bounding toward zero gravity, taking his longest arc into the bullet and the finality and terror of all you have made of the world, the finality you know that you share even with your babies with their inherited and ambiguous dentition, the finality that any minute now you will meet as well.

He slid a hundred yards in a rush of snow. I dressed him and skidded him by one antler to the horse. I made a slit behind the last ribs, pulled him over the saddle and put the horn through the slit, lashed the feet to the cinch dees, and led the horse downhill. The horse had bells of clear ice around his hoofs, and when he slipped, I chipped them out from under his feet with the point of a bullet.

I hung the buck in the open woodshed with a lariat over a rafter. He turned slowly against the cooling air. I could see the intermittent blue light of the television against the bedroom ceiling from where I stood. I stopped the twirling of the buck, my hands deep in the sage-scented fur, and thought: This is either the beginning or the end of everything.

In Fields Near Home

BY VANCE BOURJAILY

W HAT HAPPENS WHEN a distinguished novelist takes a literary look around the great American heartland where he lives, works and hunts? A book called *The Unnatural Enemy* is what happens.

Vance Bourjaily had already written four novels (and would go on to write others) when his book of hunting stories was published by The Dial Press in 1963. Critics and readers alike embraced Bourjaily's eloquent and moving prose as something new and exciting in the realm of hunting literature.

During my years as editor of *Sports Afield* in the '70's, I was determined to bring this wonderful story to our readers, even though the magazine in the main only published original pieces. I arranged to reprint a shorter version of "In Fields Near Home" and also managed to get Vance Bourjaily to do some original stories for *Sports Afield*.

Here is a story I regard as one of the greatest pieces of hunting literature ever written, shorter than the full original story in *The Unnatural Enemy,* presented just as we ran it in *Sports Afield* in October, 1970.

Any autumn. Every autumn, so long as my luck holds and my health, and if I win the race. The race is a long slow one that has been going on since I started to hunt again. The race is between my real competence at hunting gradually developing, and, gradually fading, the force of the fantasies which have sustained me while the skills are still weak. If the fantasies fade before the competence is really mine, I am lost as a hunter because I cannot enjoy disgust. I will have to stop, after all, and look for something else.

So I shan't write of any autumn, or every autumn, but of last autumn, the most recent and the most skilled. And not of any day, but a particular day, when things went really well.

7:45   No clock need wake me.

7:55   While I am pulling on my socks, taking simple-minded satisfaction in how clean my feet are from last night's bath, relishing the feel against them of heavy, close-knit wool, fluffed and warmed and freshly washed, the phone rings downstairs. I go down to answer it, stocking-footed and springy-soled, but I am not wondering particularly who the caller is. I am still thinking about clean feet and socks. Even 20 years after infantry training, I can remember what it is like to walk too far with wet lint, cold dirt, and calluses between the flesh and the matted stocking sole, and what it is like to long for the sight of one's own unfamiliar feet and for the opportunity to make them comfortable and unrepulsive.

It is Mr. Burton on the phone.

"Hello?"

"Yeah. Hi, Mr. Burton."

"Say, I've got some news. I called a farmer friend of mine, up north of Waterloo last night. He says there're lots of birds, his place hasn't been hunted for a week."

"Uh-huh."

"I thought we'd go up there instead."

Mr. Burton is a man in his late 50s whom I've known for two or three years. He took me duck hunting once, to a privately leased place, where we did quite well. I took him pheasant hunting in return, and he has a great admiration for my dog Moon. He wants his nephew to see Moon work. The kid has a day off from school today.

But: "The boy can't go after all," Mr. Burton says. "His mother won't let him. But say, I thought we might pick up Cary Johnson—you know him don't you? The attorney. He wants to go. We'll use his car."

Boy, I can see it. It's what my wife calls the drive-around. Mr. Burton will drive to my house; he will have coffee. We will drive to Johnson's house. We will have coffee while Johnson changes to different boots—it's colder than he expected. Johnson will meet a friend who doesn't want to hold us fellows up, but sure would like to go if we're sure there's room. We will have coffee at the drugstore while Johnson's friend goes home, to check with his wife and change. It will be very hot in the drugstore in hunting clothes; the friend will phone and say he can't go after all. Now nothing will be holding us up but the decision to change back to my car, because Johnson's afraid my dog's toenails will rip his seat covers. Off for Waterloo, two hours away (only an hour and a half if Mr. Burton knew exactly how to find the farm). The farmer will have given us up and gone to town. Now that we're here, though, we will drive into town to the feed store, and . . .

"Hell, Mr. Burton," I say. "I'm afraid I can't go along."

"Sure you can. We have a date, don't we?"

"I'll be glad . . ."

"Look, I know you'll like Johnson. That's real hunting up there—I'll bet you five right now we all get limits."

I will not allow myself to think up an excuse. "I'm sorry," I say. "I'll be glad to take you out around here." I even emphasize you a little to exclude Johnson, whoever he is.

"I pretty much promised my farmer friend . . . Oh, look now, is it a matter of having to be back or something?"

"I'm sorry."

"Well, I told him we'd come to Waterloo. There are some things I have to take up to him."

Not being among the things Mr. Burton has to take to his farmer friend, nor my dog either, I continue to decline. Hot damn. Boy, boy, boy. A day to myself.

Ten months a year I'm a social coward, but it's hard to bully me in hunting season, especially with clean socks on.

8:05   Shaving: Unnecessary. Shaving for fun, with a brand new blade.

Thinking: Mr. Burton, sir, if your hunting is good, and you

get a limit of three birds, in two hours 2
& it takes two hours driving to get there 2
& an hour of messing around on arrival 1
& an hour for lunch. 1
& two hours to get back and run people home 2
                                                                                    ___
                                                                                     8

you will call it a good hunt, though the likelihood is, since you are no better shot than I, that other men will have shot one or more of your three birds. There is a shoot-as-shoot-can aspect to group hunts; it's assumed that all limits are combined, and it would be considered quit boorish to suggest that one would somehow like to shoot one's own birds.

Thinking: suppose I spend the same eight hours hunting, and it takes me all that time to get three pheasants. In my eccentric mind, that would be four times as good a hunt, since I would be outdoors four times as long. And be spared all that goddamn conversation.

Chortling at the face behind the lather: pleasant fellow, aren't you?

Thinking: God I like to hunt near home. The known covert, the familiar trail. And in my own way, and at my own pace, and giving no directions, nor considering any other man's. Someday I'll own the fields behind my house, and there'll be nothing but a door between me and the game—pick up a gun, call a dog, slip out. They'll know where I've gone.

Thinking as I see the naked face, with no lather to hide behind now: I'll take Mr. Burton soon. Pretty nice man. I'll find him birds, too, and stand aside while he shoots, as I did for Jake, and Grannum, and that short guy, whatever his name was, looked so good. Moon and I raised three birds for him, one after another, all in nice range, before he hit one. Damn. That's all right. I don't mind taking people. It's a privilege to go out with a wise hunter; a pleasure to go out with one of equal skill, if he's a friend; and a happy enough responsibility to take an inexperienced one sometimes. Eight or 10 pheasants given away like that this season? Why not? I've got 12 already myself, more than in any season before and this one's barely 10 days old. And for the first time, missed fewer than I've hit.

Eggs?

8:15 Sure! Eggs! Three of them! Fried in that olive oil, so they puff up. With lemon juice. Tabasco. Good. Peppery country sausage, and a stack of toast. Yes, hungry. Moon comes in.

"Hey, boy. Care to go?"

Wags.

"Wouldn't you just rather stay home today and rest up?"

Wags, grins.

"Yeah, wag. If you knew what I said you'd bite me."

Wags, stretches, rubs against me.

"You'd better have some breakfast, too." I go to the refrigerator. Moon is a big dog, a Weimaraner, and he gets a pound of hamburger mornings when he's going to be working. I scoop out cold ground meat from its paper carton, and pat it between my hands into a ball. I roll it across the floor, under his dignified nose. This is a silly game we play; he follows it with his eyes, then pounces as if it really were a ball, trapping it with a paw. My wife, coming in from the yard, catches us.

"Having a game of ball," I say.

"What is it you're always telling the children about not making the same joke twice?"

"Moon thinks it's funny."

"Moon's a very patient dog. I see you're planning to work again today."

I smile. I know this lady. "I really should write letters," I say.

"They can wait, can't they?" She smiles. She likes me to go hunting. She's still not really convinced that I enjoy it—when we were first married I liked cities—but if I do enjoy it, then certainly I must go.

Yes, letters can wait. Let them ripen a few more days. It's autumn. Maybe some of them will perish in the frost if I leave them another week or two—hell, even the oldest ones are barely a month old.

8:45 I never have to tell Moon to get in the car. He's on his hind legs, with his paws on the window, before I reach it. As I get in, start the car, and warm it up, an image comes into my mind of a certain hayfield. It's nice the way this happens; no reasoning, no weighing of one place to start against another. As if the image were projected directly by the precise feel of a certain temperature, a certain wind strength—from sensation to picture without intervening thought. As we drive, I can see just how much the hay should be waving in the wind, just how the shorter grass along the highway will look, going from white to wet as the frost melts off—for suddenly the sun's quite bright.

8:55 I stop, and look at the hayfield, and if sensation projected an image of it into my mind, now it's as if my mind could project this same image, expanded, onto a landscape. The hay is waving, just that much. The frost is starting to melt.

"Whoa, Moon. Stay."

I have three more minutes to think it over. Pheasant hunting starts at nine.

"Moonie. Quiet, boy."

He is quivering, whining, throwing his weight against the door.

I think they'll be in the hay itself—tall grass, really, not a seeded crop; anyway, not in this shorter stuff that grows in the first 100 yards or so along the road. Right?

8:58 Well. Yeah. Whoa.

The season's made its turn at last. Heavy frost every morning now. No more mosquitoes, flies. Cold enough so that it feels good to move, not so cold that I'll need gloves: perfect. No more grasshoppers, either. A sacrifice, in a way—pheasants that feed on hoppers, in open fields, are wilder and taste better than the ones that hang around corn.

The season's made its turn in another sense—the long progression of openings is over: Rabbits, squirrels, September 15. Geese, October 5. Ducks, snipe, October 27. Quail, November 3. Pheasants, November 10. That was 10 days ago. Finally, everything that's ever legal may be hunted. The closings haven't started yet. Amplitude. Best time of the year. Whoa.

8:59: Whoa! Now it's me quivering, whining, but I needn't throw my weight against the door—open it. I step out, making Moon stay. I uncase the gun, look at it with love, throw the case in the car; load. Breathe cold air. Good. Look around. Fine.

"Come on, Moonie. Nine o'clock."

9:00 I start on the most direct line through the short grass, toward the tall, not paying much attention to Moon, who must relieve himself. I think this is as much a matter of nervous tension as it is of regularity.

"Come on, Moon," I call, keeping to my line. "This way, boy."

He thinks he's got a scent back here, in the short grass; barely enough for a pheasant to hide in, and much too thin for cold-day cover.

"Come, Moon. Hyeahp."

It must be an old scent. But he disregards me. His stub of a tail begins to go as he angles off, about 30 yards from where I am; his body lowers just a little and he's moving quickly. I am ignorant in many things about hunting, but there's one thing I know after eight years with this dog, if you bother to hunt with a dog at all, believe what he tells you. Go where he says the bird is, not where you think it ought to be.

I move that way, going pretty quickly myself, still convinced it's an old foot-trail he's following, and he stops in a half-point, his head sinking down while his nose stays up, so that the gray neck is almost in a shallow S-curve.

A cock, going straight up, high, high, high. My gun goes up with him and is firm against my shoulder as he reaches the top of his leap. He seems to hang there as I fire, and he drops perfectly, two or three yards from where Moon waits.

"Good dog. Good boy, Moon," I say as he picks the heavy bird up in his mouth and brings it to me. "Moonie, that was perfect." The bird is thoroughly dead, but I open my pocket knife, press the blade into the roof of its mouth so that it will bleed properly. Check the spurs—they're stubby and almost rounded at the tip. This year's pheasant, probably. Young. Tender. Simply perfect.

Like a book pheasant, I think, and how seldom it happens. In the books, pheasants are said to rise straight up as this one did, going for altitude first, then pausing in the air to swing downwind. The books are quite wrong; most pheasants I see take straight off, without a jump, low and skimming, curving if they rise much, and never hanging at all. I wonder about evolution: among pheasant generations in this open country, did the ones who went towering into the air and hung like kites get killed off disproportionately? While the skulkers and skimmers and curvers survived, to transmit crafty genes?

"Old-fashioned pheasant, are you? You just set a record for me. I never dreamed I'd have a bird so early in the day," I check my watch.

9:15 The device I was so hopeful of is not working out too well. It is a leather holder which slides onto the belt, and has a set of rawhide loops. As I was supposed to, I have hooked the pheasant's legs into a loop, but he swings against my own leg at the knee. Maybe the thing was meant for taller men.

"Moon. This way. Come around, boy." I feel pretty strongly that we should hunt the edge.

The dangling bird is brushing grass tops. Maybe next time I should bring my trout creel, which is oversized, having been made by optimistic Italians. No half-dozen trout would much more than cover the bottom, but three cock pheasants might lie nicely in the willow, their tails extending backwards through the crack between lid and body, the rigidity of the thing protecting them as a game bag doesn't.

"Moon. Come back here. Come around." He hasn't settled down for the day. Old as he is, he still takes a wild run, first thing.

I'm pretty well settled, myself (it's that bird bumping against my leg). Now Moon does come back into the area I want him in, the edge between high grass and low; there's a distinction between following your dog when he's got something and trusting him to weigh odds. I know odds better, and here is one of those things that will be a cliché of hunting in a few years, since the game-management men are telling it to one another now and it's started filtering into outdoor magazines: the odds are that most game will be near the edge of cover, not in the center of it. The phrase for this is "edge factor."

"Haven't you heard of the edge factor?" I yell at Moon. "Get out along the edge here, boy." And in a few steps he has a scent again. When he's got the tail factor going, the odds change, and I follow him, almost trotting to keep up, as he works from edge to center, back toward edge, after what must be a running bird. He slows a little, but doesn't stop; the scent is hot, but apparently the bird is still moving. Moon stops, points, holds. I walk as fast as I can, am in range—and Moon starts again. He is in a crouch now, creeping forward in his point. The unseen bird must be shifting; he is starting to run again, for Moon moves out of the point and stars to lope; I move, fast as I can and still stay collected enough to shoot—gun held in both hands out in front of me—exhilarated to see the wonderful mixture of exuberance and certainty with which Moon goes. To make such big happy moves, and none of them a false one, is something only the most extraordinary human athletes can do, after years of training—it comes naturally to almost any dog. And that pheasant out there in front of us—how he can go! Turn and twist through the tangle of stems, never showing himself, moving away from Moon's speed and my calculations. But we've got him—I think we do—Moon slows, points. Sometimes we win in a run down—usually not—usually the pheasant picks the right time, well out and away, to flush out of range—but this one stopped. Yes. Moon's holding again. I'm in range. I move up, beside the rigid dog. Past him. WHIRR-PT. The gun rises, checks itself, and I yell at Moon, who is ready to bound forward:

"Hen!"

Away she goes, and away goes Moon, and I yell: "Whoa. Hen, hen," but it doesn't stop him. He's pursuing, as if he could get up enough speed to rise onto the air after her. "Whoa." It doesn't stop him. WHIRRUPFT. That stops him. Stops me too. A second hen. WHIRRUPFT. WHIRRUPFT. Two more. And another, that makes five who were sitting tight. And then, way out, far from this little group, through which he must have passed, and far from us, I see the cock, which is almost certainly the bird we were chasing (hens don't run like that), fly up silently, without a cackle, and glide away, across the road and out of sight.

9:30 "There's got to be another," I say to Moon. A man I know informed me quite vehemently a week ago that one ought never to talk to a dog in the field except to give commands; distracts him, the man said, keeps him too close. Tell you what, man: you run your dogs your way, and I'll run my dog mine. Okay?

We approach a fence, where the hayfield ends; the ground is clear for 20 feet before the fence line. Critical place. If birds have been moving ahead of us, and are reluctant to fly, this is where they'll hide. They won't run into the open. And just as I put this card in the calculator, one goes up. CUK CUK CUK, bursting past Moon full speed and low, putting the dog between me and him so that, while my gun is ready, I can't shoot immediately; he rises only enough to clear the fence, sweeping left between two bushes as I fire, and I see the pellets agitate the leaves of the right-hand bush, and I know I shot behind him.

Moon, in the immemorial way of bird dogs, looks back to me with what bird hunters who miss have immemorially taken for reproach.

We turn along the edge paralleling the fence. He may not have been the only one we chased down here—Moon is hunting, working from fence to edge, very deliberate. Me to. I wouldn't like to miss again. Moon swerves to the fence row, tries some likely brush. Nope. Lopes back to the edge, lopes along it. Point. Very stiff. Very sudden. Ten yards, straight ahead.

This is a beautifully awkward point, Moon's body curved into it, shoulders down, rear up, head almost looking back at me; this one really caught him. As now we'll catch the pheasant? So close. Dog so steady. I have the impression Moon's looking a bird straight in the eye. I move slowly. No need for speed, no reason to risk being off balance. Let's be so deliberate, so cool, so easy.

The gun is ready to come up—I never have the feeling that I myself bring it up. Don't be off balance. He'll go now. Now. Nope—when he does, I try to tell myself, don't shoot too fast, let the bird get out a little, but I'm not really that good and confident in my shooting. Thanks be for brush loads. Ought to have them in both barrels for this situation. Will I have to kick the pheasant out? I am within two steps of Moon, who hasn't stirred except for the twitching of his shoulder and haunch muscles, when the creature bolts. Out he comes, under Moon's nose, and virtually between my legs if I didn't jump aside—a rabbit, tearing for the fence row. I could recover and shoot, it's an easy shot, but not today; I smile, relax, and sweat flows. I am not that desperate for game yet.

I yell "Whoa" at Moon, and for some dog's reason he obeys this time. I should punish him, now; for pointing fur? But it's my fault—sometimes, being a one-dog man, I shoot fur over him, though I recognize it as a genuine error in bird-dog handling. But with the long bond of hunting and mutual training between us (for Moon trained me no less than I did him), my taking a rabbit over him from time to time—or a mongoose, or a kangaroo—is not going to change things between us.

In any case, my wife's never especially pleased to see me bring a rabbit home, though the kids and I like to eat them. I pat Moon, who whoaed for the rabbit. "Whoa, big babe," I say softly. "Whoasie-posner, whoa-daboodle-dog, big sweet posner baby dog . . ." I am rubbing his back.

10:40   Step out of the car, look around, work it out: the birds slept late this morning, because of the wind and frost, and may therefore be feeding late. If so, they're in the field itself, which lies beyond two fallow fields. They roost here in this heavy cover, fly out to the corn—early on nice mornings; later, if I'm correct, on a day like this. When they're done feeding, they go to what game experts call loafing cover—relatively thin cover, near the feeding place, and stay in it till the second feeding in the afternoon; after which they'll be back here where they started, to roost again.

The wind is on my left cheek, as Moon and I go through the roosting cover, so I angle right. This will bring us to where we can turn and cross the popcorn field, walking straight into the wind. This will not only be better for Moon, for obvious reasons, but will also be better for shooting; birds in open rows, hearing us coming, can sail away out of range very fast with the wind behind them. If it blows towards me, they'll either be lifted high, going into the wind, or curve off to one side or the other.

The ragweed, as we come up close to it and Moon pauses before choosing a spot at which to plunge in, is eight feet high—thick, dry, brittle, gray-stemmed stuff which pops and crackles as he breaks into it. I move a few feet along the edge of the draw, shifting my position as I hear him working through, to stay as well in range of where he is as possible. I am calmly certain there's a bird in there, even that it's a cock. I think he moved in ahead of us as we were coming up the field, felt safe when he saw us apparently about to pass by, and doesn't want to leave the defense overhead protection now.

But he must. Moon will send him up in a moment, perhaps out the far side where the range will be extreme. It will be a long shot, if that happens, and Moon is now at the far edge, is turning along it, when I hear the cackle of the cock rising. For a moment I don't know where, can't see him, and by the time I do he's going out to my right, almost back towards me, having doubled away from the dog. Out he comes, already in full flight and low, with the wind behind him for speed. And yet I was so well set for this, for anything, that it all seems easy—to pivot, mounting the gun as I do, find it against my cheek and the bird big and solid at the end of the barrel, swing, taking my time, and shoot. The bird checks, fights air, and tumbles, and in my sense of perfection I make an error: I am so sure he's perfectly hit that I do not take the second shot, before he falls in some waist-high weeds. I mark the place by keeping my eye on a particular weed, a little taller than the others, and walk slowly, straight towards it, not letting my eye move away, confident he'll be lying right by it. Moon, working the ragweed, would neither see the rise nor mark the fall and he comes bounding out to me now, coming to the sound of the shot. I reach the spot first, so very carefully marked, and there's no bird there.

Hunters make errors; dogs correct them. While I am still standing there, irritated with myself for not having shot twice, Moon is circling me, casting, inhaling those great snuffs, finding the ground scent. He begins to work a straight line, checks as I follow him, starts again in a slightly different direction; I must trust him, absolutely, and I do. I remind myself that once he trailed a crippled bird more than half a mile in the direction opposite from that in which I had actually seen the bird start off. I kept trying to get him to go the other way, but he wouldn't; and he found the pheasant. It was by the edge of a dirt road, so that Max Morgan and I could clock the distance afterwards by car speedometer.

Our present bird is no such problem. Forty feet from where the empty shell waves gently back and forth on top of the weed, Moon hesitates, points. Then, and I do not know how he knows that this particular immobile pheasant will not fly (unless it's the smell of fresh blood), Moon lunges. His head darts into matted weeds, fights spurs for a moment, tosses the big bird once so that he can take it by the back, lifts it; and he comes to me proudly, trotting, head as high as he can hold it.

11:00 Iowa hunters are obsessed with corn. If there are no birds in the cornfields, they consider the situation hopeless. This may come from the fact that most of them hunt in drives—a number of men spread out in line, going along abreast through standing corn, with others blocking the end of the field. My experience, for I avoid that kind of hunt every chance I get, is quite different; I rarely find pheasants in cornfields, except along the edges. More than half of those I shoot, I find away from corn, in wild cover, and sometimes the crops show that the bird has not been eating grain at all but getting along on wilder seeds.

But as I start to hunt the popcorn field, something happens that shows why driving often works out. We start into the wind, as planned, moving down the field the long way, and way down at the other end a farm dog sees us. He starts towards us, intending to investigate Moon, I suppose. I see him come towards the field; I see him enter it, trotting our way, and the wind carries the sound of his barking. And then I see—the length of a football field away, reacting to the farm dog—pheasants go up; not two or three, but a flock, 12 or 14, and another and another and another, cocks and hens, flying off in all directions, sailing down wind and out of sight. Drivers and blockers would have had fast shooting with that bunch—but suppose I'd got up? Well, this gun only shoots twice. And, well again, boy. Three's the limit, dunghead. And you've got two already.

11:30 Two birds before lunch? I ought to limit out, I ought to limit out soon. And stop looking for pheasants, spend the afternoon on something else. Take Moon home to rest, maybe, and know that the wind's going down and the sun's getting hot, go into the woods for squirrels, something I like but never get around to.

Let's get the other one. Where?

We are walking back to the car, the shortest way, no reason to go through the popcorn field after what happened. Where? And I think of a pretty place, not far away.

11:45 Yes, it's pretty. Got a bird here last year, missed a couple, too, why haven't I been here this season? It's a puzzle, and the solution, as I stop the car once more, is a pleasure: I know a lot of pretty places near home, 20 or 30 of them, all quite distinct, and have gotten or missed birds at all of them, one season or another.

There are no pheasants this time, only signs of pheasant; roosting places, full of droppings. Some fresh enough so that they were dropped this morning. A place for the next windy morning; I put that idea in a safe place, and move back, after Moon—he's pretty excited with all the bird scent, but not violently; it's not that fresh—towards the fence along the soybean field. We turn from the creek, and go along the fence line, 20 or 30 feet out, towards an eight-acre patch of woods where I have often seen deer, and if I were a real reasoner or a real instinct man, not something in between, what happens would not find me unprepared. Moon goes into a majestically rigid point, foreleg raised, tail out straight, aimed at low bushes in the fence row. I hardly ever see him point so rigidly without first showing the signs he gives while the quarry is still shifting. I move in rather casually, suspecting a hen, but if it's a cock rather confident, after my last great shot, and there suddenly comes at me, buzzing angrily, a swarm of—pheasants? Too small—hornets? Sparrow? Quail! drilling right at me, the air full of them, whirring, swerving to both sides.

Much too late, surprised, confused—abashed, for this is classic quail cover—I flounder around, face back the way I came, and pop off a pair of harmless shots, more in valediction than in hope of hitting. Turn back to look at Moon, and up comes a straggler, whirring all by himself, also past me. There are no easy shots on quail, but I could have him, I think, if both barrels weren't empty. He's so close that I can see the white on neck and face, and know him for a male. Jock though I am, at least I mark him down, relieved that he doesn't cross the creek.

Moon works straight to the spot where I marked the straggler, and sure enough he flushes, not giving the dog a chance to point, flushes high and I snap-shoot and he falls. Moon bounds after him and stops on the way, almost pitching forward, like a car when its brakes lock. Another bird. Ready. I hope I have my down bird marked. Careful. *Whirr*—I damn near stepped on him, and back he goes behind me. I swing 180 degrees, and as he angles away have him over the end of the barrel. As I fire, it seems almost accidental that I should be on him so readily, but it's not of course—it's the one kind of shot that never misses, the unplanned, reflexive shot, when conditioning has already operated before self-consciousness could start up. This quail falls in the soft maple seedlings, in a place I won't forget, but the first one may be hard.

He's not. I find him without difficulty, seeing him on the ground at just about the same time that Moon finds him too. Happy to have him, I bring Moon back to the soft maple seedlings, but we do not find the second bird.

12:30 Lunch is black coffee in the thermos, an apple and an orange, and the sight of two quail and two pheasants, lying in a neat row on the car floor. I had planned to go home for lunch; and it wouldn't take so very much time; but I would talk with my family, of course, and whatever it is this noon that they're concerned with, I would be concerned with. And that would break the spell, as an apple and an orange will not.

12:45 Also

1:45 and, I'm afraid

2:45 these hours repeat one another, and at the end of them I have: two pheasants, as before; two quail; and an afterthought.

The afterthought shouldn't have run through my mind, in the irritable state that it was in.

The only shots I took were at domestic pigeons, going by fast and far up, considered a nuisance around here; I missed both times. But what made me irritable were all the mourning doves.

There are doves all over the place in Iowa, in every covert that I hunt—according to the last Audubon Society spring census at Des Moines, doves were more common even than robins and meadow larks. In my three hard hours of barren pheasant hunting, I could have had shots at 20 or 25 doves (a game bird in 30 states, a game bird throughout the history of the world), and may not try them. Shooting doves is against the law in Iowa. The harvesting of our enormous surplus (for nine out of 10 will die before they're a year old anyway) is left to cats and owls and—because the dove ranges get so crowded—germs.

Leaving the half-picked cornfield, I jump yet another pair of doves, throw up my gun and track them making a pretended double, though I doubt that it would work.

Three hours of seeing doves, and no pheasants, has made me pettish, and perhaps I am beginning to tire.

A rabbit jumps out behind the dog, unseen by Moon but not by me. At first I assume that I want to let him go, as I did the earlier one; then he becomes the afterthought: company, dinner—so you won't let me shoot doves, eh rabbit? He's dead before he can reach cover.

3:00 Now I have only an hour left to get my final bird, for pheasant hunting ends at four. This is a symbolic bird: a good hunter gets his limit. At noon it seemed almost sure I would; suddenly it's doubtful.

I sit in the car, one hand on Moon who is lying on the seat beside me. We've reached the time of the day when he rests when he can.

3:10 On my way to someplace else, I suddenly brake the car.

"Hey, did you see that?" I am talking to Moon again. He has a paw over his nose, and of course saw nothing. I look over him, eagerly, out the window and down into a big marsh we were about to pass by. We were on our way to the place I'd thought of, an old windbreak of evergreens near an abandoned farmhouse site, surrounded by overgrown pasture, and not too far from corn. It's an ace-in-the-hole kind of place for evening shooting, for the pheasants come in there early to roost; I've used it sparingly, shown it to no one.

Going there would be our best chance to fill out, I think, but look: "Damn, Moon, snipe. Snipe, boy, I'm sure of it."

On the big marsh, shore birds are rising up and setting down, not in little squadrons like killdeer—which are shore birds about the same size, and very common—but a bird here, a bird there. Becoming instantly invisible when they land, too, and so not among the wading shore birds. I get out the glasses and step out of the car, telling Moon to stay. I catch one of the birds in the lenses, and the silhouette is unmistakable—the long, comic beak, the swept-back wings.

"You are snipe," I say, addressing—well, them, I suppose. "Where've you boys been?"

Two more whiz in and out of the image, too quickly to follow, two more of my favorite of all game birds. Habitat changes around here so much from year to year, with the great fluctuations in water level from the dam, that this marsh, which was full of snipe three years ago, has shown none at all so far this year. What snipe hunting I've found has been in temporarily puddled fields, after rains, and in a smaller marsh.

"I thought you'd never come," I say. "Moon!" I open the car door. "Moon, let's go." My heartiness is a little false, for snipe are my favorite bird, not Moon's. He'll flush them, if he must, but apparently they're distasteful to him, and when I manage to shoot one, he generally refuses even to pick it up, much less retrieve it for me.

Manage to shoot one? Last year, on the first day I hunted snipe, I shot 16 shells before I hit my first. That third pheasant can wait there in the hole with the other aces.

Remembering the 16 straight misses, I stuff my pockets with shells—brush loads still for the first shot but, with splendid consistency, high-brass 7½s for the second, full-choke shot. I won't use them on a big bird, like a pheasant; I will on a tiny bird, like a snipe. The snipe goes fast, and by the second shot you need all the range you can get.

I should have hip boots now. Go back and get them? Nuts. Get muddy.

Down we go, Moon with a certain silly enthusiasm for the muskrats he smells and may suppose are now to be our quarry. I see that the marsh water is shallow, but the mud under it is always deep—thigh-deep in some places; the only way to go into it is from hummock to hummock of marsh grass. Actually, I will stay out of it if I can, and so I turn along the edge, Moon hunting out in front. A snipe rises over the marsh at my right, too far to shoot at, scolding us anyway: *scaip, scaip.* Then two more, which let the dog get by them, going up between me and

Moon—a chance for a double, in a highly theoretical way. I shoot and miss at the one on the left as he twists low along the edge. He rises, just after the shot, going up in a tight turn, and I shoot again, swinging up with him, and miss again.

At my first shot, the other snipe—the one I didn't shoot at—dove, as if hit. But I know he wasn't; I've seen the trick before. I know about where he went in, and I decide not to bother with Moon, who is chasing around in the mud, trying to convince himself that I knocked down a pheasant or something decent like that.

I wade in myself, mud to ankles, mud to calves, up to the tops of the low boots I'm wearing; no bird? What the hell, mud over the boot tops, and I finally climb a hummock. This puts up my diving snipe, 10 yards further out and scolding, but the hummocks are spaced too far apart in this part of the swamp so there's no point shooting. I couldn't recover him and I doubt that Moon would. I let him rise, twist, swoop upwards, and I stand as still as I can, balanced on the little mound of grass; I know a trick myself. It works; at the top of his climb the snipe turns and comes streaking back, 40 yards up, directly overhead. I throw up the gun for the fast overhead shot, and miss.

I splash back to the edge and muck along. A snipe goes up, almost at my feet, and his first swerve coincides with my snap shot—a kind of luck that almost seems like skill. Moon, bounding back, has seen the bird fall and runs to it—smells it, curls his lip and slinks away. He turns his head to watch me bend to pick it up, and as I do, leaps back and tries to take it from me.

"Moondog," I say, addressing him severely by his full name. "I'm not your child to punish. I like this bird. Now stop it."

We start along again, come to the corner where the marsh dies out, and turn. Moon stops, sight-pointing in a half-hearted way, and a snipe goes up in front of him. This one curves towards some high weeds; I fire and miss, but stay on him as he suddenly straightens and goes winging straight out, rising very little. He is a good 40 yards away by now, but he tumbles when I fire, and falls on open ground. It takes very little to kill a snipe. I pace the distance, going to him, and watch Moon, for Moon picks this one up. Then, when I call to him to bring it, he gradually, perhaps sulkily, lowers his head and spits it out again. He strolls off as if there were nothing there. I scold him as I come up, but not very hard; he looks abashed, and makes a small show of hunting dead in a bare spot about 10 yards from where we both know the snipe is lying. I pick up the bird, and tell Moon that he is probably the worst dog that ever lived, but not in an unkind voice for I wouldn't want to hurt his feelings.

This a pleasanter area we are crossing now: firm mud, patches of swamp weeds, frequent puddles. Moon, loping around aimlessly, blunders into a group of five or six snipe at the far side of a puddle, and I put trying to get a double out of my mind; I try to take my time; pick out an individual, follow him as he glides toward some high reeds and drop him.

Now we go along, towards the back of the marsh, shooting and missing, hitting just twice. One shot in particular pleases me: a snipe quite high, in full flight coming towards me. I shoot, remembering a phrase I once read: "A shotgun is a paint brush." I paint the snipe blue, to match the sky, starting my brush stroke just behind him, painting evenly along his body, completing the stroke about three lengths in front where I fire, and follow through. This is a classic shot, a memorable one, so much so that there are just two others I can put with it—one on a faraway pheasant last year, one on a high teal in Chile. They sky is all blue now, for the snipe is painted out of it and falls, almost into my hand.

It is just 3:55.

There is magic in this. The end of the legal pheasant hunting day is four o'clock.

4:00 Just after the pheasant, I kill another snipe, the sixth. He is along the stream, too, and so I follow it, awed at the thought that I might even get a limit on these. But on the next chance, not a hard one, I think too hard, and miss the first shot, as he twists, and the rising one as well.

We leave the watercourse for a tiny marsh, go back to it (or a branch) through government fields I've never crossed before, by strange potholes and unfamiliar willow stands. We flush a woodcock, cousin to the snipe, but shooting him is not permitted here. We turn away in a new direction—snipe and woodcock favor different sorts of cover. And sometime along in there, I walk up two snipe, shoot one very fast, and miss a perplexing but not impossible shot at the other, as he spirals up.

"There he goes," I think. "My limit bird." He flies into the east, where the sky is getting dark; clouds have come to the western horizon and the sun is gone for the day, behind them.

5:03 In this remnant of perfect habitat, the sky is empty. It is five minutes till sunset, but it is dusk already, when my last snipe does go up, I hear him before I see him. I crouch down, close to the ground, trying to expand the area of light against which he will show up, and he appears now, winging for the upper sky; but I cannot decide to shoot, shouldering my gun in that awkward position. And in another second it is too late, really too late, and I feel as if the last hunter in the world has let the last snipe go without a try.

I straighten up reluctantly, unload gun, and wonder where I am. Suddenly I am tired, melancholy, and very hungry. I know about which way to go, and start along, calling Moon, only half lost dragging a little. The hunting is over and home an hour away.

I think of quail hunting in Louisiana, when we crouched, straining for shots at the final covey, as I did just now for the final snipe.

I find a little road I recognize, start on it the wrong way, correct myself and turn back along it. A touch of late sun shows now, through a rift, enough to cast a pale shadow in front of me—man with gun—on the sand road.

We were on an evening march, in some loose company formation, outside of training camp. We were boys.

I watched our shadows along the tall clay bank at the side of the road. We were too tired to talk, even garrulous Bobby Hirt, who went AWOL later and spent two years, so we heard, in military prison. He was a boy. We all were. But the helmeted shadows, with packs and guns in silhouette, were the shadows of soldiers—faceless, menacing, expendable. No one shadow different from the other. I could not tell you, for after training we dispersed, going out as infantry replacements, which of those boys, whose misery and defiance and occasional good times I shared for 17 unforgotten weeks, actually were expended. Several, of course, since statistics show what they do of infantry replacements. Statistics are the representation of shadows by numbers.

My shadow on the sand road is of a different kind. I have come a little way in 19 years, whatever the world has done. I am alone, in a solitary place, as I wish to be, accountable only as I am willing to be held so, therefore no man's statistic. Melancholy for the moment, but only because I am weary, and coming to the end of this day which, full of remembering, will be itself remembered.

Moon is beside me, tired now too, throwing his own pale dog-shadow ahead. And the hunter-shadow with him, the pheasant hanging from the hunter's belt, sniper bulging in the jacket—the image teases me. It is not the soldiers, but some other memory. An image, failing because the sun is failing, the rift closing very slowly. An image of. A hunter like. A dream? Not a dream, but the ghost of a dream, my old, hunter-and-his-dog-at-dusk dream. And the sun goes down, and the ghost with it, and the car is in sight which will carry us home.

Race At Morning

BY WILLIAM FAULKNER

ALTHOUGH HE WAS a highly prolific and critically acclaimed writer at the time, when William Faulkner went to work in Hollywood as a scriptwriter in the '30s, his name was simply not well known. Nor did he have very much money, the real reason for his enlistment in the studios of Jack Warner. Turning his creative talents away from the legendary Yoknapatawpha County he had created in his novels and stories, Faulkner was forced to leave his Oxford, Mississippi home and his prose to try his hand at writing for the silver screen. In the years ahead would be the Nobel Prize, many more internationally praised books and stories, and immense fame. But there in Hollywood, slogging through writing cash-and-carry screen treatments and screenplays, William Faulkner was not a happy camper.

As if he needed being reminded of his condition, there occurred an incident now famous among literary anecdotes.

Southerner and hunter that he was, Faulkner anticipated the month of September with a passion. September meant dove hunting. And California had plenty of it back then. As Faulkner was headed for the dove fields with a Hollywood friend one day, a third member joined the party. He was the actor Clark Gable, also an avid hunter. Faulkner had never met Gable. After he had settled into the car, Gable turned to Faulkner and said, "What do you do, Mister Faulkner?"

"I'm a writer," Faulkner shot back, instantly. "And what do you do, Mister Gable?"

Mr. Gable looked at Mr. Faulkner like he had been kicked in the groin.

In retelling that story, my sense of fairness compels me to add that from many things I have heard and read, Clark Gable was a warm and generous

4 3

man in person. While I was editor of *Sports Afield,* the legendary duck hunter and clay-bird authority, Jimmy Robinson, told me some wonderful stories about Clark Gable visiting his duck camp in Manitoba. From guides to cooks, everybody loved the real Clark Gable. It's too bad the world of hunting lost such a figure when Gable succumbed to coronary artery disease at such a relatively young age.

"Race At Morning" is a William Faulkner story that originally appeared in the *Saturday Evening Post* and was later collected with many of his other stories that have hunting backgrounds in the book *Big Woods,* published by Random House in 1955. Among the tales included are "Delta Autumn" and a condensed version of the Faulkner classic, "The Bear."

Although Faulkner was of an inquiring mind and quite experienced in international travel—he served as a pilot in the Lafayette Escadrille in World War One—William Faulkner's most famous literary works are set in the Mississippi he loved and knew so well. Books like *The Sound and the Fury, As I Lay Dying, The Bear* are established literary landmarks. Short stories such as "Delta Autumn," "Two Soldiers," and "That Evening Sun" will be included in anthologies of classics as long as such books are published.

I can't resist closing this with another Faulkner Hollywood anecdote. It seems that one day Faulkner phoned his boss, Jack Warner, and said, "Jack, I'm not feeling well. Do you mind if I try to work at home for a while?"

"Of course not, Bill," Warner said. "I hope you feel better soon."

A week or so later Warner happened to be looking for Faulkner. After some confusion it was learned that Faulkner was back in Oxford, Mississippi. When he had asked to "go home," he really meant home.

Oh well. I guess the poet T. S. Eliot was right, when he said, "Home is where you start from."

I was in the boat when I seen him. It was jest dust-dark; I had jest fed the horses and clumb back down the bank to the boat and shoved off to cross back to camp when I seen him, about half a quarter up the river, swimming; jest his head above the water, and it no more than a dot in that light. But I could see that rocking chair he toted on it and I knowed it was him, going right back to that canebrake in the fork of the bayou where he lived all year until the day before the season opened, like the game wardens had give him a calendar, when he would clear out and disappear, nobody knowed where, until the day after the season closed. But here he was, coming back a day ahead of time, like maybe he had got mixed up and was using last year's calendar by mistake. Which was jest too bad for him, because me and Mister

Ernest would be setting on the horse right over him when the sun rose to-morrow morning.

So I told Mister Ernest and we et supper and fed the dogs, and then I holp Mister Ernest in the poker game, standing behind his chair until about ten o'clock, when Roth Edmonds said, "Why don't you go to bed, boy?"

"Or if you're going to set up," Willy Legate said, "why don't you take a spelling book to set up over? He knows every cuss word in the dictionary, every poker hand in the deck and every whisky label in the distillery, but he can't even write his name. Can you?" he says to me.

"I don't need to write my name down," I said. "I can remember in my mind who I am."

"You're twelve years old," Walter Ewell said. "Man to man now, how many days in your life did you ever spend in school?"

"He ain't got time to go to school," Willy Legate said. "What's the use in going to school from September to middle of November, when he'll have to quit then to come in here and do Ernest's hearing for him? And what's the use in going back to school in January, when in jest eleven months it will be November fifteenth again and he'll have to start all over telling Ernest which way the dogs went?"

"Well, stop looking into my hand, anyway," Roth Edmonds said.

"What's that? What's that?" Mister Ernest said. He wore his listening button in his ear all the time, but he never brought the battery to camp with him because the cord would bound to get snagged ever time we run through a thicket.

"Willy says for me to go to bed!" I hollered.

"Don't you never call nobody 'mister'?" Willy said.

"I call Mister Ernest 'mister'," I said.

"All right," Mister Ernest said. "Go to bed then. I don't need you."

"That ain't no lie," Willy said. "Deaf or no deaf, he can hear a fifty-dollar raise if you don't even move your lips."

So I went to bed, and after a while Mister Ernest come in and I wanted to tell him again how big them horns looked even half a quarter away in the river. Only I would 'a' had to holler, and the only time Mister Ernest agreed he couldn't hear was when we would be setting on Dan, waiting for me to point which way the dogs was going. So we jest laid down, and it wasn't no time Simon was beating the bottom of the dishpan with the spoon, hollering, "Raise up and get your four-o'clock coffee!" and I crossed the river in the dark this time, with the lantern, and fed Dan and Roth Edmondziz horse. It was going to be a fine day, cold and bright; even in the dark I could see the white frost on the leaves and bushes—jest exactly the kind of day that big old son of a gun laying up there in that brake would like to run.

Then we et, and set the stand-holder across for Uncle Ike McCaslin to put them on the stands where he thought they ought to be, because he was the oldest one in camp. He had been hunting deer in these woods for about a hundred years, I reckon, and if anybody would know where a buck would pass, it would be him. Maybe with a big old buck like this one, that had been running the woods for what would amount to a hundred years in a deer's life, too, him and Uncle Ike would sholy manage to be at the same place at the same time this morning—provided, of course, he managed to git away from me and Mister Ernest on the jump. Because me and Mister Ernest was going to git him.

Then me and Mister Ernest and Roth Edmonds sent the dogs over, with Simon holding Eagle and the other old dogs on leash because the young ones, the puppies, wasn't going nowhere until Eagle let them, nohow. Then me and Mister Ernest and Roth saddled up, and Mister Ernest got up and I handed him up his pump gun and let Dan's bridle go for him to git rid of the spell of bucking he had to git shut of ever morning until Mister Ernest hit him between the ears with the gun barrel. Then Mister Ernest loaded the gun and give me the stirrup, and I got up behind him and we taken the fire road up toward the bayou, the four big dogs dragging Simon along in front with his single-barrel britchloader slung on a piece of plow line across his back, and the puppies moiling along in ever'body's way. It was light now and it was going to be jest fine; the east already yellow for the sun and our breaths smoking in the cold still bright air until the sun would come up and warm it, and a little skim of ice in the ruts, and ever leaf and twig and switch and even the frozen clods frosted over, waiting to sparkle like a rainbow when the sun finally come up and hit them. Until all my insides felt light and strong as a balloon, full of that light cold strong air, so that it seemed to me like I couldn't even feel the horse's back I was straddle of—jest the hot strong muscles moving under the hot strong skin, setting up there without no weight atall, so that when old Eagle struck and jumped, me and Dan and Mister Ernest would go jest like a bird, not even touching the ground. It was jest fine. When that big old buck got killed today, I knowed that even if he had put it off another ten years, he couldn't 'a' picked a better one.

And sho enough, as soon as we come to the bayou we seen his foot in the mud where he had come up out of the river last night, spread in the soft mud like a cow's foot, big as a cow's, big as a mule's, with Eagle and the other dogs laying into the leash rope now until Mister Ernest told me to jump down and help Simon hold them. Because me and Mister Ernest knowed exactly where he would be—a little canebrake island in the middle of the bayou, where he could lay up until whatever doe or little deer the dogs had happened to jump could go up or down the bayou in either direction and take the dogs on away, so he could steal out and creep back down the bayou to the river and swim it, and leave the country like he always done the day the season opened.

Which is jest what we never aimed for him to do this time. So we left Roth on his horse to cut him off and turn him over Uncle Ike's standers if he tried to slip back down the bayou, and me and Simon, with the leashed dogs, walked on up the bayou until Mister Ernest on the horse said it was fur enough; then turned up into the woods about half a quarter above the brake because the wind was going to be south this morning when it riz, and turned down toward the brake, and Mister Ernest give the word to cast them, and we slipped the leash and Mister Ernest give me the stirrup again and I got up.

Old Eagle had done already took off because he knowed where that old son of a gun would be laying as good as we did, not making no racket atall yet, but jest boring on through the buck vines with the other dogs trailing along behind him, and even Dan seemed to know about that buck, too, beginning to souple up and jump a little through the vines, so that I taken my holt on Mister Ernest's belt already before the time had come for Mister Ernest to touch him. Because when we got strung out, going fast behind a deer, I wasn't on Dan's back much of the time nohow, but mostly jet strung out from my holt on Mister Ernest's belt, so that Willy Legate said that when we was going through the woods fast, it looked like Mister Ernest had a boy-size pair of empty overalls blowing out of his hind pocket.

So it wasn't even a strike, it was a jump. Eagle must 'a' walked right up behind him or maybe even stepped on him while he was laying there still thinking it was day after tomorrow. Eagle jest throwed his head back and up and said, "There he goes," and we even heard the buck crashing through the first of the cane. Then all the other dogs was hollering behind him, and Dan give a squat to jump, but it was against the curb this time, not jest the snaffle, and Mister Ernest let him down into the bayou and swung him around the brake and up the other bank. Only he never had to say, "Which way?" because I was already pointing past his shoulder, freshening my holt on the belt jest as Mister Ernest touched Dan with that big old rusty spur on his nigh heel, because when Dan felt it he would go off jest like a stick of dynamite, straight through whatever he could bust and over or under what he couldn't, over it like a bird or under it crawling on his knees like a mole or a big coon, with Mister Ernest still on him because he had the saddle to hold on to, and me still there because I had Mister Ernest to hold on to; me and Mister Ernest not rid-ing him, but jest going along with him, provided we held on. Because when the jump come, Dan never cared who else was there neither; I believe to my soul he could 'a' cast and run them dogs by hisself, without me or Mister Ernest or Simon or nobody.

That's what he done. He had to; the dogs was already almost out of hearing. Eagle must 'a' been looking right up that big son of a gun's tail until he finally decided he better git on out of there. And now they must 'a' been getting pretty close to Uncle Ike's standers, and Mister Ernest reined Dan back and held him, squatting and bouncing and trembling like a mule having his tail roached, while we listened for the shots. But never none come, and I hollered to Mister Ernest we better go on while I could still hear the dogs, and he let Dan off, but still there wasn't no shots, and now we knowed the race had done already passed the standers, like that old son of a gun actually was a hant, like Simon and the other field hands said he was, and we busted out of a thicket, and sho enough there was Uncle Ike and Willy standing beside his foot in a soft patch.

"He got through us all," Uncle Ike said. "I don't know how he done it. I just had a glimpse of him. He looked big as a elephant, with a rack on his head you could cradle a yellin' calf in. He went right on down the ridge. You better get on, too; that Hog Bayou camp might not miss him."

So I freshened my holt and Mister Ernest touched Dan again. The ridge run due south; it was clear of vines and bushes so we could go fast, into the wind, too, because it had riz now, and now the sun was up, too; though I hadn't had time to notice it, bright and strong and level through the woods, shining and sparking like a rainbow on the frosted leaves. So we would hear the dogs again any time now as the wind got up; we could make time now, but still holding Dan back to a canter, because it was either going to be quick, when he got down to the standers from that Hog Bayou camp eight miles below ourn, or a long time, in case he got by them, too. And sho enough, after a while we heard the dogs; we was walking Dan now to let him blow a while, and we heard them, the sound coming faint up the wind, not running now, but trailing because the big son of a gun had decided a good piece back, probably, to put a end to this foolishness, and picked hisself up and soupled out and put about a mile between hisself and the dogs—until he run up on them other standers from that camp below. I could almost see him stopped behind a bush, peeping out and saying, "What's this? What's this? Is this whole durn country full of folks this morning?" Then looking back over his shoulder at where old Eagle and the others was hollering along after him while he decided how much time he had to decide what to do next.

Except he almost shaved it too fine. We heard the shots; it sounded like a war. Old Eagle must 'a' been looking right up his tail again and he had to bust on through the best way he could. "Pow, pow, pow, pow" and then "Pow, pow, pow, pow," like it must 'a' been three or four ganged right up on him before he had time even to swerve, and me hollering, "No! No! No! No!" because he was ourn. It was our beans and oats he et and our brake he laid in; we had been watching him every year, and it was like we had raised him, to be killed at last on our jump, in front of our dogs, by some strangers that would probably try to beat the dogs off and drag him away before we could even git a piece of the meat.

"Shut up and listen," Mister Ernest said. So I done it and we could hear the dogs; not just the others, but Eagle, too, not trailing no scent now and not baying no downed meat neither, but running hot on sight long after the shooting was over. I jest had time to freshen my holt. Yes, sir, they was running on sight. Like Willy Legate would say, if Eagle jest had a drink of whisky he would ketch that deer; going on, done already gone when we broke out of the thicket and seen the fellers that had done the shooting, five or six of them, squatting and crawling around, looking at the ground and the bushes, like maybe if they looked hard enough, spots of blood would bloom out on the stalks and leaves like frogstools or hawberries, with old Eagle still in hearing and still telling them that what blood they found wasn't coming out of nothing in front of him.

"Have any luck, boys?" Mister Ernest said.

"I think I hit him," one of them said. "I know I did. We're hunting blood now."

"Well, when you find him, blow your horn and I'll come back and tote him in to camp for you," Mister Ernest said.

So we went on, going fast now because the race was almost out of hearing again, going fast, too, like not jest the buck, but the dogs, too, had took a new leash on life from all the excitement and shooting.

We was in strange country now because we never had to run this fur before, we had always killed before now; now we had come to Hog Bayou that runs into the river a good fifteen miles below our camp. It had water in it, not to mention a mess of down trees and logs and such, and Mister Ernest checked Dan again, saying, "Which way?" I could just barely hear them, off to the east a little, like the old son of a gun had give up the idea of Vicksburg or New Orleans, like he first seemed to have, and had decided to have a look at Alabama, maybe, since he was already up and moving; so I pointed and we turned up the bayou hunting for a crossing, and maybe we could 'a' found one, except that I reckon Mister Ernest decided we never had time to wait.

We come to a place where the bayou had narrowed down to about twelve or fifteen feet, and Mister Ernest said, "Look out, I'm going to touch him" and done it; I didn't even have time to freshen my holt when we was already in the air, and then I seen the vine—it was a loop of grapevine nigh as big as my wrist, looping down right across the middle of the bayou—and I thought he seen it, too, and was jest waiting to grab it and fling it up over our heads to go under it, and I know Dan seen it because he even ducked his head to jump under it. But Mister Ernest never seen it atall until it skun back along Dan's neck and hooked under the head of the saddle horn, us flying on through the air, the loop of the vine gitting tighter and tighter until something somewhere was going to have to give. It was the saddle girth. It broke, and Dan going on and scrabbling up the other bank bare nekkid except for the bridle, and me and Mister Ernest and the saddle, Mister Ernest still setting in the saddle holding the gun, and me still holding onto Mister Ernest's belt, hanging in the air over the bayou in the tightened loop of that vine like in a drawed-back loop of a big rubber-banded slingshot, until it snapped back and shot us back across the bayou and flang us clear, me still holding onto Mister Ernest's belt and on the bottom now, so that when we lit I would 'a' had Mister Ernest and the saddle both on top of me if I hadn't clumb fast around the saddle and up Mister Ernest's side, so that when we landed, it was the saddle first, then Mister Ernest, and me on top, until I jumped up, and Mister Ernest still laying there with jest the white rim of his eyes showing.

"Mister Ernest!" I hollered, and then clumb down to the bayou and scooped my cap full of water and clumb back and throwed it in his face, and he opened his eyes and laid there on the saddle cussing me.

"God dawg it," he said, "why didn't you stay behind where you started out?"

"You was the biggest!" I said. "You would 'a' mashed me flat!"

"What do you think you done to me?" Mister Ernest said. "Next time, if you can't stay where you start out, jump clear. Don't climb up on top of me no more. You hear?"

"Yes, sir," I said.

So he got up then, still cussing and holding his back, and clumb down to the water and dipped some in his hand onto his face and neck and dipped some more up and drunk it, and I drunk some, too, and clumb back and got the saddle and the gun, and we crossed the bayou on the down logs. If we could jest ketch Dan; not that he would have went them fifteen miles back to camp, because, if anything, he would have went on by hisself to try to help Eagle ketch that buck. But he was about fifty yards away, eating buck vines, so I brought him back, and we taken Mister Ernest's galluses and my belt and the whang leather loop off Mister Ernest's horn and tied the saddle back on Dan. It didn't look like much, but maybe it would hold.

"Provided you don't let me jump him through no more grapevines without hollering first," Mister Ernest said.

"Yes, sir," I said. "I'll holler first next time—provided you'll holler a little quicker when you touch him next time, too." But it was all right; we jest had to be a little easy getting up. "Now which-a-way?" I said. Because we couldn't hear nothing now, after wasting all this time. And this was new country, sho enough. It had been cut over and growed up in thickets we couldn't 'a' seen over even standing up on Dan.

But Mister Ernest never even answered. He jest turned Dan along the bank of the bayou where it was a little more open and we could move faster again, soon as Dan and us got used to that homemade cinch strop and got a little confidence in it. Which jest happened to be east, or so I thought then, because I never paid no particular attention to east then because the sun—I don't know where the morning had went, but it was gone, the morning and the frost, too—was up high now, even if my insides had told me it was past dinnertime.

And then we heard him. No, that's wrong; what we heard was shots. And that was when we realized how fur we had come, because the only camp we knowed about in that direction was the Hollyknowe camp, and Hollyknowe was exactly twenty-eight miles from Van Dorn, where me and Mister Ernest lived—jest the shots, no dogs nor nothing. If old Eagle was still behind him and the buck was still alive, he was too wore out now to even say, "Here he comes."

"Don't touch him!" I hollered. But Mister Ernest remembered that cinch strop, too, and he jest let Dan off the snaffle. And Dan heard them shots, too, picking his way through the thickets, hopping the vines and logs when he could and going under them when he couldn't. And sho enough, it was jest like before—two or three men squatting and creeping among the bushes, looking for blood that Eagle had done already told them wasn't there. But we never stopped this time, jest trotting on by with Dan hopping and dodging among the brush and vines dainty as a dancer. Then Mister Ernest swung Dan until we was going due north.

"Wait!" I hollered. "Not this way."

But Mister Ernest jest turned his face back over his shoulder. It look tired, too, and there was a smear of mud on it where that ere grapevine had snatched him off the horse.

"Don't you know where he's heading?" he said. "He's done done his part, give everybody a fair open shot at him, and now he's going home, back to that brake in our bayou. He ought to make it exactly at dark."

And that's what he was doing. We went on. It didn't matter to hurry now. There wasn't no sound nowhere; it was that time in the early afternoon in November when don't nothing move or cry, not even birds, the pecker-woods and yellowhammers and jays, and it seemed to me like I could see all three of us—me and Mister Ernest and Dan—and Eagle, and the other dogs, and that big old buck, moving through the quiet woods in the same direction, headed for the same place, not running now but walking, that had all run the fine race the best we knowed how, and all three of us now turned like on a agreement to walk back home, not together in a bunch because we didn't want to worry or tempt one another, because what we had all three spent this morning doing was no play-acting jest for fun, but was serious, and all three of us was still what we was—that old buck that had to run, not because he was skeered, but because running was what he done the best and was proudest at; and Eagle and the dogs that chased him, not because they hated or feared him, but because that was the thing they done the best and was proudest at; and me and Mister Ernest and Dan, that run him not because we wanted his meat, which would be too tough to eat anyhow, or his head to hang on a wall, but because now we could go back and work hard for eleven months making a crop, so we would have the right to come back here next November—all three of us going back home now, peaceful and separate, but still side by side, until next year, next time.

Then we seen him for the first time. We was out of the cut-over now; we could even 'a' cantered, except that all three of us was long past that, and now you could tell where west was because the sun was already halfway down it. So we was walking, too, when we come on the dogs—the puppies and one of the old ones—played out, laying in a little wet snag, panting, jest looking up at us when we passed, but not moving when we went on. Then we come to a long open glade, you could see about half a quarter, and we seen the three other old dogs and about a hundred yards ahead of them Eagle, all walking, not making no sound; and then suddenly, at the fur end of the glade, the buck his-self getting up from where he had been resting for the dogs to come up, get-ting up without no hurry, big, big as a mule, tall as a mule, and turned without no hurry still, and the white underside of his tail for a second or two more be-fore the thicket taken him.

It might 'a' been a signal, a good-bye, a farewell. Still walking, we passed the other three old dogs in the middle of the glade, laying down, too, now jest where they was when the buck vanished, and not trying to get up neither when we passed; and still that hundred yards ahead of them, Eagle, too, not laying down, because he was still on his feet, but his legs was spraddled and his head was down; maybe jest waiting until we was out of sight of his shame, his eyes saying plain as talk when we passed, "I'm sorry, boys, but this here is all."

Mister Ernest stopped Dan. "Jump down and look at his feet," he said.

"Ain't nothing wrong with his feet," I said. "It's his wind has done give out."

"Jump down and look at his feet," Mister Ernest said.

So I done it, and while I was stooping over Eagle I could hear the pump gun go, "Snick-cluck. Snick-cluck. Snick-cluck" three times, except that I never thought nothing then. Maybe he was jest running the shells through to be sho it would work when we seen him again or maybe to make sho they was all buckshot. Then I got up again, and we went on, still walking; a little west of north now, because when we seen his white flag that second or two before the thicket hid it, it was on a beeline for that notch in the bayou. And it was evening, too, now. The wind had done dropped and there was a edge to the air and the sun jest touched the tops of the trees now, except jest now and then, when it found a hole to come almost level through onto the ground. And he was taking the easiest way, too, now, going straight as he could. When we seen his foot in the soft places he was running for a while at first after his rest. But soon he was walking, too, like he knowed, too, where Eagle and the dogs was.

And then we seen him again. It was the last time—a thicket, with the sun coming through a hole onto it like a searchlight. He crashed jest once; then he was standing there broadside to us, not twenty yards away, big as a statue and red as gold in the sun, and the sun sparking on the tips of his horns—they was twelve of them—so that he looked like he had twelve lighted candles branched around his head, standing there looking at us while Mister Ernest raised the gun and aimed at his neck, and the gun went, "Click. Snick-cluck. Click. Snick-cluck. Click. Snick-cluck" three times, and Mister Ernest still holding the gun aimed while the buck turned and give one long bound, the white underside of his tail like a blaze of fire, too, until the thicket and the shadows put it out; and Mister Ernest laid the gun slow and gentle back across the saddle in front of him, saying quiet and peaceful, and not much louder than jest breathing, "God dawg. God dawg."

Then he jogged me with his elbow and we got down, easy and careful because of that ere cinch strop, and he reached into his vest and taken out one of the cigars. It was busted where I had fell on it, I reckon, when we hit the ground. He throwed it away and taken out the other one. It was busted, too, so he bit off a hunk of it to chew and throwed the rest away. And now the sun was gone even from the tops of the trees and there wasn't nothing left but a big red glare in the west.

"Don't worry," I said. "I ain't going to tell them you forgot to load your gun. For that matter, they don't need to know we ever seed him."

"Much oblige," Mister Ernest said. There wasn't going to be no moon tonight neither, so he taken the compass off the whang leather loop in his buttonhole and handed me the gun and set the compass on a stump and stepped back and looked at it. "Jest about the way we're headed now," he said, and taken the gun from me and opened it and put one shell in the britch and taken up the compass, and I taken Dan's reins and we started, with him in front with the compass in his hand.

And after a while it was full dark; Mister Ernest would have to strike a match ever now and then to read the compass, until the stars come out good and we could pick our one to follow, because I said, "How fur do you reckon it is?" and he said, "A little more than one box of matches." So we used a star when we could, only we couldn't see it all the time because the woods was too dense and we would git a little off until he would have to spend another match. And now it was good and late, and he stopped and said, "Get on the horse."

"I ain't tired," I said.

"Get on the horse," he said. "We don't want to spoil him."

Because he had been a good feller ever since I had knowed him, which was even before that day two years ago when maw went off with the Vicksburg roadhouse feller and the next day pap didn't come home neither, and on the third one Mister Ernest rid Dan up to the door of the cabin on the river he let us live in, so pap could work his piece of land and run his fish line, too, and said, "Put that gun down and come on here and climb up behind."

So I got in the saddle even if I couldn't reach the stirrups, and Mister Ernest taken the reins and I must 'a' went to sleep, because the next thing I knowed a buttonhole of my lumberjack was tied to the saddle horn with that ere whang cord off the compass, and it was good and late now and we wasn't fur, because Dan was already smelling water, the river. Or maybe it was the feed lot itself he smelled, because we struck the fire road not a quarter below it, and soon I could see the river, too, with the white mist laying on it soft and still as cotton. Then the lot, home; and up yonder in the dark, not no piece akchully, close enough to hear us unsaddling and shucking corn prob'ly, and sholy close enough to hear Mister Ernest blowing his horn at the dark camp for Simon to come in the boat and git us, that old buck in his brake in the bayou; home, too, resting, too, after the hard run, waking hisself now and then, dreaming of dogs behind him or maybe it was the racket we was making would wake him, but not neither of them for more than jest a little while before sleeping again.

Then Mister Ernest stood on the bank blowing until Simon's lantern went bobbing down into the mist; then we clumb down to the landing and Mister Ernest blowed again now and then to guide Simon, until we seen the lantern in the mist, and then Simon and the boat; only it look like ever time I set down and got still, I went back to sleep, because Mister Ernest was shaking me again to git out and climb the bank into the dark camp, until I felt a bed against my knees and tumbled into it.

Then it was morning, tomorrow; it was all over now until next November, next year, and we could come back. Uncle Ike and Willy and Walter and Roth and the rest of them had come in yestiddy, soon as Eagle taken the buck out of hearing and they knowed that deer was gone, to pack up and be ready to leave this morning for Yoknapatawpha, where they lived, until it would be November again and they could come back again.

So, as soon as we et breakfast, Simon run them back up the river in the big boat to where they left their cars and pickups, and now it wasn't nobody but jest me and Mister Ernest setting on the bench against the kitchen wall in the sun; Mister Ernest smoking a cigar—a whole one this time that Dan hadn't had no chance to jump him through a grapevine and bust. He hadn't washed his face neither where that vine had throwed him into the mud. But that was all right, too; his face usually did have a smudge of mud or tractor grease or beard stubble on it, because he wasn't jest a planter; he was a farmer, he worked as hard as ara one of his hands and tenants—which is why I knowed from the very first that we would git along, that I wouldn't have no trouble with him and he wouldn't have no trouble with me, from that very first day when I woke up and maw had done gone off with that Vicksburg roadhouse feller without even waiting to cook breakfast, and the next morning pap was gone, too, and it was almost night the next day when I heard a horse coming up and I taken the gun that I had already throwed a shell into the britch when pap never come home last night, and stood in the door while Mister Ernest rid up and said, "Come on. Your paw ain't coming back neither."

"You mean he give me to you?" I said.

"Who cares?" he said. "Come on. I brought a lock for the door. We'll send the pickup back tomorrow for whatever you want."

So I come home with him and it was all right, it was jest fine—his wife had died about three years ago—without no women to worry us or take off in the middle of the night with a durn Vicksburg roadhouse jake without even waiting to cook breakfast. And we would go home this afternoon, too, but not jest yet; we always stayed one more day after the others left because Uncle Ike always left what grub they hadn't et, and the rest of the homemade corn whisky he drunk and that town whisky of Roth Edmondziz he called Scotch that smelled like it come out of a old bucket of roof paint; setting in the sun for one more day before we went back home to git ready to put in next year's crop of cotton and oats and beans and hay; and across the river yonder, behind the wall of trees where the big woods started, that old buck laying up today in the sun, too—resting today, too, without nobody to bother him until next November.

So at least one of us was glad it would be eleven months and two weeks before he would have to run that fur that fast again. So he was glad of the very same thing we was sorry of, and so all of a sudden I thought about how maybe planting and working and then harvesting oats and cotton and beans and hay wasn't jest something me and Mister Ernest done three hundred and fifty-one days to fill in the time until we could come back hunting again, but it was something we had to do, and do honest and good during the three hundred and fifty-one days, to have the right to come back into the big woods and hunt for the other fourteen; and the fourteen days that old buck run in front of dogs wasn't jest something to fill his time until the three hundred and fifty-one when he didn't have to, but the running and the risking in front of guns and dogs was something he had to do for fourteen days to have the right not to be bothered for the other three hundred and fifty-one. And so the hunting and the farming wasn't two different things atall—they was jest the other side of each other.

"Yes," I said. "All we got to do now is put in that next year's crop. Then November won't be no time away atall."

"You ain't going to put in the crop next year," Mister Ernest said. "You're going to school."

So at first I didn't even believe I had heard him. "What?" I said. "Me? Go to school?"

"Yes," Mister Ernest said. "You must make something out of yourself."

"I am," I said. "I'm doing it now. I'm going to be a hunter and a farmer like you."

"No," Mister Ernest said. "That ain't enough any more. Time was when all a man had to do was just farm eleven and a half months, and hunt the other half. But not now. Now just to belong to the farming business and the hunting business ain't enough. You got to belong to the business of mankind."

"Mankind?" I said.

"Yes," Mister Ernest said. "So you're going to school. Because you got to know why. You can belong to the farming and hunting business and you can learn the difference between what's right and what's wrong, and do right.

And that used to be enough—just to do right. But not now. You got to know why it's right and why it's wrong, and be able to tell the folks that never had no chance to learn it; teach them how to do what's right, not just because they know it's right, but because they know now why it's right because you just showed them, told them, taught them why. So you're going to school."

"It's because you been listening to that durn Will Legate and Walter Ewell!" I said.

"No," Mister Ernest said.

"Yes!" I said. "No wonder you missed that buck yestiddy, taking ideas from the very fellers that let him git away, after me and you had run Dan and the dogs durn night clean to death! Because you never even missed him! You never forgot to load that gun! You had done already unloaded it a purpose! I heard you!"

"All right, all right," Mister Ernest said. "Which would you rather have? His bloody head and hide on the kitchen floor yonder and half his meat in a pickup truck on the way to Yoknapatawpha County, or him with his head and hide and meat still together over yonder in that brake, waiting for next November for us to run him again?"

"And git him, too," I said. "We won't even fool with no Willy Legate and Walter Ewell next time."

"Maybe," Mister Ernest said.

"Yes," I said.

"Maybe," Mister Ernest said. "The best word in our language, the best of all. That's what mankind keeps going on: Maybe. The best days of his life ain't the ones when he said 'Yes' beforehand: they're the ones when all he knew to say was 'Maybe.' He can't say 'Yes' until afterward because he not only don't know it until then, he don't want to know 'Yes' until then. . . . Step in the kitchen and make me a toddy. Then we'll see about dinner."

"All right," I said. I got up. "You want some of Uncle Ike's corn or that town whisky of Roth Edmondziz?"

"Can't you say Mister Roth or Mister Edmonds?" Mister Ernest said.

"Yes, sir," I said. "Well, which do you want? Uncle Ike's corn or that ere stuff of Roth Edmondziz?"

Spirit of the North

BY THOMAS MCINTYRE

DURING HIS EDITORSHIP of *Sports Afield* throughout the 1980s and well into the 1990s, my friend Tom Paugh was responsible for upgrading the quality of the magazine in many areas, ranging from the graphics to the prose. New painters and photographers were introduced to the magazine's pages and many new writers, including Tom McIntyre.

Now moved on to *Field & Stream,* Tom McIntyre has been one of my favorite writers for years, and I can assure you that I am far from alone in my regard for his prose. Many of Tom's best stories, ranging from bird hunting in the West to big and dangerous game in Africa, have been included in the collection *Dreaming the Lion,* published by Countrysport Press of Traverse City, Michigan, in 1993.

In this one, Tom takes us up North and then downriver in some of the great moose country of the Canadian bush.

In the tent the hunters come and go, talking of the Windigo—although Windigos would probably be among the very last thing anybody would care to talk about in the moose country of the North.

Moose country is by nature the most remote of all hunting countries we may ever experience. This moose country, experienced in mid-September, was the world's largest swamp, the Hudson Bay lowlands of Manitoba, Canada. To be precise, it lay along the course of the Bigstone River, the Bigstone a tributary of the Fox, the Fox a tributary of the Hayes. These rivers were once part of a famous fur-trading route, the Middle Track, that ran 570 miles from The Pas in the interior out to the bay at York Factory, which for the two-and-a-half centuries that it was a Hudson's Bay Company post was the capital of the northern fur trade.

Though the fur trade continues, the days of the great bundle-laden birch-bark canoes transporting the season's pelts are long passed, and now the only canoes you are likely to meet on these waters are those of such individuals as my hunting companions Gren and Harold who each September venture into this backcountry to paddle along and hunt moose. Yet even with two other individuals present—friendly individuals with considerable bush sense to boot—I still could never be certain what kind of hearts they might have. This could, quite justifiably, make one feel like the last human alive, especially while hunting moose and worrying about the Windigo in a distant wilderness like this.

The remoteness of moose country is not contingent upon how far away from everywhere else it may be. Caribou (and muskox) country, for instance, can be a much more distant place. But the tundra spaces the caribou click across in their vast herds are usually wide-open ones and in their way rather pleasant, making caribou the plains game of the North and putting one in mind of other sunlighted Pleistocene expanses with names like Serengeti. For the moose's part, he quite often abides in dense willow thickets and spruce jungles of almost oppressive darkness and damp.

In such locales the moose, who unlike the caribou is definitely not a herd animal, can seem as solitary as a tiger. In moose country entire days can go by with hunters never seeing a single one of the animals they are in pursuit of, and without seeing another member of their own species either. This was precisely the sort of circumstance in which I found myself as I hunted by canoe on the Bigstone with Gren and Harold.

It was the time of the rut for moose; at first light on a typical hunting day Gren and I might paddle the big aluminum canoe a mile or more upstream from camp on the fog-wooled river, beaching it on a muddy bank where there would be the deep hoof prints of a moose who had swum the river and moved on into the bush. We would hunker on the canoe thwarts then and wait for the long, plaintive early-morning grunting of a cow moose to break the silence, to be answered by the equally low, short, harsh grunting of a bull. Gren, cupping his hands around his mouth and pinching closed his nostrils with his index fingers, would imitate these grunts and listen for a response. Yet even when his call did receive an answer there was no guarantee that a moose would appear. After an hour or two of shivering, we would paddle back to camp where Harold would have piping bowls of Red River cereal awaiting us.

With breakfast eaten we would head out onto the river again, covering as much of the remote territory as we could, hoping to catch a moose when he stepped out onto the shore to leave his tracks once more in the mud.

The landscape in that season was patched by the yellow of willows as their leaves turned, seemingly, before our eyes. Almost as soon as we paddled past a clump of shimmering-green bush it would begin to blaze like the top of some octogenarian's birthday cake. While the needles of the tamaracks died off in their own fiery-yellow manner, the always-dark spruces stood reservedly back from it all, looking down on this spectacle of deciduousness and having none of it.

As the canoe glided noiselessly through the water faster than a man could jog along the shore, we could slip up on beavers the dimensions of Clumber spaniels who had constructed stick houses the dimensions of palazzos. The huge rodents, humped up on the shore, gnawing at lengths of poplar, would stare at us pig-eyed as we drew near, before waddling into the river. They would cut a clean V through the water as they swam, eyeing the canoe's approaching prow with suspicion, then dive, slapping their flat hairless tails on the surface as loudly as someone doing a belly flop off a springboard. Looking down into the clear flow, you might catch sight of them torpedoing sleekly past, as if in the fantasy of some *voyageur* from York Factory's first days.

We would see Canada geese ahead of us, their heads rising alertly on their long necks as we hove into view; then the ludicrous honking would begin as we approached, concluding with flapping sprints across the water and boisterous liftoffs. Ducks followed suit. Bald eagles, already airborne, demonstrated a different technique to show us we were not to be trusted, gaining altitude over the river above us by kicking downward with their taloned feet as their wings pulled them upward.

Minks, who must surely possess brains no larger than the tip of a finger, were as erratic as pinballs, first swimming away from us, then zigging directly back at us, then diving under us at the last instant. The river otters, on the other hand, would tread water and watch us curiously but with transcendent indifference while making a purring hum. On one occasion we even spotted a fisher, big as a housecat, with a cat's long tail, standing on the bedrock shore, bobbing his open-mouthed head in weasel fashion before turning and slipping away from our sight.

Nonetheless, it was moose we were after and moose we would be thinking about as we paddled back in at night with the moon bright as a street lamp behind us. The water was satin beneath the moon, and the paddle would dip into it with a tearing sound as it was pulled, spraying drops in a pearled arc as it was lifted out, only to be dipped in again in the seemingly endless cycle of paddling that made up our day until we were back at the lantern-lit camp.

In the tent, heated at night by the airtight wood stove, I would still be thinking of moose while Gren and Harold read about famous battles and military heroes. Eventually they would mark the pages in their books and sit up on their cots to tell me about the Windigo, again.

Even today in the Hudson Bay lowlands the Windigo is as tangible and frightening to the Ojibwa and Cree as a Jeffrey Dahmer is to us. The Windigo often takes the form of a ten-foot giant, and though he breathes fire his heart is a ball of solid ice. He flies through the air at night, looking for lone humans so he can commit that still most heinous of all crimes, cannibalism, surviving on a diet of his victims' flesh and blood. A shaman, with the aid of other spirits, has a chance of killing a Windigo, but for an ordinary man the task is nearly impossible. If he should manage to cut off the Windigo's head, that head will only reunite with the monstrous body. Any bullet other than a silver one would be useless against him. A human bitten by a Windigo will unavoidably become one, and simply dreaming of the creature can effect the transformation.

Finishing their nightly recitation of the tale of the Windigo, Gren or Harold would turn off the lantern and in the faltering glow of the mantle would both wish me pleasant dreams.

In the morning, none of us apparently having been devoured or transformed in the night, we would be out after moose once more. Canoeing for game was something of a novel experience for me, with its own set of rules to be memorized. First there was the necessity of absolute silence. Sound seemed to travel an infinite distance across the water, so speech could never rise above a whisper. Then there was the problem of banging a paddle against the hull, the resulting sound to our ears approximating the bells of Notre Dame. Early on in the hunt I had learned how to paddle—leaning back with each stroke, rather than tiring myself by pulling with my arms alone—without letting the paddle touch the gunwale. If we ever spotted a moose while I was paddling in my bow seat, I was not to worry about trying to place my paddle back into the canoe, but was simply to lay it gently on the water where it would float and get my rifle ready. (In this part of Manitoba it was legal to hunt from a canoe as long as it was not being powered by a motor.) Finally there was the problem I had with "right" and "left."

When we came to white water we had several options. In many places we would get out and portage the canoe around the rapids. In others we might try to "line" it up- or downriver. This entailed our hopping from rock to rock ahead of the canoe, holding a rope tied to it, and pulling it through like packers leading a mule through a bad place on the trail. But wherever the water permitted we decided that honor demanded we paddle our way through.

As we would approach white water, Gren, or Harold when I was hunting with him, would outline the upcoming campaign for me.

"Now at Radio Rapids . . ." the instructions would begin. Or, "If we have to go through Antler Rapids . . ."

Where do those names come from, I asked, instinctively regretting the question about as soon as it left my lips.

"Well," Gren or Harold would reply, studiously avoiding eye contact, "Radio Rapids is where we turned over the canoe one year and lost the radio. And Antler Rapids . . ." But enough of that, he would say and quickly go on to explain that at the next stretch of white water I would have to pull hard to the right or left as per his shouted command to keep us heading straight. Then we would be racing through the rapids—always much sooner than I had anticipated—and I would hear *"Right"* from behind me and begin to paddle furiously.

"Right, RIGHT!" would come the shout again and I knew I was paddling on the wrong side and would hastily switch.

After one such rock-banging run, Harold asked me the question I had been dreading.

"You don't have some sort of trouble with 'right' and 'left', do you?" he asked mildly.

I slumped visibly.

One of the darkest secrets of my life had been revealed, because, truth to tell, I had never had the damnedest idea which was right or left. It was a long story about being born left-handed and being made right-handed, more or less; the end result was a form of dyslexia in which my right hand not only never knew what my left was up to, it didn't even know it *was* my "right."

Harold listened in silence and after a moment of thought merely nodded. At the next set of rapids I sat taut as fence wire, hoping I could respond properly this time to the command so there would not be a Tom Rapids or McIntyre Maelstrom added to the map. As we started into the chute of boiling water I was waiting for the indecipherable shout of *"Right,"* when instead I heard Harold shouting *"Rifle side."* We sailed through as delicately as a fallen leaf.

Yet in spite of several ten- and twelve-hour days of canoeing on the Bigstone, we had, with the exception of one cow and her calf, yet to see a moose, and it was hard not to feel the deep lonesomeness of moose country when the object of your pursuit cannot be seen. I could feel the lonesomeness most when we would stand by a tumbled-down trapper's cabin on the bank where a man would have wintered in a low, windowless room, supplied with tea, flour, baking powder, and salt; two-pound tins of Roger's Golden Syrup and seventeen-cent ones of Club Chewing Tobacco; and whatever his rifle, traps, fishing line, nets, and berry bucket might provide, without the sound of a human voice other than his own from freeze up to spring thaw and with thoughts of the Windigo becoming all too real. I think even Harold and Gren, far more used to moose country than I, were feeling it, too, in their own ways.

On one of the last days all three of us were out in the canoe together. In the distance we heard a plane, and I remembered that it had been over a week since I had last heard one. Harold, keen student of military history that he was, lifted his paddle from the water and squinted skyward.

"What do you think, Grendel," I heard him ask. "Cargo plane? Or," he brightened noticeably, "maybe a heavy bomber come to put us out of our misery by dropping five-hundred-pound women on us!?" They both laughed, and so did I. Then the thought, Did I actually hear him say, *"Grendel"*? stopped me in midguffaw. I listened, then, to their laughter, and wondered if Windigos' sounded like that.

In spite of the lonesomeness, there were still moose to be found in this country. But like so many other wild animals, they were to be found mostly on their own terms.

A day before we were scheduled to fly out, Harold and I made one of our long moose-hunting circuits along the river. After a day of paddling, portaging, and running rapids, of driving and still-hunting through the nearly impenetrable mossy-floored stands of timber and tall willows, we found our way back to the last bend above camp. For an hour we sat while Harold called.

It was nearing last light and cloud cover had moved in to turn the day gray and misty—if this was not Windigo weather, then I didn't know what was. Having heard no answer to Harold's calling, we finally decided to make our way back to camp.

We were five or six hundred yards downriver when we heard the loud, splashing, boggy sound from the shore behind us. I had no idea what could make such a sound; but as we turned the canoe back upriver, I was wishing I had a few 300-grain silver bullets to complement the lead-and-gilding-metal ones loaded in my .375.

Then far ahead of us I could see a small feeder creek that ran into the Bigstone, with a beaver dam across its mouth. From the deep mud behind the dam that he had stumbled through with that loud noise, a perfectly fine bull moose pulled himself onto the bank. He stood a moment, dripping, then walked into the willows, moving upstream along the Bigstone.

Every so often a hump of brown fur or the oaken color of a wide antler palm could be seen above the yellow leaves, until about two hundred yards farther the bull walked out onto the open bank and stared across the river to the other side where several minutes before we had been sitting while Harold had called.

We were still out of range, but as I hooked my elbows over my knees and watched the bull through my 2½ Xscope, Harold's soundless paddling drew us incrementally closer.

"If he turns and looks at us," Harold whispered, "he'll be gone."

Still I waited. We had to get closer to make the shot sure. With agonizing slowness 500 yards was shrunk to 475. Then 450. At 425 the bull turned his giant head toward us and I could see the wide spread of his antlers. He was still too far. At 400 yards the bull turned away from us and the last I saw of him in the slow dying light of the North—having no choice but to let him go—was his heavy haunches as he walked off into the willows and the thick spruces beyond, gone with the Windigo into the most remote country of all.

Mister Howard Was a Real Gent

BY ROBERT C. RUARK

L IKE JACK LONDON, Robert Ruark was destined to become a writer of prodigious literary output, widespread popularity, and an early demise. When Ruark died of illness at age 50 in 1965, he had written five novels, a nonfiction safari account (*Horn of the Hunter*), enough magazine articles to fill a couple of anthologies, and the classic "The Old Man and the Boy" series that appeared in *Field & Stream* and was later collected into two books.

It is a fact that the "Old Man and the Boy" column in *Field & Stream* helped Ruark chuck his newspaper syndication column and pursue his research in Africa that produced the bestselling novel, *Something Of Value,* about the Mau-Mau uprising.

Set in North Carolina, where Ruark was raised and educated, all the "Old Man and the Boy" pieces are imminently readable, but this particular tale about the boy, his grandfather, and an interesting visitor is one of my favorites.

The week before Thanksgiving that year, one of the Old Man's best buddies came down from Maryland to spend a piece with the family, and I liked him a whole lot right from the start. Probably it was because he looked like the Old Man—ragged mustache, smoked a pipe, built sort of solid, and he treated me like I was grown up too. He was interested in 'most everything I was doing, and he admired my shotgun, and he told me a whole lot about the dogs and horses he had up on his big farm outside of Baltimore.

He and the Old Man had been friends for a whole lot of years, they had been all over the world, and they were always sitting out on the front porch, smoking and laughing quiet together over some devilment they'd been up to before I was born. I noticed they always shut up pretty quick when Miss

Lottie, who was my grandma, showed up on the scene. Sometimes, when they'd come back from walking down by the river, I could smell a little ripe aroma around them that smelled an awful lot like the stuff that the Old Man kept in his room to keep the chills off him. The Old Man's friend was named Mister Howard.

They were planning to pack up the dogs and guns and a tent and go off on a camping trip for a whole week, 'way into the woods behind Allen's Creek, about fifteen miles from town. They talked about it for days, fussing around with cooking gear, and going to the store to pick up this and that, and laying out clothes. They never said a word to me; they acted as if I wasn't there at all. I was very good all the time. I never spoke at the table unless I was spoken to, and I never asked for more than I ate, and I kept pretty clean and neat, for me. My tongue was hanging out, like a thirsty hound dog's. One day I couldn't stand it any longer.

"I want to go too," I said. "You promised last summer you'd take me camping if I behaved myself and quit stealing your cigars and didn't get drowned and—"

"What do you think, Ned?" Mister Howard asked the Old Man. "Think we could use him around the camp, to do the chores and go for water and such as that?"

"I dunno," the Old Man said. "He'd probably be an awful nuisance. Probably get lost and we'd have to go look for him, or shoot one of us thinking we were a deer, or get sick or bust a leg or something. He's always breaking something. Man can't read his paper around here for the sound of snapping bones."

"Oh, hell, Ned," Mister Howard said, "let's take him. Maybe we can teach him a couple of things. We can always get Tom or Pete to run him back in the flivver, if he don't behave."

"Well," the Old Man said, grinning, "I'd sort of planned to fetch him along all along, but I was waiting to see how long it'd take him to ask."

We crowded a lot of stuff into that old tin Liz. Mister Howard and the Old Man and me and two bird dogs and two hound dogs and a sort of fice dog who was death on squirrels and a big springer spaniel who was death on ducks. Then there were Tom and Pete, two kind of half-Indian backwoods boys who divided their year into four parts. They fished in the summer and hunted in the fall. They made corn liquor in the winter and drank it up in the spring. They were big, dark, lean men, very quiet and strong. Both of them always wore hip boots, in the town and in the woods, on the water or in their own back yards. Both of them worked for the Old Man when the fishing season was on and the pogies were running in big, red, fat-backed schools. They knew just about everything about dogs and woods and water and game that I wanted to know.

The back seat was full of dogs and people and cooking stuff and guns. There were a couple of tents strapped on top of the Liz, a big one and a small one. That old tin can sounded like a boiler factory when we ran over the bumps in the corduroy clay road. I didn't say anything as we rode along. I was much too excited; and anyhow, I figured they might decide to send me back home.

It took us a couple of hours of bumping through the long, yellow savanna-land hills before we came up to a big pond, about five hundred yards from a swamp, or branch, with a clear creek running through it. We drove the flivver up under a group of three big water oaks and parked her. The Old Man had camped there lots before, he said. There was a cleared-out space of clean ground about fifty yards square between the trees and the branch. And there was a small fireplace, or what had been a small fireplace, of big stones. They were scattered around now, all over the place. A flock of tin cans and some old bottles and such had been tossed off in the bush.

"Damned tourists," the Old Man muttered, unloading some tin pots and pans from the back of the car. "Come in here to a man's best place and leave it looking like a hogwallow. You, son, go pick up those cans and bury them some place out of my sight. Then come back here and help with the tents."

By the time I finished collecting the mess and burying it, the men had the tents laid out flat on the ground, the flaps fronting south, because there was a pretty stiff northerly wind working, and facing in the direction of the pond. Tom crawled under the canvas with one pole and a rope, and Pete lifted the front end with another pole and the other end of the rope. Mister Howard was behind with the end of Tom's rope and a peg and a maul. The Old Man was at the front with the end of Pete's rope and another stake and maul. The boys in the tent gave a heave, set the posts, and the two old men hauled taut on the ropes and took a couple of turns around the pegs.

The tent hung there like a blanket on a clothesline until Tom and Pete scuttled out and pegged her out stiff and taut from the sides. They pounded the pegs deep into the dirt, so that the lines around the notches were clean into the earth. It was a simple tent, just a canvas V with flaps fore and aft, but enough to keep the wet out. The other one went up the same way.

We didn't have any bedrolls in those days, or cots either. The Old Man gave me a hatchet and sent me off to chop the branches of the longleaf pine saplings that grew all around—big green needles a foot and a half long. While I was gone he cut eight pine stakes off an old stump, getting a two-foot stake every time he slivered off the stump, and then he cut four long oak saplings. He hammered the stakes into the ground inside the tent until he had a wide rectangle about six by eight feet. Then he split the tops of the stakes. He wedged two saplings into the stakes lengthwise, jamming them with the flat of the ax, and then he jammed two shorter saplings into the others, crosswise. He took four short lengths of heavy fishing cord and tied the saplings to the stakes, at each of the four corners, until he had a framework, six inches off the ground.

"Gimme those pine boughs," he said to me, "and go fetch more until I tell you to stop."

The Old Man took the fresh-cut pine branches, the resin still oozing stickily off the bright yellow slashes, and started shingling them, butt to the ground. He overlapped the needles like shingles on a house, always with the leaf end up and the branch end down to the ground. It took him about fifteen minutes, but when he finished he had a six-by-eight mattress of the spicy-smelling pine boughs. Then he took a length of canvas tarpaulin and arranged it neatly over the top. There were little grommet holes in each of the four corners, and he pegged the canvas tight over the tops of the saplings that confined the pine boughs. When he was through, you could hit it with your hand and it was springy but firm.

"That's a better mattress than your grandma's got," the Old Man said, grinning over his shoulder as he hit the last lick with the ax. "All it needs is one blanket under you and one over you. You're off the ground, and dry as a bone, with pine needles to smell while you dream. It's just big enough for two men and a boy. The boy gets to sleep in the middle, and he better not thrash around and snore."

By the time he was through and I had spread the blankets, Tom and Pete had made themselves a bed in the other tent, just the same way. The whole operation didn't take half an hour from stopping the car until both tents and beds were ready.

While we were building the beds Mister Howard had strung a line between a couple of trees and had tied a loop in the long leash of each dog, running the loop around the rope between the trees and jamming it with a square knot. The dogs had plenty of room to move in, but not enough to tangle up with each other, and not enough to start to fight when they got fed. They had just room enough between each dog to be sociable and growl at each other without starting a big rumpus. Pretty soon they quit growling and lay down quietly.

We had two big canvas water bags tied to the front of the flivver, and the Old Man gestured at them. "Boys have to handle the water detail in a man's camp," he said. "Go on down to the branch and fill 'em up at that little spillway. Don't roil up the water. Just stretch the necks and let the water run into the bags."

I walked down through the short yellow grass and the sparkleberry bushes to the branch, where you could hear the stream making little chuckling noises as it burbled over the rocks in its sandy bed. It was clear, brown water, and smelled a little like the crushed ferns and the wet brown leaves around it and in it. When I got back, I could hear the sound of axes off in a scrub-oak thicket, where Tom and Pete had gone to gather wood. Mister Howard was sorting out the guns, and the Old Man was puttering around with the stones where the fire marks were. He didn't look up.

"Take the hatchet and go chop me some kindling off that lighterd-knot stump," he said. "Cut 'em small, and try not to hit a knot and a chop off a foot. Won't need much, 'bout an armful."

When I got back with kindling, Tom and Pete were coming out of the scrub-oak thicket with huge, heaping armfuls of old dead branches and little logs as big as your leg. They stacked them neatly at a respectable distance from where the Old Man had just about finished his oven. It wasn't much of an oven—just three sides of stones, with one end open and a few stones at intervals in the middle. I dumped the kindling down by him, and he scruffed up an old newspaper and rigged the fat pine on top, in a little sharp-pointed tepee over the crumbled paper.

He put some small sticks of scrubby oak crisscross over the fat pine, and then laid four small logs, their ends pointing in to each other until they made a cross, over the stones and over the little wigwam of kindling he had erected. Then he touched a match to the paper, and it went up in a poof. The blaze licked into the resiny lightwood, which roared and crackled into flame, soaring in yellow spurts up to the other, stouter kindling and running eager tongues around the lips of the logs. In five minutes it was roaring, reflecting bright red against the stones.

The Old Man got up and kicked his feet out to get the cramp out of his knees. It was just on late dusk. The sun had gone down, red over the hill, and the night chill was coming. You could see the fog rising in snaking wreaths out of the branch. The frogs were beginning to talk, and the night birds were stirring down at the edge of the swamp. A whippoorwill tuned up.

" 'Bout time we had a little snort, Howard," the Old Man said. "It's going to be chilly. Pete! Fetch the jug!"

Pete ducked into his tent and came out with a half-gallon jug of brown corn liquor. Tom produced four tin cups from the nest of cooking utensils at the foot of the tree on which they had hung the water bags, and each man poured a half-measure of the whisky into his cup. I reckoned there must have been at least half a pint in each cup. Tom got one of the water bags and tipped it into the whisky until each man said, "Whoa." They drank and sighed. The Old Man cocked an eye at me and said, "This is for when you're bigger."

They had another drink before the fire had burned down to coal, with either Tom or Pete getting up to push the burning ends of the logs closer together. When they had a solid bed of coal glowing in the center of the stones, the Old Man heaved himself up and busied himself with a frying pan and some paper packages. He stuck a coffee pot off to one side, laid out five tin plates, dribbled coffee into the pot, hollered for me to fetch some water to pour into the pot, started carving up a loaf of bread, and slapped some big thick slices of ham into the frying pan.

When the ham was done, he put the slices, one by one, into the tin plates, which had warmed through from the fire, and laid slices of bread into the bubbling ham grease. Then he broke egg after egg onto the bread, stirred the whole mess into a thick bread-egg-and-ham-grease omelet, chopped the omelet into sections, and plumped each section onto a slice of ham. He poured the steaming coffee into cups, jerked his thumb at a can of condensed milk and a paper bag of sugar, and announced that dinner was served.

He had to cook the same mess three more times and refill the coffee pot before we quit eating. It was black dark, with no moon, when we lay back in front of the fire. The owls were talking over the whippoorwills, and the frogs were making an awful fuss.

The Old Man gestured at me. "Take the dirty dishes and the pans down to the branch and wash 'em," he said. "Do it now, before the grease sets. You won't need soap. Use sand. Better take a flashlight, and look out for snakes."

I was scared to go down there by myself, through that long stretch of grass and trees leading to the swamp, but I would have died before admitting it. The trees made all sorts of funny ghostly figures, and the noises were louder. When I got back, Mister Howard was feeding the dogs and the Old Man had pushed more logs on the fire.

"You better go to bed, son," the Old Man said. "Turn in in the middle. We'll be up early in the morning, and maybe get us a turkey."

I pulled off my shoes and crawled under the blanket. I heard the owl hoot again and the low mutter from the men, giant black shapes sitting before the fire. The pine-needle mattress smelled wonderful under me, and the blankets were warm. The fire pushed its heat into the tent, and I was as full of food as a tick. Just before I died I figured that tomorrow had to be heaven.

It was awful cold when the Old Man hit me a lick in the ribs with his elbow and said, "Get up, boy, and fix that fire." The stars were still up, frosty in the sky, and a wind was whistling round the corners of the tent. You could see the fire flicker just a mite against the black background of the swamp. Mister Howard was still snoring on his side of the pine-needle-canvas bed, and I remember that his mustache was riffling, like marsh grass in the wind. Over in Tom and Pete's tent you could hear two breeds of snores. One was squeaky, and the other sounded like a bull caught in a bob-wire fence. I crawled out from under the covers, shivering, and jumped into my hunting boots, which were stiff and very cold. Everything else I owned I'd slept in.

The fire was pretty feeble. It had simmered down into gray ash, which was swirling loosely in the morning breeze. There was just a little red eye blinking underneath the fine talcumy ashes. After kicking some of the ashes aside with my boot, I put a couple of lightwood knots on top of the little chunk of glowing coal, and then I dragged some live-oak logs over the top of the lightwood and waited for her to catch. She caught, and the tiny teeth of flame opened wide to eat the oak. In five minutes I had a blaze going, and I was practically in it. It was mean cold that morning.

When the Old Man saw the fire dancing, he woke up Mister Howard and reached for his pipe first and his boots next. Then he reached for the bottle and poured himself a dram in a tin cup. He shuddered some when the dram went down.

"I heartily disapprove of drinking in the morning," he said. "Except some mornings. It takes a man past sixty to know whether he can handle his liquor good enough to take a nip in the morning. Howard?"

"I'm past sixty too," Mister Howard said. "Pass the jug."

Tom and Pete were coming out of the other tent, digging their knuckles into sleepy eyes. Pete went down to the branch and fetched a bucket of water, and everybody washed their faces out of the bucket. Then Pete went to the fire and slapped some ham into the pan and some eggs into the skillet, set some bread to toasting, and put the coffee pot on. Breakfast didn't take long. We had things to do that day.

After the second cup of coffee—I can still taste that coffee, with the condensed milk sweet and curdled on the top and the coffee itself tasting of branch water and wood smoke—we got up and started sorting out the guns.

"This is a buckshot day," the Old Man said, squinting down the barrel of his pump gun. "I think we better get us a deer today. Need meat in the camp, and maybe we can blood the boy. Tom, Pete, you all drive the branch. Howard, we'll put the boy on a stand where a buck is apt to amble by, and then you and I will kind of drift around according to where the noise seems headed. One, t'other of us ought to get a buck. This crick is populous with deer."

The Old Man paused to light his pipe, and then he turned around and pointed the stem at me.

"You, boy," he said. "By this time you know a lot about guns, but you don't know a lot about guns and deer together. Many a man loses his wits when he sees a big ol' buck bust out of the bushes with a rockin' chair on his head. Trained hunters shoot each other. They get overexcited and just bang away into the bushes. *Mind* what I say. A deer ain't a deer unless it's got horns on its head and you can see all of it at once. We don't shoot does and we don't shoot spike bucks and we don't shoot each other. There ain't no sense to shootin' a doe or a young'un. One buck can service hundreds of does, and one doe will breed you a mess of deer. If you shoot a young'un, you haven't got much meat, and no horns at all, and you've kept him from breedin' to make more deer for you to shoot. If you shoot a man, they'll likely hang you, and if the man is me I will be awful gol-damned annoyed and come back to ha'nt you. You mind that gun, and don't pull a trigger until you can see what it is and *where* it is. *Mind,* I say."

Tom and Pete picked up their pump guns and loaded them. They pushed the load lever down so there'd be no shell in the chamber, but only in the magazine. The Old Man looked at my little gun and said, "Don't bother to load it until you get on the stand. You ain't likely to see anything to shoot for an hour or so."

Tom and Pete went over to where we had the dogs tethered on a line strung between two trees, and he unleashed the two hounds, Bell and Blue. Bell was black-and-tan and all hound. Blue was a kind of a sort of dog. He had some plain hound, some Walker hound, and some bulldog and a little beagle and a smidgen of pointer in him. He was ticked blue and brown and black and yellow and white. He looked as if somebody spilled the eggs on the checkered tablecloth. But he was a mighty dandy deer dog, or so they said. Old Sam Watts, across the street, used to say there wasn't no use trying to tell Blue anything, because Blue had done forgot more than you knew and just got annoyed when you tried to tell him his business.

Tom snapped a short lead on Blue, and Pete snapped another one on Bell. They shouldered their guns and headed up the branch, against the wind. We let 'em walk, while the Old Man and Mister Howard puttered around, like old people and most women will. Drives a boy crazy. What I wanted to do was go and shoot myself a deer. *Now.*

After about ten minutes the Old Man picked up his gun and said, "Let's go." We walked about half a mile down the swamp's edge. The light had come now, lemon-colored, and the fox squirrels were beginning to chase each other through the gum trees. We spied one old possum in a persimmon tree, hunched into a ball and making out like nobody knew he was there. We heard a turkey gobble away over yonder somewheres, and we could hear the doves beginning to moan—*oooh—oohoo—oooooh.*

All the little birds started to squeak and chirp and twitter at each other. The dew was staunchly stiff on the grass and on the sparkleberry and gallberry bushes. It was still cold, but getting warmer, and breakfast had settled down real sturdy in my stomach. Rabbits jumped out from under our feet. We stepped smack onto a covey of quail just working its way out of the swamp, and they like to have scared me to death when they busted up under our feet. There was a lot going on in that swamp that morning.

We turned into the branch finally, and came up to a track that the Old Man said was a deer run. He looked around and spied a stump off to one side, hidden by a tangle of dead brush. From the stump you could see clear for about fifty yards in a sort of accidental arena.

"Go sit on that stump, boy," the Old Man said. "You'll hear the dogs after a while, and if a deer comes down this branch he'll probably bust out there, where that trail comes into the open, because there ain't any other way he can cross it without leaving the swamp. Don't let the dogs fool you into not paying attention. When you hear 'em a mile away, the chances are that deer will be right in your lap. Sometimes they travel as much as two miles ahead of the dogs, just slipping along, not running; just slipping and sneaking on their little old quiet toes. And stay still. A deer'll run right over you if you stay still and the smell is away from him. But if you wink an eye, he can see it two hundred yards off, and will go the other way."

I sat down on the stump. The Old Man and Mister Howard went off, and I could hear them chatting quietly as they disappeared. I looked all around me. Nothing much was going on now, except a couple of he-squirrels were having a whale of a fight over my head, racing across branches and snarling squirrel cuss words at each other. A chickadee was standing on its head in a bush and making chickadee noises. A redheaded woodpecker was trying to cut a live-oak trunk in half with his bill. A rain crow—a kind of cuckoo, it is—was making dismal noises off behind me in the swamp, and a big old yellowhammer was swooping and dipping from tree to tree.

There were some robins hopping around on a patch of burnt ground, making conversation with each other. Crows were cawing, and two doves looped in to sit in a tree and chuckle at each other. A towhee was scratching and making more noise than a herd of turkeys, and some catbirds were meowing in the low bush while a big, sassy old mocker was imitating them kind of sarcastically. Anybody who says woods are quiet is crazy. You learn how to listen. The Tower of Babel was a study period alongside of woods in the early morning.

It is wonderful to smell the morning. Anybody who's been around the woods knows that morning smells one way, high noon another, dusk still another, and night most different of all, if only because the skunks smell louder at night. Morning smells fresh and flowery and little-breezy, and dewy and spanking new. Noon smells hot and a little dusty and sort of sleepy, when the breeze has died and the heads begin to droop and anything with any sense goes off into the shade to take a nap. Dusk smells scary. It is getting colder and everybody is going home tired for the day, and you can smell the turpentine scars on the trees and the burnt-off ground and the bruised ferns and the rising wind. You can hear the folding-up, I'm-finished-for-the-day sounds all around, including the colored boys whistling to prove they ain't scared when they drive the cows home. And in the night you can smell the fire and the warm blankets and the coffee a-boil, and you can even smell the stars. I know that sounds silly, but on a cool, clear, frosty night the stars have a smell, or so it seems when you are young and acutely conscious of everything bigger than a chigger.

This was as nice a smelling morning as I can remember. It smelled like it was going to work into a real fine-smelling day. The sun was up pretty high now and was beginning to warm the world. The dew was starting to dry, because the grass wasn't clear wet any more but just had little drops on top, like a kid with a runny nose. I sat on the stump for about a half-hour, and then I heard the dogs start, a mile or more down the swamp. Bell picked up the trail first, and she sounded as if church had opened for business. Then Blue came in behind her, loud as an organ, their two voices blending—fading sometimes, getting stronger, changing direction always.

Maybe you never heard a hound in the woods on a frosty fall morning, with the breeze light, the sun heating up in the sky, and the "aweful" expectancy that something big was going to happen to you. There aren't many things like it. When the baying gets closer and closer and still closer to you, you feel as if maybe you're going to explode if something doesn't happen quick.

And when the direction changes and the dogs begin to fade, you feel so sick you want to throw up.

But Bell and Blue held the scent firmly now, and the belling was clear and steady. The deer was moving steady and straight, not trying to circle and fool the dogs, but honestly running. And the noise was coming straight down the branch, with me on the other end of it.

The dogs had come so close that you could hear them panting between their bays, and once or twice one of them quit sounding and broke into a yip-yap of barks. I thought I could hear a little tippety-tappety noise ahead of them, in between the belling and the barking, like mice running through paper or a rabbit hopping through dry leaves. I kept my eyes pinned onto where the deer path opened into the clearing. The dogs were so close that I could hear them crash.

All of a sudden there was a flash of brown and two does, flop-eared, with two half-grown fawns skipped out of the brush, stopped dead in front of me, looked me smack in the face, and then gave a tremendous leap that carried them halfway across the clearing. They bounced again, white tails carried high, and disappeared into the branch behind me. As I turned to watch them go there was another crash ahead and the buck tore through the clearing like a race horse. He wasn't jumping. This boy was running like the wind, with his horns laid back against his spine and his ears pinned by the breeze he was making. The dogs were right behind him. He had held back to tease the dogs into letting his family get a start, and now that they were out of the way he was pouring on the coal and heading for home.

I had a gun with me and the gun was loaded. I suppose it would have fired if the thought had occurred to me to pull the trigger. The thought never occurred. I just watched that big buck deer run, with my mouth open and my eyes popped out of my head.

The dogs tore out of the bush behind the buck, baying out their brains and covering the ground in leaps. Old Blue looked at me as he flashed past and curled his lip. He looked as if he were saying, "This is man's work, and what is a boy doing here, spoiling my labor?" Then he dived into the bush behind the buck.

I sat there on the stump and began to shake and tremble. About five minutes later there was one shot, a quarter-mile down the swamp. I sat on the stump. In about half an hour Tom and Pete came up to my clearing.

"What happened to the buck?" Pete said. "Didn't he come past here? I thought I was going to run him right over you."

"He came past, all right," I said, feeling sick-mean, "but I never shot. I never even thought about it until he was gone. I reckon you all ain't ever going to take me along any more." My lip was shaking and now I *was* about to cry.

Tom walked over and hit me on top of the head with the flat of his hand. "Happens to everybody," he said. "Grown men and boys, both, they all get buck fever. Got to do it once before you get over it. Forget it. I seen Pete here shoot five times at a buck big as a horse last year, and missed him with all five."

There were some footsteps in the branch where the deer had disappeared, and in a minute Mister Howard and the Old Man came out, with the dogs leashed and panting.

"Missed him clean," the Old Man said cheerfully. "Had one whack at him no farther'n thirty yards and missed him slick as a whistle. That's the way it is, but there's always tomorrow. Let's us go shoot some squirrels for the pot, and we'll rest the dogs and try again this evenin'. You *see* him, boy?"

"I *saw* him," I said. "And I ain't ever going to *forget* him."

We went back to camp and tied up the hounds. We unleashed the fice dog, Jackie, the little sort of yellow fox terrier kind of nothing dog with prick ears and a sharp fox's face and a thick tail that curved up over his back. I was going with Pete to shoot some squirrels while the old gentlemen policed up the camp, rested, took a couple of drinks, and started to prepare lunch. It was pretty late in the morning for squirrel hunting, but this swamp wasn't hunted much. While I had been on the deer stand that morning the swamp was alive with them—mostly big fox squirrels, huge old fellers with a lot of black on their gray-and-white hides.

"See you don't get squirrel fever," the Old Man hollered over his shoulder as Pete and I went down to the swamp. "Else we'll all starve to death. I'm about fresh out of ham and eggs."

"Don't pay no 'tention to him, son," Pete told me. "He's a great kidder."

"Hell with him," I said. "He missed the deer, didn't he? At least *I* didn't miss him."

"That's right," Pete agreed genially. "You got to shoot at 'em to miss 'em."

I looked quick and sharp at Pete. He didn't seem to be teasing me. A cigarette was hanging off the corner of his lip, and his lean, brown, Injun-looking face was completely straight. Then we heard Jackie, yip-yapping in a querulous bark, as if somebody had just insulted him by calling him a dog.

"Jackie done treed hisself a squirrel," Pete said. "Advantage of a dog like Jackie is that when the squirrels all come down to the ground to feed, ol' Jackie rousts 'em up and makes 'em head for the trees. Then he makes so much noise he keeps the squirrel interested while we go up and wallop away at him. Takes two men to hunt squirrels this way. Jackie barks. I go around to the other side of the tree. Squirrel sees me and moves. That's when you shoot him, when he slides around on your side. Gimme your gun."

"Why?" I asked. "What'll I use to shoot the—"

"*Mine,*" Pete answered. "You ain't going to stand there and tell me you're gonna use a shotgun on a squirrel? Anybody can hit a pore little squirrel with a shotgun. Besides, shotgun shells cost a nickel apiece."

I noticed Pete's gun for the first time. He had left his pump gun in camp and had a little bolt-action .22. He took my shotgun from me and handed me the .22 and a handful of cartridges.

" 'Nother thing you ought to know," Pete said as we walked up to the tree, a big blue gum under which Jackie seemed to be going mad, "is that when you're hunting for the pot you don't belong to make much more noise with guns than is necessary. You go booming off a shotgun, blim-blam, and you spook ever'thing in the neighborhood. A .22 don't make no more noise than a stick crackin', and agin the wind you can't hear it more'n a hundred yards or thereabouts. Best meat gun in the world, a straight-shootin' .22, because it don't make no noise and don't spoil the meat. Look up yonder, on the fourth fork. There's your dinner. A big ol' fox squirrel, near-about black all over."

The squirrel was pasted to the side of the tree. Pete walked around, and the squirrel moved with him. When Pete was on the other side, making quite a lot of noise, the squirrel shifted back around to my side. He was peeping at Pete, but his shoulders and back and hind legs were on my side. I raised the little .22 and plugged him between the shoulders. He came down like a sack of rocks. Jackie made a dash for him, grabbed him by the back, shook him once and broke his spine, and sort of spit him out on the ground. The squirrel was dang near as big as Jackie.

Pete and I hunted squirrels for an hour or so, and altogether we shot ten. Pete said that was enough for five people for a couple of meals, and there wasn't no sense to shootin' if the meat had to spoil. "We'll have us some venison by tomorrow, anyways," he said. "One of us is bound to git one. You shot real nice with that little bitty gun," he said. "She'll go where you hold her, won't she?"

I felt pretty good when we went into camp and the Old Man, Mister Howard, and Tom looked up inquiringly. Pete and I started dragging fox squirrels out of our hunting coats, and the ten of them made quite a sizable pile.

"Who shot the squirrels?" the Old Man asked genially. "The dog?"

"Sure," Pete grinned. "Dog's so good we've taught him to shoot, too. We jest set down on a log, give Jackie the gun, and sent him off into the branch on his lonesome. We're planning to teach him to skin 'em and cook 'em, right after lunch. This is the best dog I ever see. Got more sense than people."

"Got more sense than *some* people," the Old Man grunted. "Come and git it, boy, and after lunch you and Jackie can skin the squirrels."

The lunch was a lunch I loved then and still love, which is why I'm never going to be called one of those epicures. This was a country hunting lunch, Carolina style. We had Vienna sausages and sardines, rat cheese, gingersnaps and dill pickles and oysterettes and canned salmon, all cold except the coffee that went with it, and that was hot enough to scald clean down to your shoes. It sounds horrible, but I don't know anything that tastes so good together as Vienna sausages and sardines and rat cheese and gingersnaps. Especially if you've been up since before dawn and walked ten miles in the fresh air.

After lunch we stretched out in the shade and took a little nap. Along about two I woke up, and so did Pete and Tom, and the three of us started to skin the squirrels. It's not much trouble, if you know how. Pete and I skinned 'em and Tom cleaned and dressed 'em. I'd pick up a squirrel by the head, and Pete would take his hind feet. We'd stretch him tight, and Pete would slit him down the stomach and along the legs as far as the feet. Then he'd shuck him like an ear of corn, pulling the hide toward the head until it hung over his head like a cape and the squirrel was naked. Then he'd just chop off the head, skin and all, and toss the carcass to Tom.

Tom made a particular point about cutting the little castor glands. Squirrel with the musk glands out is as tasty as any meat I know, but unless you take out those glands an old he-squirrel is as musky as a billy goat, and tastes like a billy goat smells. Tom cut up the carcasses and washed them clean, and I proceeded to bury the heads, hides, and guts.

The whole job didn't take forty-five minutes with the three of us working. We put the pieces of clean red meat in a covered pot, and then woke up the Old Man and Mister Howard. We were going deer hunting again.

The dogs had rested too; they had had half a can of salmon each and about three hours' snooze. It was beginning to cool off when Tom and Pete put Blue and Bell on walking leashes and we struck off for another part of the swamp, which made a Y from the main swamp and had a lot of water in it. It was a cool swamp, and Tom and Pete figured that the deer would be lying up there from the heat of the day, and about ready to start stirring out to feed a little around dusk.

I was in the process of trying to think about just how long forever was when the hounds started to holler real close. They seemed to be coming straight down the crick off to my right, and the crick's banks were very open and clear, apart from some sparkleberry and gallberry bushes. The *whoo-whoo-ing* got louder and louder. The dogs started to growl and bark, just letting off a *woo-woo* once in a while, and I could hear a steady swishing in the bushes.

Then I could see what made the swishing. It was a buck, a big one. He was running steadily and seriously through the low bush. He had horns—my Lord, but did he have horns! It look to me like he had a dead tree lashed to his head. I slipped off the safety catch and didn't move. The buck came straight at me, the dogs going crazy behind him.

The buck came down the water's edge, and when he got to about fifty yards I stood up and threw the gun up to my face. He kept coming and I let him come. At about twenty-five yards he suddenly saw me, snorted, and leaped to his left as if somebody had unsnapped a spring in him. I forgot he was a deer. I shot at him as you'd lead a duck or a quail on a quartering shot—plenty of lead ahead of his shoulder.

I pulled the trigger—for some odd reason shooting the choke barrel—right in the middle of a spring that had him six feet off the ground and must have been wound up to send him twenty yards, into the bush and out of my life. The gun said *boom!* but I didn't hear it. The gun kicked but I didn't feel it. All I saw was that this monster came down out of the sky like I'd shot me an airplane. He came down flat, turning completely over and landing on his back, and he never wiggled.

The dogs came up ferociously and started to grab him, but they had sense and knew he didn't need any extra grabbing. I'd grabbed him real good, with about three ounces of No. 1 buckshot in a choke barrel. I had busted his shoulder and busted his neck and dead-centered his heart. I had let him get so close that you could practically pick the wads out of his shoulder. This was *my* buck. Nobody else had shot at him. Nobody else had seen him but me. Nobody had advised or helped. This monster was mine.

And monster was right. He was huge, they told me later, for a Carolina whitetail. He had fourteen points on his rack, and must have weighed nearly 150 pounds undressed. He was beautiful gold on his top and dazzling white on his underneath, and his little black hoofs were clean. The circular tufts of hair on his legs, where the scent glands are, were bright russet and stiff and spiky. His horns were as clean as if they'd been scrubbed with a wire brush, gnarled and evenly forked and the color of planking on a good boat that's just been holy-stoned to where the decks sparkle.

I had him all to myself as he lay there in the aromatic, crushed ferns—all by myself, like a boy alone in a big cathedral of oaks and cypress in a vast swamp where the doves made sobbing sounds and the late birds walked and talked in the sparkleberry bush. The dogs came up and lay down. Old Blue laid his muzzle on the big buck's back. Bell came over and licked my face and wagged her tail, like she was saying, "You did real good, boy." Then she lay down and put her face right on the deer's rump.

This was our deer, and no damn bear or anything else was going to take it away from us. We were a team, all right, me and Bell and Blue.

I couldn't know then that I was going to grow up and shoot elephants and lions and rhinos and things. All I knew then was that I was the richest boy in the world as I sat there in the crushed ferns and stroked the silky hide of my first buck deer, patting his horns and smelling how sweet he smelled and admiring how pretty he looked. I cried a little bit inside about how lovely he was and how I felt about him. I guess that was just reaction, like being sick twenty-five years later when I shot my first African buffalo.

I was still patting him and patting the dogs when Tom and Pete came up one way and the Old Man and Mister Howard came up from another way. What a wonderful thing it was, when you are a kid, to have four huge, grown men—everything is bigger when you are a boy—come roaring up out of the woods to see you sitting by your first big triumph. "Smug" is a word I learned a lot later. Smug was modest for what I felt then.

"Well," the Old Man said, trying not to grin.

"Well," Mister Howard said.

"Boy done shot hisself a horse with horns," Pete said, as proud for me as if I had just learned how to make bootleg liquor.

"Shot him pretty good, too," Tom said. "Deer musta been standing still, boy musta been asleep, woke up, and shot him in self-defense."

"Was not, either," I started off to say, and then saw that all four men were laughing.

They had already checked the sharp scars where the buck had jumped, and they knew I had shot him on the fly. Then Pete turned the buck over and cut open his belly. He tore out the paunch and ripped it open. It was full of green stuff and awful smelly gunk. All four men let out a whoop and grabbed me. Pete held the paunch and the other men stuck my head right into—blood, guts, green gunk, and all. It smelled worse than anything I ever smelled. I was bloody and full of partly digested deer fodder from my head to my belt.

"That," the Old Man said as I swabbed the awful mess off me and dived away to stick my head in the crick, "makes you a grown man. You have been blooded, boy, and any time you miss a deer from now on we cut off your shirt tail. It's a very good buck, son," he said softly, "one of which you can be very, very proud."

Tom and Pete cut a long sapling, made slits in the deer's legs behind the cartilage of his knees, stuck the sapling through the slits, and slung the deer up on their backs. They were sweating him through the swamp when suddenly the Old Man turned to Mister Howard and said, "Howard, if you feel up to it, we might just as well go get *our* deer and lug him into camp. He ain't but a quarter-mile over yonder, and I don't want the wildcats working on him in that tree."

"What deer?" I demanded. "You didn't shoot this afternoon, and you missed the one you—"

The Old Man grinned and made a show of lighting his pipe. "I didn't miss him, son," he said. "I just didn't want to give you an inferiority complex on your first deer. If you hadn't of shot this one—and he's a lot better'n mine—I was just going to leave him in the tree and say nothing about him at all. Shame to waste a deer; but it's a shame to waste a boy, too."

I reckon that's when I quit being a man. I just opened my mouth and bawled. Nobody laughed at me, either.

Slim Boggins' Mistake

A LTHOUGH IT MAY safely be said of many college English pro-
fessors that while they may know a great deal about literature and
writers, few are capable of writing sprightly prose themselves.
"Cash and carry" prose, I choose to call it—the kind people will
pay money to read.

Such a charge cannot be laid at the desk of the late Havilah Babcock,
who wrote many of the most popular tales in outdoor literature during his years
as the head of the English Department of the University of South Carolina. Best
known for the many stories inspired by his passion for quail hunting, Babcock
also wrote interesting yarns on subjects ranging from chiggers to dogfish. His
popular collections of stories have been republished several times and include
Tales of Quail 'n Such and *My Health Is Better in November,* among others.

"Slim Boggins' Mistake" is a charming tale about a quail hunter who
learns what the father of choke boring, Fred Kimball, meant when he said, "To
hit is history. To miss is mystery."

A big covey exploded from the brown fern and went corkscrewing
through the tree-tops. Only a jumping-jack could have drawn bead on those
pettifogging politicians. I got one bird and thanked providence for its kindly
intercession.

"How did you come out?" I turned to my companion.

"Short and simple are the annals of the poor," he answered, glancing
wryly at the interlacing tree-tops. "When I zigged, they zagged. And vice versa.
There are too many bones in the human body for that sort of shooting. Even
my head got in my way."

Then as we stood by, explaining our misses to each other's entire
satisfaction, a fat cock lifted leisurely from the fern and loafed tantalizingly

away through the only opening in the thicket. We looked ruefully at our empty guns.

"Could have knocked him down with a second-hand washboard," was Cliff's unhappy comment. "Third time that's happened this morning. Hereafter I'm going to save a shell for the sleeper, so help me Hannah!"

I have never figured out the psychology of the sleeper, that saucy jackanapes who gets up belatedly and flies provokingly low and straight away while the gunner stands like a simpleton with an empty gravel-shooter. Is his tardy take-off due to wariness or to unwariness? Is he a dastardly fellow who deliberately lets his compatriots take the rap? Is he a slow-coach and addle-pated dunce who requires an extra interval to think things out? Or is he the Phi Beta Kappa of the class who figures thus to disadvantage the gunner?

That morning I was shooting indifferently because of the sleepless night I had spent. Regularly, for a quarter of a century, inability to sleep the night before has made a wreck of me on Thanksgiving, the traditional opening day for quail in South Carolina. I doubt that I have slept twenty-five winks in twenty-five years during that particular night.

I count everything that can jump a fence or go through a gap, and wear out every sleep-inducing device known. "I could be bounded in a nut-shell and count myself a king of infinite space were it not that I had bad dreams," I quote Shakespeare, who was something of a hunter himself.

"Tomorrow is an important day," I spend the night reminding myself. "If I don't get some sleep, I'll feel like the wreck of the Hesperus and shoot worse than a constipated owl with a crooked shotgun." Maybe I make it too important. I'm a bird hunter, not a psychologist. Finally, I deliver an ultimatum to my uncooperative body: "Now, damn your hide, you can sleep or stay awake just as you like, but you are going to catch the devil tomorrow and you needn't expect any sympathy from me. So if I were you—"

You'd think an old codger like me would have too much gumption to behave like this. But if you are a born bird hunter and had rather hunt birds than do anything else on this slightly flattened and somewhat cock-eyed globe, you might discover in your heart a modicum of sympathy.

For twenty-five years I have hunted with the same companion, which must establish some sort of record for mutual tolerance! Now, there are both advantages and disadvantages in having the same side-kick so long. We know the idiosyncrasies of our dogs, which enhances the pleasure of the hunt. We also know the idiosyncrasies of each other, which *sometimes* enhances the pleasure of the hunt.

During twenty-five years of companionship any two men will accumulate a fund of experiences to talk about, but long association tends to reduce the necessity of conversation. We know each other so well that we don't have to talk. A monosyllable may effect a meeting of minds, a meaningful glance may recall some experience memorable to both. Even a wide grin becomes an adequate reminder.

But such intimate companionship makes bragging next to impossible. How can you embroider some past exploit with glowing details if your audience was there when it happened? It's like gilding the lily in the presence of your mother-in-law, like having an extra conscience always following you around.

"No man is a hero to his valet," remarked Carlyle. And seldom to his hunting companion. When I inventory my deficiencies as a side-kick, I realize that only a great and magnanimous gentleman would put up with me for twenty-five years. But calling Cliff a gentleman doesn't keep him from bossing me around at times.

"Havilah!" his voice boomed through the flatwoods. "Why don't you quit wool-gathering and look after your dog?"

Fleet, my sedate little setter, was trailing in a patch of beggar's-lice near a cornfield. Cliff's slim-legged pointer raced in, verified Fleet's discovery, and seconded the motion. But neither was dead yet. Every quail dog has some mannerism that advertises the proximity of game and tells the discerning owner how the quest is progressing.

I never cock a gun over Fleet, however imminent things look, until her merry tail stiffens and curls at the tip. Cliff never slips the safety over Carrie until her right hind foot is lifted gingerly from the ground. The beggar's-lice was seven feet tall and seed showered down as we passed through.

"Why do people import food for birds when this native beggar's-lice is unbeatable? There's enough food here for ten coveys," remarked Cliff.

"True," I replied. "But in a few weeks it will be plowed under. After all, that's the greatest single enemy of quail—the plow."

At the far end of the patch both dogs dropped dead, a big bevy hurtled up, and we downed three birds on the rise. One of the secrets of bird hunting is marking the flight of a decamping covey, an art at which Cliff is especially adept. But this time we both saw it: fully twenty birds deploying beautifully in the broomstraw 350 yards away.

"Lovely! Lovely!" rhapsodized Cliff. "The enchanted dream of every bird hunter. Your masterpieces of art, your fabled beauties of the boudoir, your deathless symphonies—what can hold a candle to a picture like this?"

"First one like that I've seen for quite a spell," I admitted, "except on a patent-medicine calendar."

"Button up your shootin' britches and shake a leg," Cliff relapsed into English. "Let's go down and take up collection before they start socializin' and get together."

We did. And that's one of the things I like about quail shooting in the Carolina low country: You can usually see where your birds go down. That is, approximately where. I don't mean you can saunter nonchalantly down and spit on their tails, and I'm not guaranteeing you can hit them when you get there. That's a horse of another complexion.

But the gunner's vision is often unobstructed for a quarter of a mile, and he gets at least a general idea as to the line of flight. He doesn't have to tramp over half a county to exhaust the possibilities, as he must often do in broken terrain where singles shooting is little more than a process of elimination: you just look everywhere they *could* have flown.

This flat country is also friendly to my aging legs. Indeed, my old underpinnings have a deep affection for the gentle terrain of this half-forgotten kingdom. But how they do argue and upbraid me when they have to propel my *corpus delicti* up and down the red hills of my native Virginia, as they do ten days every season! Yes, mine is definitely a flat-country species of leg.

I like the low-country too because it is unfenced—one of the few unenclosed and unspoiled provinces left on the map. It is said that barbed-wire did more to tame the Wild West than did the six-guns of the United States marshals, but I don't want anything tamed. Don't fence me in! On the sprawling plantations I can walk or ride the livelong day without encountering a single fence. Yes, sir, I've hunted bobwhite over a fair segment of his range, and I'll take mine in the South Carolina low-country every time.

"By the way," I asked after we had pocketed enough singles from the beggar's-lice bevy, "where was Timrod while the other dogs were trailing back there? I completely forgot the pup."

"Timrod was excusin' himself from the proceedings," laughed Cliff. "He stalked stiff-legged forty yards behind the other dogs, with his ears pricked up and an awfully worried look on his face. He figured something was going to pop, and he didn't want to be caught with his suspenders down."

Carrie is Cliff's dog, and Fleet is mine, but Timrod, a six-month-old setter pup, is *our* dog. We had taught him the backyard rudiments before the season opened, but this was his first day in school, his maiden voyage afield. Nearly every season we have a stripling coming along, not only as an eventual replacement, but for the pleasure of watching a youngster discover himself. We have a theory too that teaching a pup his a-b-c's keeps a hunter's heart young.

A mighty hunter is Timrod, and the world is full of wonderful things to be pointed. During the morning he must have pointed a full twenty times, stretching out on everything from stink sparrows to terrapins. And at noon he wound up in a blaze of glory by dropping as dead as chiseled granite on a yoke of oxen plowing in a field.

Not only have I hunted for twenty-five years with the same companion, but over the same territory, and in many instances the identical coveys themselves. Indeed, it would not be inaccurate to say that I have been shooting at the same birds for a quarter of a century! Successive generations have brought me both pleasure and embarrassment. Bob is a durable fellow and a great begetter of his kind. And he is a stable freeholder who sticks to the old homestead as long as it remains congenial to his tenancy.

Down through the years many of these coveys have earned pet names for themselves, such as Lazy Mule, Barking Dog, Foolish Virgins, Mother-in-Law, Po' Chance and Handshake. Years ago—it must have been in the late 'twenties—Cliff and I each downed three birds with a single shot and spent the rest of the afternoon admiring each other. It was an epic event, one enshrined in the memory of two men who are no longer spring chickens. Thus the covey we still call Handshake won a niche in our affections.

There are practical advantages in hunting the same territory and the same coveys year after year. We have learned the flight habits of many families, and how to dispose ourselves to best advantage before a rise. We have learned their range, their probable feeding ground and their sanctuaries, because we have read their diaries from season to season. We know when and where to hunt a particular covey. Such information can be a very present help in time of need.

It was in the Po' Chance country that we found ourselves on Thanksgiving afternoon, and here we ran into one Slim Boggins, a neighborhood character, famed for his shooting prowess and not in the least averse to demonstrating it.

"Have you gents ever heard of a fellow who can drap fo' birds on a rise?" he pushed his cap back and asked.

We didn't think we had. With an occasional fluke shot maybe, but certainly not with any measure of consistency. Was there such a fellow?

"You air talkin' to him now. Slim Boggins by name. My ole she-bitch is trailin' yonder. Come on over and I'll give y'all a demonstratin'."

Striding loose-jointedly behind his dog, he kicked up a covey and neatly dropped four birds on a simultaneous flush. Furthermore, he made it look easy, almost inevitable, in fact.

"That air is what I mean, gents. And I ain't usin' no fancy autymatic neither. Jes' this here ole flippity-flop pump gun. Shucks, 'tain't nothin'," he discounted.

I looked at Cliff and Cliff looked at me, and we conveyed a lot without saying anything. This cocky, self-contained and unbookish fellow, this gangling son of the swamp, was the nearest thing to a natural shot we had ever seen. And the ancient pump which he fondled was as nerveless and supple-jointed as its owner. Never tell me that a repeater can't compete with an automatic in speed!

"Two birds fromped down in that broomstraw yonder. Come on over and I'll give you gents another demonstratin'," our uninvited guest announced.

A few minutes later the gaunt "ole she-bitch" pointed and her gangling master beckoned to us. "Now I'll th'ow this ole gun on the ground till the birds get up. Then I'll grab her and politely drap 'em both."

Two birds hurtled away toward a pine thicket. Slim swooped down, retrieved his gun and dropped them both. And they were as dead as a quarter past four when they hit.

" 'Taint' nothin'," he manfully deprecated. "Also shoots 'em from the hip. If you gents want a free sample—"

Cliff and I were impressed by this backwoods paragon. We were also scared. If this "demonstratin' " kept up, there would be precious few birds left in Po' Chance. This two-legged epidemic that called himself Slim Boggins had to be curbed in some way.

With his usual resourcefulness, Cliff launched the attack. A flank attack it proved to be, and its very simplicity at first baffled me.

"Most wonderful shooting we have ever seen, and we are indebted to you for the exhibition," Cliff laid the groundwork. "It probably won't improve our shooting any, but may I ask you one question?"

"Shore, shore. Anything to oblige," expansively offered our Mr. Boggins.

"Do you practice monocular or binocular shooting?"

"Says how much?" Slim blinked.

"Do you shoot with one eye closed, or with both open?" Cliff pursued.

"Aw, that. Funny thing, I ain't never noticed. Never crossed my mind till you brung it up. Funny, ain't it? Tell you what, I'll take notice and let you gents know. It mout help y'all some. That's me, Slim Boggins."

Fleet had a single at the base of a cypress stump. I raised my gun, but Cliff shook his head. The bird flew as straight as a martin to its gourd. Slim raised his gun and confidently banged away. Then he banged again, but the bird reached the haven of the swamp untouched. A frown of perplexity gathered on Slim's face, but it was quickly dissipated.

"Shucks. Had my left eye closed that time. That ain't the way I been doing it. I shoot with both eyes open. It's come to me now. Show you gents next time," he quickly reassured himself.

A few minutes later Carrie froze at the edge of a pea-patch. Two birds got up and sauntered straight down main street. Slim pumped away four times, but nary a feather did he cut. Stock-still he stood, enveloped in an awful silence. The shadow of amazed disbelief crept over his face. Picking up an empty cartridge, he absently fingered it, then shook his head as if to dispel a grisly vision.

"Great balls of fire! I helt both eyes open that time. That must not be the way I do it either!"

An awful doubt had insinuated itself into the soul of Slim Boggins. He eyed his dog distrustfully and regarded his faithful old pump with new-found suspicion, as if the wife of his bosom had unaccountably betrayed him.

"Jes' happened to think," he explained limply. "Got fo' cows to milk when I get home. If you gents will excuse me—" And he sloped off across the field.

That's the last we saw of Slim Boggins. But not the last we heard. A hundred yards away he must have stepped into a single, because we heard a rapid succession of shots and then, "Great balls of fire!" Three hundred yards away another fusillade rent the air, and the word "fire!" resounded through the hushed flatwoods and died away in the swamp.

"Cliff, the devil's going to get you for sure!" I said. "For a trick like that, your carcass should be hanged, quartered and dried on a 'simmen bush. Besides, there's a constitutional amendment about cruel and unusual punishments."

"I haven't done a thing, not a blessed thing!" Cliff protested with a twinkle discernible at fifty feet. "Our Mister Boggins just made the mistake of thinking. He shot well because he shot unconsciously, in a manner of speaking. He was not handicapped by a college education. But he made the mistake of thinking, and that's sometimes fatal. Now let that teach you a lesson, son," he admonished with a solemn chuckle.

"Well, our friend will recover in time, but chances are he won't insist on demonstrating to us again," I said. "And these Po' Chance birds will give you the thanks of the republic. They've had enough for one day. We have only an hour or so before dark. Let's amble over to the Mother-in-Law covey and see how they fared this summer."

It was in the Mother-in-Law country that Timrod won his spurs. These birds are great gadabouts, and it was nearing nightfall before Carrie and Fleet found their names on the society page. Then they trailed across a bog, through a field of wild partridge-peas, and into an uncultivated strip fingering out from the swamp. There both dogs came to a peremptory halt.

But we instantly lowered our guns and looked at each other for swift confirmation. There, slightly ahead of the other dogs, was little Timrod on point. He had intercepted the homeward-bound covey and pinned it down in the brown cinnamon fern, under whose friendly canopy Bob so loves to doze. And there stood Timrod, with both eyes resolutely shut, rigid as a bisque figurine.

"I'll just be damned!" breathed Cliff. "Do you see what I see?"

"Shut up! Ain't you got no manners?" I grinned back.

As we eased forward Timrod covertly opened his eyes and glanced at Carrie, his guardian and preceptor. Her right hind foot delicately scorned the ground. Carefully Timrod lifted his foot to conform. Carrie's muzzle angled sharply to the left. Timrod, who had been manfully pointing the whole world more or less, shifted his muzzle to match. Then he sort of looked over his glasses at us and ventured: "Is this something like it, *mister?*"

Lowering his gun, Cliff nodded to me and lifted one finger. I shot once at the scudding bevy, and we held the other dogs while Timrod proudly retrieved the bird. Then we danced a jig around the newest member of our family, playfully pommeled him in the fern and called him "old horse." The starry-eyed Timrod pranced around and yipped his great pleasure. "Come on, let's find some more!" he barked.

"We've got a dog in the family now," Cliff said. "When you get home, write that down in your diary."

And I did. I wrote: "On this day Timrod, a pup of whom I have high hopes, graduated from the first grade and received his diploma."

It was nightfall now, and the hunt was over. Another Thanksgiving had come and gone. It had been a pleasant but somewhat arduous day, and as I climbed gratefully into the car I fervently sighed: "May the Lord be thanked for putting a night between every two days!"

The Black Death

BY PETER HATHAWAY CAPSTICK

A MONG THE COUNTLESS books of African big game hunting adventures, none that I can ever remember have vaulted into best-sellerdom with the kind of leap Peter Capstick's *Death in the Long Grass* achieved back in 1977. Splendidly written, bristling with the drama of very real hunting danger, Capstick's book sold like no other. Then, decisively proving that *Long Grass* was no fluke, Peter Capstick followed through with *Death in Silent Places, Death on the Dark Continent, Death in a Lonely Land,* and several other titles, published by St. Martin's Press. All were eagerly snapped up by readers won over by Capstick's engaging prose.

"The Black Death" is about the animal many white hunters have always considered the most dangerous of all, the Cape buffalo. The piece is included in *Death in a Lonely Land,* published by St. Martin's in 1990. That book also includes a piece Peter wrote for me when I was editing *Sports Afield* in 1973 called, "Anything the 20-Gauge Can Do, the 12 Can Do Better." That one really made the fur fly!

As corpses go, it was a real humdinger, the kind even a big-city coroner wouldn't forget in a hurry. It hung fifteen feet in the air above me, draped like a torn mannequin over the spiked branch of yellow acacia. My thumb instinctively slipped onto the safety of the Evans .470 Nitro Express double rifle. Literally dead center, smack through the solar plexus, was a hole large enough to accommodate a fair-sized pumpkin if you shooed off the hundreds of iridescent green flies and white maggots swarming over the torn mess. Two days of hanging in the searing sun and spring humidity hadn't been especially beneficial to the general odor of the immediate area.

I started Invisible, my Number Two man, scraping away a shallow grave. Silent, my ancient, gnome-like Awiza gunbearer cut a sapling and pushed the dead man from his grisly perch to land with a foul thump beneath the tree. The ground was mostly rockless, sandy clay, so we covered the grave with staked-down mounds of the meanest thorn bushes we could find to keep the hyenas and jackals from invading the poor man's privacy.

The spoor told the whole tale as simply and clearly as a Dick-and-Jane book. A mangled, smooth-bore muzzle-loader lay fifty yards away, the fired percussion cap still pinched in place between the hammer and nipple. The wire-bound stock and barrel looked ready to be stamped into scrap. We retraced the big, splayed hoofprints easily to a shadowy stand of thick mopane, where the two old Cape buffalo bulls had stood, dozing away the afternoon heat. The splintered end of a sap-oozing twig showed where the bullet had clipped it before it went on to slam into meat—too far back, by the look of the dried blood. Probably guts or stomach. The wounded bull had immediately charged, while the second had run off a few yards and stood, confused. The hunter, a Senga tribesman whose name we later learned was Fantastic, had dropped the gun and run for the shelter of the big tree. He was still ten feet short when the bull smashed into him, shoving what was probably the right horn completely through the man's chest, back to front. The unbelievable power of the charge's impact had, by the look of the wound's diameter, pushed the horn clear up to the base. Then the toss had thrown him free, straight up to where he happened to land across the branch, probably already dead of a crushed spine.

Then the bull had stopped, probably perplexed that the man was no longer in sight. For what must have been several minutes, he charged here and there before he smelled or saw the blood leaking down and spotted the body. From a point some four feet above the trampled ground, the bark had been bludgeoned and torn from the tree where the bull charged it, repeatedly trying to knock the man free. But the cruel thorns held the dead man, and the bull gave up, returning to the dropped gun, which he proceeded to pulverize until he wandered off with his pal to nurse the terrible pain in his guts.

It was now my job to track him down, root him out of the thick stuff, and stamp him "canceled." As Game and Elephant Control Officer of the district, it was my responsibility to kill him before he bumped into some poor beggar and put on his act again. Having been in on the demise of something around one thousand Cape buffalo, or *M'bogo,* as he's called in KiSwahili, or *Inyati* in Fanagalo, the central and southern African equivalent catchall language, I knew enough not to be very keen on the idea.

At first light the next morning, we broke camp and immediately made for the Lundazi River on foot. As is my custom, I carried the .470 myself at any time visibility was less than one hundred yards. Silent tracked ahead, looking for spoor, while I covered him by watching the sides and far front. Invisible, just behind me, carried the water bag and my extra cartridges and iron ration provisions for at least one night in case we had to sleep on the trail.

We cut spoor after about an hour of hunting, that of a pair of bulls for sure, leading from the water's edge and then back at a lazy angle into the heavy bush. I very much wish somebody would come up with a more appropriate term that I could plagiarize. "Heavy bush" simply does not fairly describe the vegetable morass of almost solid growth that lines the Lundazi to a depth of three hundred yards from its banks. It's rather like calling Rocky Marciano a sissy. Visibility is not measured in yards, but often in fractions of feet.

My tracker has found a lovely pile of near-steaming pasture-patty, not even glazed over. You stick your finger into it and discover it's not fifteen minutes old. It also contains, you note with no little interest, large, dark clots of blood mixed in with the fecal material. Guess who.

We follow the spoor for another forty yards until a very convenient, thigh-thick sapling appears. As you cover the bush ahead, Silent, who is well named, sneaks silently up the trunk until he is twenty feet above the tops of the surrounding ground cover. An errant swirl of wind doesn't do much for your confidence as you steal a glance up at him. He's staring hard at something, obviously indistinct, about fifty yards off. It seems like two weeks before he points with his chin and holds out two fingers; then a single finger up and another down. One bull is standing, the other lying down. Pointing a line of direction, he looks expectantly down at you. Go get 'em, boy. Oh, me, oh, my. Silent, who is not stupid, will stay in the tree where you can see him, giving signals if the buffalo move. Like straight at you.

Following his pointed azimuth, you snick the safety off the Evans and begin creeping forward, picking each step in slow motion, walking on the outside edges of your sockless desert boots. After ten yards, you look back at Silent, who simply nods. Still there. Ahead, there is nothing but the shadowy tangles of branches, leaves, and grass woven more densely than an Oriental rug. Every few yards you lie flat, trying to pick out the silhouette of a leg or the movement of a flicked tail or ear. Nope. You'd think that a couple of critters that push a ton or so would at least crack a twig or swish a leaf; maybe even break wind or something. Not bloody likely. You pause for a moment to persuade your heart to stop pounding so loud you couldn't hear an express train if it was coming right at you. Fear and raw nerves make you sweat, and your legs feel like spaghetti. You're not scared, you're terrified motherless.

Then an astonishingly familiar bovine odor smacks you in the face. And you realize you can hear the flies! You freeze into an idiotic statue, one foot off the ground. When you can smell them and even hear the flies, you have a fair hunch they're not awfully far away. Your sweat-stinging eyes probe every inch of alternating light and shadow ahead and to the sides as you try to lower your leg without losing your balance. That would be cute! A step. Another. Where are they? You want to shoot them, not take them prisoner!

Then it's there, its very size making it nearly invisible in the dappled play of sun. But what is it? Well, you reason, if it smells like a Cape buffalo, makes tracks and droppings like one, draws flies and has a big slab of grayish-black hide with sparse bristles near enough to count, then it is fairly reasonable to assume it *is* a Cape buffalo. Or, at the very least, *part* of a Cape buffalo. But which part and which one? You don't want to cash in the unwounded one unless you have to. Long, very long, seconds creak and crawl by as you strain to figure out what you are looking at and whether it's the end that bites. Maybe just another few steps closer. At six yards—African yards are much shorter than the ones used to measure American football fields—your brain slips into panic overdrive. From between two leaves, a single, baleful eye is staring right at the center of your stomach. That's all, boys. You don't get paid *that* much. At eighteen feet, you couldn't give a howl in hell which bull it is. Hopefully, he doesn't yet realize what he's looking at either, so now's your chance. With the sneakiest possible movement, you level the Evans. The ivory bead mates with the vee of the single express rear leaf; hold slightly over the eye and squeeze off.

The muzzle blast smothers any sound of bullet strike, and for an incredible millisecond there is silence. It is, however, a mini-millisecond because now the air is alive with shouts from Silent, very unsociable grunts from a couple of feet away, and the noise of the radical rearrangement of some local flora. The second bull, whichever one he is, has unquestionably had his attention gotten and is charging, bearing down invisibly through the heavy bush with an irresistible power that is hair-raisingly awesome. You jump a few yards to your left as he breaks cover, exactly where you were standing, attacking the sound of the hated gun. He is clearly not very happy with you.

The reflex that has kept you alive through all these uninsurable years in a never exactly dull business has the .470 doing its little act all by itself. As he swings toward you—head high, changing direction—a charming, white-edged hole appears between his eyes, right at the base of his big, black, wet nose. He's hardly hit the ground, blood pouring from his ears, before the Evans is broken and new rounds chambered. Another solid throws a puff of dust from the back of his neck. Sure he's down for the count, you spin and level the rifle back at the place where that spooky eye was, holding it in its marvelous balance by the pistol grip, index finger on the second trigger, while you fish out another cigar-sized cartridge from your pocket with your left hand and reload the fired chamber.

You need not have bothered. The first bull is lying where he dropped, the solid slug neatly through his left eye as he looked at you. He's as dead as your innocence and the tax shelter combined, but, even though .470 Kynochs are worth their weight in sterling silver, you stick to the rule that's kept you ambulatory and swat him in the nape of the neck anyway.

The urge for a cigarette and a long, absolutely obscene scotch are overwhelming as you sit down ten yards away. You manage the cigarette on the third try, just as Silent and Invisible come up wholesaling the usual *"eeeeehhhs"* and *"aaaaahhhhs"* of the excited bush African.

When we had the bulls rolled over, and the fat, red ticks were beginning to drop off the crotch area, sensing death, we were able to determine that it was the second bull that had been wounded. Silent dug out a wicked chunk of iron reinforcing rod that had passed through five coils of intestine and lodged against the far skin's inside. The people in this part of the world have great imagination when it comes to ammunition. A couple of feet forward, and it would have been a fine lung shot and the late, lamented Fantastic would have been the village hero.

By the time we had taken the interior fillets and tails for table fare, as well as the ears to turn in to the government, the circle of human vultures had moved in. They had likely been following us from the village all day, waiting for the sound of my shots. When we finished the walk back to the Rover, I took a healthy belt of scotch, grilled some of the fillets, and spent the rest of the day driving back to base camp. I certainly hadn't enjoyed the business of following up somebody else's wounded buffalo, I reflected as the hunting car rocked and scraped along the light bush track, but it sure as hell beat the *real* fight for survival, back in civilization.

Out On the Land

BY CHARLES FERGUS

WHEN LYONS AND Burford published Charles Fergus' *A Rough Shooting Dog* in 1991, I immediately told Nick Lyons that I thought the book was very special. A collection of warm and insightful chronicles of Fergus' hunts with his springer spaniel, the book today has lost none of the enchantment I first felt when I discovered it.

The "Rough Shooting" title is derived from the English hunting expression "Rough Shoot," which is what the Brits call the type of shoot where one works a piece of country to bag whatever legal game one can kick up.

This particular chapter is typical of what you can expect throughout the book and happens to be one of my favorites.

To be out on the land in all weathers, the gun barrels warm in the sun or shelved with snow or beaded with rain, the light wan or blazing, the wind rattling leaves down the hollow that yesterday brimmed with fog; to be out among stones and trees and streams, among the animals who reside here day in and day out: grouse and pheasants, deer and bear, rabbits and squirrels—and the ones who steal in mysteriously, the ducks and the woodcock, arriving by night from unknown origins and bound for unknown destinations; to be out on the land with a silent companion whose boundless, instinctive energy clarifies and intensifies one's own; to listen as fall segues into winter, to walk upon one short segment of the ever-repeating cycle; to come home fully spent, empty-handed or bearing food for the table; to sit by the fire and feel the day dying down: This is what it is to hunt. This is what it is to live.

On the way in the truck, in thick fog, the radio warned: "Watch your step out there."

John's Quarter was dotted with dried chalk and devoid of woodcock. We left and drove back through Port Matilda, the town's shabbiness effaced by the fog, a golden yellow light wreathing Lyken's Market, where shadowy figures attended the gas pumps. We drove past fields, the harvest equipment silent, looming—past country churches with their bordering cemeteries—past muddy farmyards where white chickens huddled—and turned up a side road toward Bogsucker Flats.

The old house stood shuttered up. It looked like an outcropping in the fog, beneath the two giant spruces that were once tame front-yard plantings but now towered up and over the small dwelling, shutting it away from the light. I loaded up. At the wave of my hand, she was hunting. All was well. Dew covered the ground, and the fog trapped the scent near the earth. We went among aspen and alder and musclewood; the trees, coated with mist, looked like they were sweating.

Things had settled between us. Jenny did not always perform as I wanted her to, and she was still a lot of dog to handle, but we had begun communicating more clearly. I had not defeated her impetuosity, and she had not defeated my insistence on rules and order. We were in something of a convivial stalemate out of which a certain efficiency was arising. Concerning the matter of heeling, for instance: We had reached agreement that "heel" in the bird coverts was different from "heel" on the sidewalk; on the hunting ground it was permissible to mess around in a circle some ten yards in diameter, with the master at the center, and still be considered at heel. I had gotten her to quit running after missed birds, and had even hupped her on the hot trail of a grouse, that I might get ready for the shot.

We hunted through the dripping goldenrod and thistle. The fog swirled. I glanced back toward the house, but only the sentinel spruces could be discerned, twin dark shafts tapering into a milk sky.

Bogsucker Flats. Simply my name for it; if others hunt the covert, no doubt they know it by different cognomens. Ten years ago, a friend and I had driven up the winding gravel road, prospecting for new hunting grounds. The colors were falling in earnest, and my friend's large, unruly pointer kept lunging and snapping at the spinning orange and yellow leaves as they slapped the pickup's windshield.

We both knew it for woodcock cover the moment we saw it: alders and aspens in a wet swale with a stream running through it.

The chimney was smoking, so we stopped to ask permission. The house was sided with red and green asphalt octagons, many of them curling. We picked our way across a porch strewn with yellowing stacks of newspapers, a rusted bicycle, crates, grimy canning jars, overturned chairs. I reached in through the torn screen of the outer door and knocked on the inner one. Scrapes and bumpings could be heard from inside. The door opened and an old man peered out, blinking against the light. He was stooped and thin, clad in slippers and a frayed bathrobe. On his head sat a straw hat consisting mainly of a brim, the crown having raveled away. White whiskers covered his chin and issued from the vents of his ears. Above sunken cheeks, his eyes were clouded and suspicious.

"We were wondering," I said, "if we could hunt for woodcock out back."

"Wood cock?" He said it slowly, mistrustfully, a tentative weight on each word.

"Woodcock. The little brown birds—" I held my thumb and forefinger apart "—with the long bills."

The old man pursed his lips. Slowly they parted in a sneer. "Bogsuckers?" He dismissed us with a wave of his bony hand. "Go ahead. Clean 'em out."

We did not clean them out, not that day, although we did bag several woodcock and were outsmarted by a big cock grouse. Every year since, I've gone back. I've never stopped at the house, not wishing to meet that troubled and troubling old soul. Recently I told this to my neighbor, who said he had known the old man. A drunkard, a hellion in his younger days, never married, finally left alone in his dotage; a year or more ago, he wandered down to the highway one night and was killed.

Halfway into the covert, we had found no birds and no chalk. I sat on a log and told Jenny to take a rest. "Where are they, girl? Where are those bogsuckers?" She turned up her face, her tail sweeping the leaves.

I scratched behind her ears, and she rubbed against my leg. She did not really want affection, though, and left to begin making short sorties into the brush. I let her persuade me to stir my stumps. We hunted on, and her manner cheered me.

She knew nothing of loneliness or death or human longing. She was simply herself, a creature who had been allowed to become precisely what her blood directed her to be. A human hunter, I reflected, can at least partially achieve that same freed state: living out the direction of his blood, escaping—if only for scattered hours—the bounds of his thought-bombarded brain.

Bogsucker Flats was indeed empty. We hunted it the whole way out and back, and not a woodcock or a grouse did we see, not even a sparrow or a mouse. The old house, its roof blanketed with spruce needles, stood moldering into its foundation; the screen door, off its hinges, was propped against a porch support. We left there and drove to Morningstar Hollow.

On the way I had a hard time seeing. It wasn't strictly the fog. When I slammed the truck door, the sound carried flatly and quickly died out. We entered the stream bottom, mist-shrouded, dark and dense.

She plunged into the brush: The blank covert had not quelled her desire. I followed. My thoughts were elsewhere, and I stood there flatfooted when the woodcock rose. I watched it twitter away, and whistled Jenny back in. She trembled and cried to go on. I hadn't marked him down but knew he would not have flown far in the fog.

I held her in long enough to let the fever cool in her blood. Then I sent her. She rammed her way into covert, making the greenbriers shake.

The thorns plucked at my legs and elbows as I trudged deeper into the brake. I killed the woodcock—the same bird, I was sure—on the reflush. Woodcock, even when shot at, generally do not go far: fifty, sixty yards. I give myself two flushes: If I do not get the bird on the second rise, it goes free.

There by the stream, the fog lay thick. I buried myself in it. I buried myself in the hunting, to escape my grief. Death was all around. I thought of the old man gone from the shack on Bogsucker Flats. I thought of my father, healthy, vigorous, and clear of mind until his heart failed him. What had he thought, at that last lucid moment? Did he know he was dying? Did he fight it, like a drowning man fights a river—or did he let it carry him along? Did it hurt—a stunning blow to the chest? Was the pain that of self pity, or of loss? Was he afraid of the void, of extinguishment—or was it all too swift for thought? Many were the sad and demeaning and perhaps agonizing things, tied to the dwindling of life, which he had been spared. Many, too, were the joys of which he and his family had been deprived.

I called Jenny in, hooked my hand in front of her flank, and held her tight against my leg.

My wife and I had been to the hospital earlier in the week. She thought she was pregnant, and they confirmed it at the clinic, but she was having sharp pains that might signal an ectopic, or tubal, pregnancy: when the fertilized egg fails to descend to the womb, and instead attaches to the fallopian tube. It requires surgery to remove. It does not blossom into life. At the hospital they made her drink glass after glass of water to expand her bladder and render it transparent to the sound waves that would penetrate and scan beyond. The man operating the ultrasound machine was small and dark-haired, pleasant verging on wry. He placed the sound transmitter, a microphonelike device, on my wife's now-distended abdomen. He moved it around gently. He let me watch the screen, which was black-

and-white. It took him a long time to get a clear picture; what I saw was a ghostly shimmering that seemed to waver, dissipate into a fog, and become sharp again. "There." He twisted a dial, directing a black arrow that was part of the screen.

The arrow pointed at a small dot. The dot glowed like an ember in a waning fire. It was oval in shape. "That's the embryo," he said. It seemed to be centered in a flaring cone of light, which darkened as I watched. The man twirled other dials and the picture gained clarity again. He turned to my wife, lying on her back on the table; then he turned to me. "It's in the uterus," he said. "It looks like a normal pregnancy."

So I had an excuse to be less than fully engaged in my hunting. And while hunting is in many ways a surrendering to the senses, it must also remain an exercise of the intellect. Tactics—especially when one follows a hard-driving dog—are under constant, if subliminal, discussion. Go left or right of that tangle? Under or around the leaning tree? Pause here, or ten feet ahead? Don't stop now, that sapling could impede the gun.

That little patch of sedge? Get her to check it. Nothing there. Ahead. Now she is flirting with the fringe of her range. Two toots on the whistle. "Come round, come round." A flash of movement: a vole, darting through the grass underfoot; immediately the eyes dismiss it, leap back ahead. Is she making game?—Her tail has quickened, but no, the scent must be cold. Chalk on the ground—new or old? Barberry—good grouse food. *Bird!*—no!—just Jenny flapping her ears. Wings flutter in the limbs overhead, cedar waxwings feeding on grapes. Would be nice to stop and watch them but she looks birdy again. That swatch of grass, leading into the field. Worth checking? A hand signal? Not needed, she's into it already. There.

She pauses for the briefest instant before her hind legs uncoil in the accelerating charge. A clattering of wings, a raucous crowing, and the quarry is up. His white neck ring shows bright as he climbs through the foggy branches. It is the neck ring and not the treacherous tail that the eye must seize upon, and the gun speaks, seemingly unbidden at the shoulder, and the pellets swarm to their mark.

Down came the pheasant, bumping through the boughs. He thudded the ground and thrashed until Jenny pinned him. She picked him up. Her tail was high, her head as proud as she could hold it. The note, in that lonely cover tight beneath the fog, was almost unbearably pure. It wove itself together with other notes, the bubbling stream, the quavering communal buzzing of the waxwings, the swishing grass. And the song was more than all of these. It came from the earth. It came up through my feet and legs, even as it flooded down my arms and seeped from my head to my heart—to my soul. Jenny and I (and the pheasant, coming toward me in the jaws of the dog) had played the song. It was a song of life and of death, a joyful song and a threnody. It was the song I desperately needed to hear, and it filled me with hope.

She gave the pheasant up. In my hands, he relaxed in death. His beak slowly closed, the upper mandible holed by a shot. His eyes were half open. His body lay loose and warm. His plumage looked like light on running water, glints of purple, bronze, black, the lapis back feathers, the scarlet cheeks of the blue-green head, the colors all set off by the clean white encirclement of the neck, upon which a drop of blood now stood.

The fog lifted as we hunted down the hollow, the larger world coming back into view. The tamaracks were splendid in their soft golden cloaks. The hemlocks wore a blackish mantle. The sun beat down and the air became luminescent and hot; it would not be long before the scenting collapsed.

Our time in the coverts now seemed to carry new meaning. We were hunting food for a new life, a continuance of my own, my wife's, my father's; and I wanted blood and bone and eye and bowel to arise from the bodies of wild creatures, the strong dark-blooded breasts of woodcock, the fleet legs of pheasant, the wary flesh of duck and grouse.

The Ninety-Seven

BY JOHN BARSNESS

W*HAM!* . . . S*NICK,* S*NICK. WHAM!* . . . *Snick, Snick.*
"Fetch!"
The sounds you just heard—at least, I hope you heard
them—are of a pump shotgun doing its thing. Successfully, I
have tried to suggest.

For generations of hunters throughout the Twentieth Century, the
crisp, oily *snick, snick* of a pump being operated effectively has been welcome
music in countless duck and goose blinds, on pheasant drives, beside deer
trails—anywhere the hunting was good. More than likely the pump being used
was the Remington 870 Wingmaster, the Ithaca Model 37 Featherlight (with
bottom ejection!), or the exalted Winchester Model 12, arguably the most famous pump gun ever made. But before the Model 12 came the venerable Winchester Model 97, the pump with the hammer.

In this little tale, the leading character is a Winchester Ninety-Seven.
All the romance and nostalgia associated with that great gun from the end of
the 1800s well into the 1900s is captured in the wonderful prose of one of
today's finest writers, John Barsness, who lives and writes in Montana but
hunts and fishes everywhere he can.

John Barsness' best stories have been collected in two books, *Montana
Time: The Seasons of a Trout Fisherman* and *Western Skies,* from which this selection was taken.

The first time I saw the 97, I knew where it came from: that era
around the turn of the century when men still just hunted and really did not
question why. It was something they simply did. You can see it in the eyes of
the men in an old photograph from Michigan's Upper Peninsula, standing next

to a cross-pole bending with a dozen deer; in the oak-dark oils of a painting of a grouse, a dog, and a hunter; in the wagon covered with waterfowl from Chesapeake Bay. You can hear it in the rhythmic words of Roosevelt's Africa: "Had lunch today beside the carcass of a beast."

The 97 came from a closer, more western part of the era. I'd glimpsed that time and place in my grandmother's old photograph album, of the early years on the homestead in central Montana. There was Grandma B. in a white blouse, long black skirt, and Stetson, holding two sage grouse she'd shot from the sky with the little twenty-two pump in her hand. There was the grandfather I never knew with a pronghorn buck, his Savage 99 in the crook of his arm. There were friends forgotten and friends known, standing over the body of the last grizzly killed in the Judith Mountains, the mountains that overlooked the homestead. Everyone in the photographs is black and white, no shades of gray, looking steadily forward into the eye of the old Kodak, no questions in their faces. Men—and women—had guns, and they hunted. They hunted animals they ate; they hunted animals they felt threatened their new life in the wilderness; they hunted because they enjoyed hunting. It was a way of life, and they never felt compelled to defend it, because no one ever attacked it.

The 97 was almost totally without blueing, the steel the shade of a prairie September thunderstorm, the "Model 1897 Winchester" stamped into the rail behind the forearm losing its sharp edges. The wood was dark, worn by hands, dented by wagon seats and pickup doors, scratched by wild rosebushes and buffalo-berry. It had the same texture and color as the face and hands of the man who owned it, my wife's grandfather, a Sioux Indian from the Fort Peck Indian Reservation. I saw it for my first time on my first visit to the Reservation after being married, when Ben and I went hunting. We went hunting because that is what men did.

We hunted all day in the grassy hills and badlands. It was mid-afternoon when we came to a patch of chokecherry, the last cherries drying in the sun. "There's always 'chickens' here," Ben said, taking the 97 from the gun rack. "You know how to work this?" I thumbed back the hammer, then eased it down, feeling the light action of the trigger. I pulled the forearm back, then pushed it forward, moving a shell into the chamber, and eased the hammer down again.

"Yeah."

We put Ben's dog into the brush. For a moment we heard her pattering through the leaves underneath the chokecherries, and there was a time of stillness, just a moment under the prairie sky, before I heard the chatter of birds and the hard burst of wings. A sharptailed grouse flew from the brush to my right, and I brought the old shotgun to my shoulder, brought the hammer back under my thumb, everything moving easily and exactly, as if laid out in vectors and intersecting lines. I looked along the barrel as it floated toward the bird, sensing for an instant the enormity of the sky and the smallness of the grouse against it. Then the brass bead on the end of the barrel swept in front of the bird's flight, a gleaming flight in itself, and the 97 went off without my choosing it to and the bird left the sky, simply, with no after-moment of feathers floating. Then another bird came up, flying away from me, toward the hill sloping beyond the brush. There was a consciousness of the action working, the feel of steel sliding against itself, and the bead was on the bird and another shot sounded through the rush of more birds rising to my left. I saw the far bird dropping as I turned and then heard two shots, saw two more birds falling, and then silence. The last empty shell was already in the grass, the last full shell in the chamber. I looked at Ben.

"Wait," he said. The dog ran unseen in the brush below, and a single grouse rose, fighting the leaves with its wings, so far away. The shotgun moved again, locked into its movement, and then, even farther away, so far away I cannot believe it even now in my mind, the grouse fell, brown wings the color of the cured grass, its falling the curve of the hills. That was all.

Ben drew on his pipe. "Good shooting, kid." He pulled the pipe from his mouth, looked into the bowl, then knocked the burned tobacco out on his hard palm. "But you know, that's a trained gun."

He had only the one shotgun. He was from that era, that sepia-toned time, when a man only had one shotgun, one big-game rifle, and a twenty-two. Over the next three years, when I came to visit, I used it. He did not. I didn't bring any of my own shotguns. Perhaps I felt he'd be offended if I did, but perhaps more because I wanted to shoot the 97. He would just stand back and watch me shoot, or drive down to the end of a mile-long coulee to wait and pick me up with my load of sharptails.

After the third year, my wife and I moved to the Reservation. I was beginning to sense that the era I'd seen in old photographs was still at least partially alive there, in Ben and the hills he'd grown up in. For some reason I wanted to find it, to be part of it and understand that life. Perhaps it was nostalgia for the memories of my grandmother's photo album, but the desire was there.

So we hunted. We hunted for days across the open hills, hunted sharptails in the berry-brushed coulees, hunted whitetails in the wooded draws, hunted mule deer in the badlands, hunted pheasants and ducks along the sloughs of the Missouri. I learned the pattern of sharptail life across the fall, from the rosebushes along the wheatfields in September, to the buffalo-berry thickets in October, to the shortgrass along the plateau edges in November. I learned where the whitetails liked to bed and how to push the pheasants to the river's edge and then wait there, listening, shotgun held lightly, until the birds could no longer stand the silence and burst up through the snow. I learned how to pluck sharptails quickly, as soon as they'd been shot, when the feathers were easy to pull from the delicate breast-skin, and how to slice steak and roasts from a buck's hindquarter. That is what I did. I hunted and took care of game and tried to recapture an era, because that's what men did.

It was a cold evening in late November when I went to Ben's house to see if he wanted to hunt ducks in the morning. He was in his chair, puffing on his pipe, watching a football game on television.

"We'll have to wait until nine or so," he said, after I'd asked him whether he wanted to jump-shoot some farm ponds we knew, "I've gotta go to the hardware store in the morning."

"What for?"

"I'm gonna trade off that old gun."

"Which one?" All three of his guns were old.

"Oh, that shotgun. I'm getting too old to haul that thing around anymore. It's too damned heavy."

I couldn't believe what I'd heard. "You mean the 97? You're going to trade the 97? For what?"

"There's a real nice little twenty-gauge down there. Real light."

I shook my head to myself. I couldn't comprehend it. He'd told me so many stories about the old gun, about killing sharptails after his hunting partners had missed, about outshooting the trap campion of North Dakota on a pheasant hunt. I thought for a moment. "How much did they offer for it?"

He told me.

"Oh, come on. It's worth more than that."

"Hell, it's just a beat-up old gun."

"You really mean to trade it?"

He nodded, his pipe moving up and down.

"Okay. All right. Tell you what—I'll pay you that much for it."

His eyebrows came together. "Why?"

"Because I want it."

He shrugged. "If that's what you want."

My wife couldn't understand my excitement when I brought the old gun home. In reality, I didn't consider it mine, but a piece of time on loan: something of value that eventually would have to be returned. I was sure that Ben would regret his decision, especially when I placed the 97 in the line of guns in my cabinet, its gray barrel and battered stock saying so much more than the sharp new lines of the other guns.

We lived three years on the Reservation, but eventually knew we couldn't stay there forever. Life was too restricted; there were other worlds that we wanted. And I also sensed that the era I'd wanted to capture had been pushed to its limits, that its last moment there, in that remote part of Montana, was just that: something almost gone, and that perhaps its most valid place was in my mind, rather than my life. We moved to a small city in the mountains of western Montana, and I put the photos of the old life on the Reservation in a shoebox and stored them in a closet. Photos of Ben and me next to the pickup, holding two limits of sharptailed grouse, of us next to two hanging bucks, our rifles angled across our chests, of Ben taking a Canada goose from my Lab along the Missouri. Photos very similar to those old photos of the Chesapeake or the life on the old homestead, except that these were colorful Kodachrome, rather than black-and-white.

We visited the reservation each fall, and I hunted sharptails with Ben—and that was the only time I used the 97. Its full choke and thirty-inch barrel were totally impractical for mountain grouse; yet that wasn't the only reason I didn't use it in the mountains. Something had changed; the old gun was almost retired except for the prairie hunt each fall.

And then even those hunts ended. My wife and I separated, a separation much like the separation we had made with the Reservation. We each wanted other worlds. I almost acted on my original feeling then, the feeling I'd had when I first bought the gun, and almost returned it to Ben. But then I sensed that would just be a plea for the past. Perhaps I'd use it on my own sharptail hunts, wherever they were, as part of the memory of him and an era.

Then one fall the 97 never left the cabinet. I never made it east of the mountains to hunt prairie birds. It wasn't until the middle of winter, just before a trip to the trap range with two friends, that my hand impulsively took it from beside the new Remington and slid it into a case.

When I walked to the firing line, next to four men wearing vests covered with the patches of competition, carrying new guns equipped with adjustable buttplates and high ribs, and I saw the mountains beyond the traphouse turning pink with evening, a strange feeling came over me. It was as if the old shotgun and I, as its carrier, did not belong there on that concrete pad, between men dressed in bright colors and tinted glasses.

That feeling still lingered on the edges of my mind as I slid a shell into the 97's chamber, but it eased slightly as I brought the gun to my shoulder. The clay soared out against the mountains, and I swung with it; at the shot and the sight of the clay still sailing, untouched, the feeling returned. There was some-thing wrong. The gun did not feel exact, smooth, the way it had on that day when I'd stood above a chokecherry patch with an old man. In an odd way, it was the same feeling: of the shotgun being detached from me, with a sense of its own. But now the feeling was of unwillingness, as if I were forcing a saddle horse up the wrong trail.

The first five clays went untouched. I wasn't aware of the other men; their words and shots seemed something on the edge of a dream, something I had to move around but not consider. The ninth clay was barely chipped, the first hit, and I tried to concentrate, to find the rhythm of the swing. I broke two in a row, and then everything left again; only three more broke, at uncontrolled moments, during the rest of the round. As I pulled the last shell from the re-ceiver and walked away from the line, not even looking at the score sheet, I vaguely heard a slight laugh and comment from one of the other shooters. Sud-denly I was angry—not at him, not at any mockery of me or my shooting, be-cause I felt so apart from that—but at his smugness, his ignorance of what I held in my hand. I wanted to turn and tell him, coldly, of what that gun had done, of a thousand sharptails above the pale October prairie, of a pheasant dropped far off across a frozen river, of an old man with a face the color of walnut and how men once lived. I turned and looked at him; he looked away and turned toward the other men. Quickly, with that turning, all the anger drained from me. I stood for a moment, looking at the mountains, then walked slowly to the club-house, knowing I would never shoot the 97 at anything but wild prairie birds again. What it was and where it came from were something almost gone, and it should not be used in any other way. It was time to put aside illusions and live with memories. They are always much more kind.

To the Open Water

BY JESSE HILL FORD

MOST OF THE time, it's difficult to think about the dangers that can lurk in pursuing the outdoor life. In cases such as mountaineering and running whitewater rapids, the risks are very much in-your-face and obvious. In most hunting, fishing, camping, and hiking life-threatening experiences are pretty rare. And yet . . .

Here is the noted novelist and short story writer Jesse Hill Ford with the stunning tale of a hunt gone wrong. The power of "To the Open Water" reminds me very much of Jack London's classic short story, "To Build a Fire." Ford's story is from his book of short stories, *Fishes, Birds and Sons of Men,* published by Atlantic Monthly Press.

When the teal leaped from the grass it flew up so swiftly that it was already out of range by the time he fired. At the sound of the shotgun a few blackjacks put up. They rose reluctantly in the cold air and circled a moment before flying straight up channel towards the neck of the bottoms.

He quickly climbed the embankment to the road and ran to the bridge to watch the ducks. Slicing through the sky like arrows, they flew almost out of sight before they veered left, folded suddenly into a soft spiral, and went down beyond the trees.

The open water would be there, where they went down. He knew the place, a logjam island. It would be, perhaps, the only open water to be found on such a day when even the coves along the Tennessee River were frozen solid. Ice was skimming the main channel itself in places.

Even where the pale afternoon sun had shone on the windless side of the levee the air was pinching cold. Since early morning he had scouted the banks about the bottoms without venturing on the ice. Until he saw the teal he had seen only two snipe. He had killed one of them and missed the other.

He left the bridge and walked about seventy yards up the levee, then down the embankment through dead briers and dormant honeysuckle vines. The johnboat lay where he had left it, bottom upward on the bank. He stepped out on the ice.

He stamped his foot. The ice held, solid as concrete, hard as glass it seemed, too thick to break a way through it for the boat. Besides, the boat was small and of light-gauge aluminum, not meant to take the punishment of jagged, broken ice. It was made to be sculled through the bottoms on warmer days, to be ghosted along like a feather by the merest dip and twitch of the paddle, to go more quietly than man could walk or duck could fly.

He looked up. By hauling the little boat up the levee to the road he could carry it on his shoulders to the channel and put in at the bridge. He was a stout man of two hundred pounds, well used to work. Had it been morning he wouldn't have hesitated. Time, however, was against him now. Walk fast though he might, carrying the boat, and once in the channel with it, paddle swiftly though he would, there was small chance he could reach the logjam island before sundown. By that time it would be too late to shoot, and he would have labored for nothing.

His only chance was to slide the little johnboat over the ice straight out towards the logjam island, to sled along swiftly directly to his destination, pushing the little craft ahead of him and, for safety, leaning forward over the stern as he went. In that way, should he run upon rotten ice, he would fall in the boat as it cracked through.

He had gone over the ice this way many times before, but never this late in the afternoon, never with the bottoms so silent. The freeze kept other hunters close at home or sitting beside stoves in crossroads country stores. None but the most determined, not even professional guides, would try to find open water in weather such as this, even though once it was found and reached, the shooting was beyond compare. With no other place to land, the ducks would leave when jumped, only to return again and again.

The desire to be where they were this very instant made his throat ache. Once before as he slid over the ice he had cracked through in a bad place several hundred yards out and had been forced to stay where he was until after midnight, when the bottoms froze sufficiently solid for him to walk out and drag the little boat after him. Every other time, though, he had made it to the open water. There was a line of trees marking the grave of an old road buried by the winter flood. By leaping into the boat just there, it was possible to coast off the edge of the ice into the water. He had done it with never an accident, a dozen times perhaps, all before he married. Since his marriage six years ago, he had never attempted the trick.

From the time he was ten until the day of his marriage, he had hunted every day of every duck season, every day after school, even Sundays after church, though Sunday hunting was frowned upon. He had hunted them because he loved them then with the same passionate ache in his throat that he felt now for those creatures settled there on the open water by the thousands, their wild hearts calling his own, it seemed.

Marriage had pinched him down. His wife had ambitions for the farm. It wasn't enough to spend spring, summer, and fall riding a tractor, driving a cotton picker, loading and unloading his truck, working at times until long after nightfall, waiting five hours to get his cotton trailer under the suck at the gin. A wife had to have chickens and geese and cattle. Coonhounds and mules weren't creatures enough to care for, not in a wife's estimation. There must be winter duties too—even, finally, a dairy barn. God help him if he once failed to be home in time to milk.

He hadn't gone over the ice in six long years because there had been too many creatures dependent on him, nearly all of them female. First a wife, then infant daughters, and finally the wife's gentle-eyed Jerseys with their slender hips and heavy udders.

A mallard susie quacked in the distance. He turned the johnboat right side up and laid his heavy parka in it next to his gun. Besides two extra boxes of shells in the pockets of the parka, he carried twenty-three magnum loads in a shooting vest which he wore buttoned snugly about his chest for warmth. He opened his half-pint and took a drink of white moonshine whiskey. Over the bottoms the air was still.

With a practiced heave he pushed the boat out ahead of him on the ice, keeping his weight forward, ready to leap in the boat if the ice failed. As he gathered speed, his legs moving in a regular rhythm, running easily, the boat set up a screeching, thundering racket, scraping past trees and cracking through thickets. Mallards rose from the red oak thickets and flew towards the channel. Now in an open space he paused and watched them a moment. Then he pushed on, going even faster now as the open spaces between thickets got wider and wider. He began sweating a little and slowed down.

Farther out, he stopped to rest. He sat on the stern of the little boat, boots on the ice, elbows on knees, looking down at the hard, slick, olive-drab surface. He looked up at the levee, about six hundred yards away now, a long, straight elevated outline. The road was desolate in both directions. Only hunters, trappers, fishermen, or an occasional logger used it. Far down to the left, he saw the black outline of his pickup truck. He had parked it that morning before starting along the north edge of the bottoms where he had killed the snipe.

He leaned back and got the bird from the game pocket of his parka. The little body was frozen. Strangest of all were the eyes; black with life's memory, they seemed, in the instant after death, before the cold seeped into them and did its work. Frozen now, the eyes were white.

He stood up and tossed the snipe into the front of the boat, turning at the same time and leaning forward. The ice cracked. The crack ran under him and on ahead of the boat through the dark-green ice. Though a crack it most surely was, it didn't seem to be a very serious one. He held the sides of the boat, leaning forward to distribute his weight, braced like an athlete preparing to do push-ups. He waited. The ice held.

Fifty yards to the right stood a duck blind. The decoys in front of it were frozen solid into the ice and glazed with white frost. Red oak saplings shaded the ice in their direction. There the ice looked pale, almost white. It would be thicker. He could turn back now in that direction and reach the levee.

Far away to his left over the long open stretches he saw the line of trees marking the lost road. Beyond the flat glare he saw the logjam island, and around it the still blue gulf of the open water, reflecting the sky. In ten minutes he could reach the trees for the final, sliding rush.

He skidded the boat left and made straight for the trees, getting up speed first and then making only so much effort with his legs as would keep the boat sliding. Now and again the ice cracked, but the boat outran the cracks, one after the other as he pushed on, keeping his weight carefully distributed forward, over the boat.

Suddenly, with no warning the ice gave under him, and he fell into the boat just in time, just before it cracked through, and not an instant too soon, for the icy water had bitten him almost to mid-thigh, wetting him well above his insulated rubber knee boots. It had happened this way before. It was like being burned, like the sting of flames licking about his legs. He lay face down and still, waiting for his trousers to freeze. It needed only a little patience. When he sat up at last, remembering to wiggle his toes and flex his calf muscles to keep the circulation going, even the splashes had frozen. They looked like drops of candle wax.

Flared by the commotion of his fall, the ducks had flown up. Now they flocked and circled low around the edge of the open water. He slipped a magnum shell into the magazine of the automatic to replace the one fired at the teal. Then he put the parka over his head and shoulders and sat very still. He quacked with his mouth. A susie answered. He quacked again. He patted his lips, making the intimate, stuttering feed call. He tried the raucous call of the wise old susie. It all proved a false hope. The entire drove splashed in beside the island with a brisk rush of sound that set his heart beating faster.

When he put the gun down and took off the parka, his toes were numb. He moved them and rubbed his legs and finally admitted it to himself. He had cracked through; maybe the ice *was* rotten. Very well, but he had broken through only one time in several hundred yards of running, after all. He *had* managed to fall very neatly into the johnboat, hadn't he?

Though it was a ticklish sort of job, there was still a chance that he could get the boat back up on the ice. He moved back cautiously and sat on the stern, balancing his weight until the bow rose high out of the water and less than four inches of freeboard remained beneath him. Then he dipped the paddle and drove the boat hard against the edge, and moving at once, fast, before it could slide off again, he went quickly forward on all fours. The ice cracked, the long, brittle sound of a marble rolling over a glass tabletop. Crouched in the bow, he waited, holding his breath, a dull pain beating in his throat just under the Adam's apple. The ice held. Cautiously, slowly, he leaned far out over the prow and caught a willow limb in his gloved hand and pulled. The boat eased forward with him. He caught another limb and then another, getting farther and farther up on firm ice, hauling the boat painfully hand over hand until at last his arms gave out and he turned carefully and lay on his back breathing the cold, clean air through his mouth, cupping his hands and breathing into them. Lying thus, looking straight up, the depth of the clear sky was blue and magnificent. When he held his breath there was not a stir of sound anywhere to be heard. He might have been the last creature left alive on earth. A feeling of independence entered him like the slow onset of sleep.

When it was time to move again he found he was tired. He moved awkwardly, stiff in his joints, his shoulders aching in the sockets, his toes numb because he had neglected to keep moving them. He took the flat, half-pint bottle from his parka and drank it empty in three long swigs and flung the bottle away. It smashed. The clear little shards of glass slid on for several yards before they finally stopped, gleaming at rest in the waning sunlight like white jewels.

The levee had never before seemed so far away. The slanting sun perhaps added to the illusion. When he stood up he could not see the truck. Willow thickets blocked the way. In the other direction, just ahead, the island loomed from the open water, a tangled mass of roots and black tree trunks. Low in the water all around it the ducks rested, very still, as though waiting for him.

Although they were out of range, he was tempted to fire at them anyway, to put them up for the joy of seeing them fly, for the satisfaction, knowing that though they might circle the whole bottoms, they would come back. The cold air would drive them down again, here, in the last of the open water, perhaps the last open water to be found anywhere about, except in the mid-river channel.

The liquor's warmth caught hold. He hadn't eaten since before daylight. It didn't matter. He had taught himself not to want food. He had taught himself not to want anything but the beautiful joy of killing. He had always hunted this way.

Now he took the bow line, and without hesitating, stepped out on the ice and put it over his shoulder and towed the boat after him. Once started, it seemed to follow him willingly, coming after him across the patch of firm, white ice like a docile beast. When the ice shaded into olive green again, he stopped and fended his way around to the stern to rest a moment before making the final dash for trees at the edge of the open water.

Once the boat slid free he would be in range. The ducks would come up and circle, dipping their dark wings to his call, and he would lovingly kill them. He would scull coaxingly after the cripples one by one, coming so slowly on them that they would hardly know the boat was moving at all. While they flirted in that final, zigzag hesitation, he would suddenly raise the gun and shoot their heads off clean. Their blood would boil below them like a cloud into the dark, clear water.

A whistling flight of teal drove in, wings already set, and pitched in beyond the island. A susie quacked. He drew a deep breath and shoved. The boat groaned against the willows and slid forward. Faster and faster, he pushed on. Exhilaration shook him like a sudden wind among dead leaves. With less than fifty yards to go, speed was in his favor. Instinctively, at the right instant, he would leap lightly forward.

As though struck suddenly blind, however, he was groping, wet to the armpits, his breath coming so fast that his chest seemed about to burst. He saw the johnboat beside him. It had cracked through. He caught its side. Water spilled in, so he pushed back, trying to swim, his hands already so numb he could hardly feel them.

"*Still, be still!*" he commanded aloud, using words he spoke to the restless cows at milking. The cold drove in from every direction like nails, driving and driving in, searching his vitals.

He must think! Of course, only keep a clear head! Make every move carefully! Sound judgment, no wasted time or motion. "*Easy, careful,*" he said, speaking to the fiery grip of the cold, which now became more powerful than anything he had ever before imagined, for it was taking him over.

In the place of the strong, obedient body he had so long been accustomed to command, he felt a strange and foolish despair at this heaving, disquieted thing that would no longer obey.

In spite of every caution to the contrary, his body suddenly fought like a cat snared on a string. Thrashing and fighting like a dying fish, he fended himself clumsily around to the prow and threw himself hard upon it. Short of seeing it, he could never have believed such an utterly foolish panic to be possible. Already almost in the wink of an eye, he had destroyed his best hope. The incredible, the *impossible* thing happened. The boat filled almost as quickly as he had moved, and rolled down from under him.

Water covered his face. When he had fought to the surface and taken breath, he felt his hair and his eyebrows freezing.

Bottom up now and barely afloat, the boat was another creature entirely, as though it too, the docile beast of a moment before, had now lost all notion of what it was logically supposed to be, and do.

When he touched it, it rolled. When he caught at it, the weird creature shook him off; it threw him a second time, and he gentled cautiously against it, the cold biting clean through his shoulders now, like teeth. His body's least twitch made the boat heave and swing. Holding the boat, huddling on it and fighting its strange movements, he realized for the first time that the shooting vest with its cargo of magnum shells was his enemy now, the perfect weight to sink a man and kill him. Propping a hand and both knees against the boat, he tried the vest's buttons. Briefly his fingers stung back to life, but they were useless against buttons.

He tried to balance himself on the boat and rip the vest apart with both hands, no trick for a strong man in his early prime, yet each time he tried it the other creature, the rebellious animal self, seized him. His arms failed. They disobeyed. His hands groped warily forward like burned stumps, to rest against the boat and balance him.

He remained thus awhile, motionless, not even shivering, such was the marvel of it, his head just above the surface of the freezing water. The thin winter sunlight and the desolate, utter silence of the bottoms, great spanning miles of it, dinned and drummed at him.

He knew he must shout soon. It would be no use, of course. No earthly man would hear. Yet soon he would begin screaming. The body would have that too; the body would have it, though he knew shouting must only exhaust him the sooner and hasten the end. Screams began gathering in his throat like a queer nausea.

If he had only thought to take off the vest before his fingers numbed, to get out of his boots, even kick off his trousers. Then he might have gotten back in the boat. He would have wrung out his clothes and put them back on and huddled under the parka until night froze the bottoms in, and then he would have walked out to the road and gotten in the truck. He would have driven it home and tottered into the house and asked his wife to draw him a hot bath. Once he was warm and rested he would have gotten a friend or two and come back after his boat and the gun.

If they ever found it, anytime within a week or two, the gun would be all right. He kept it oiled, and with the water so cold the oil would stick. The gun wouldn't rust quickly. Perhaps they would find it. He hoped they would.

Finding the gun shouldn't be hard with the boat frozen in the ice right over it. A sudden ruthless pain in his back, above the beltline, jerked his head forward. For the first time he began shuddering. He heard himself shouting, screaming for help, the cries already hoarse though hardly even well begun. The ducks came up and began wheeling and circling above him. Their curved wings were more beautiful than any he had seen before, cupping as gently as a kiss, skimming like a long caress, each pair shaped like the touch of a woman's hands in love.

He stopped yelling and slid peacefully down into the white darkness under the surface.

Pheasants Beyond Autumn

BY JOHN MADSON

"**T**HERE IS A KEEN AND POIGNANT QUALITY in being a famished boy far afield with night coming on and miles of crusted snow yet to negotiate, the pheasants hanging over your shoulder with their legs tied with binder twine, and the little Monkey Ward double gun beginning to weigh heavy. . . . Night coming on and glory lost, for there would be no daylight in which to parade past neighbor girls' houses, the bright roosters hung from my shoulder. The girls would never know what they had missed, but I would."

This little tease from "Pheasants Beyond Autumn" is your editor's way of saying, "Don't go away! Something really good is coming."

The late John Madson was one of the finest men and best writers it has ever been my privilege to know and to read. A quiet Midwesterner who never ceased being inspired by his roots and the land he loved, John Madson wrote prose that was at once vivid but gentle, producing an aura that to this reader seems almost enchanting.

This story is from the wonderful Madson collection, *Out Home,* published by Winchester Press in 1979. In this one, the easy ringnecks that were rousted from the cornfields on an Indian-summer opening day are gone. Real pheasant hunting is about to begin.

There is a dichotomy in pheasant hunting, as in any hunting that is worth doing. There are sets of paired contrasts: two pheasant seasons, two kinds of hunters, two types of birds. Gold and gray, gay and grim, yin and yang.

One pheasant season may last no longer than opening weekend—a brief, burnished time with Indian summer still on the land, the afternoons soft and tawny and hunters with their coats open. The other pheasant season is quieter and grayer, reaching far into December. The sky is often stone-colored then, filled with prairie winds that cut with a wire edge, and even on clear days the sunlight is pale and without substance.

In that first pheasant season there were hunters by the hundreds of thousands, sweeping the fields in wide lines with deployed blockers, plaguing farmers and each other, shooting at pheasants hopelessly far away, ripping out the crotches of new hunting pants on bobwire fences, and generally having a helluva time. They head back to town with or without birds, often making a stop along the way and arriving home late and smelling like hot mince pies. They are not likely to reappear on the landscape for about one year.

The pheasant hunters who do return, and keep returning, have a singular worn quality. Their canvas coats are likely to be weatherstained and shapeless, with the main button missing and a pronounced sag in the region of the game pocket, and their gunmetal is worn to the white. They hunt without haste—dour men in twos and threes, or often alone with an old retriever at heel. Men shaped and colored by circumstance, as fitted to their environment as horseweeds and cockleburs—and just as enduring and tenacious. They must be, to match the birds that they now hunt.

The pheasants of the opening weekend were overwhelmingly birds of the year, callow juveniles that rose clattering into the air within easy gun range. Those birds went home with the opening-day hunters and, like them, will not reappear for another year. The birds that remain are either sagacious old roosters with long spurs, or smart young cocks that won their spurs during the first week of hunting. Such pheasants have much in common with the remaining hunters. Each tempers and hones the other in a process of mutual refinement.

There is some loss of pheasants with the first intense shock of cold weather. There is a marked loss of hunters as well. By then, both pheasant and hunter have evolved beyond their opening-day counterparts—for it needs a tougher breed of hunter to pit himself against the pheasant range of late December, and a tougher breed of pheasant to resist him. But somehow, the pheasant tends to harden and sharpen a bit ahead of the man who hunts him, even the very good man. There comes a point where hunter persistence is outstripped by pheasant resistance—and the roosters always win.

The December pheasant is the real pheasant and to hunt him is to hunt pheasants truly. Which is not to say that opening weekend is unworthy of serious regard. It is a very special time, a season apart, that late October or early November opening. A wedding party and honeymoon in one—green and golden preface to a hardworking marriage between bird and gunner.

Opening Day is when a small boy is allowed to tag along for the first time and maybe even carry dad's first rooster of the day, and get to keep the tail feathers. The boy will soon be carrying a 20-bore and a rooster of his own.

It is a time when the clans gather, when old hunting pards rendezvous. They come from all compass points, reaffirming the faith. I'll go home to central Iowa again and hook up with Harry Harrison or Skeeter Wheeler. Or Glen Yates—leathery, irascible, ornery, deeply regarded Yates. Sly old cuss Yates, with his bib overalls and tattered coat and Sweet Sixteen, and a profound and abiding knowledge of the ring-necked pheasant. Opening Day is playday for us. It's Gooney Bird Day, time to test the young roosters and see how all the folks are doing out there in the fields. As Yates puts it: "Of course Opening Day ain't pheasant hunting. Hell, that ain't new. But it's the start of it—and Kee-rist, Madseen, am I ready!"

It's this Opening Day that largely supports wildlife conservation in much of the Midwest—notably Iowa, Kansas, Nebraska and South Dakota. License sales soar just before the pheasant season, swelling the game and fish coffers while gun and ammunition receipts build the Pittmann-Robertson fund. In Iowa, about 300,000 residents buy hunting licenses. About 290,000 of them hunt pheasants—and probably 80 percent are out there on the great Saturday. If there were no pheasant opening in Iowa, as many as 200,000 licenses might go unsold in a given year—and the wildlife conservation program would go down the tube. It is much the same elsewhere. Let us look kindly on Opening Day.

A lot of bird hunting isn't really hunting. For example, you don't hunt waterfowl and wild turkey. You seduce and delude them. Nor do men usually hunt quail. They hunt for the dog that's hunting for the quail.

Early-season pheasant hunting isn't as likely to be hunting so much as just combing through cover. Birds are likely to be almost anywhere in the early November fields and edges, so it's usually a matter of just pointing yourself at the general landscape and grinding out mileage.

But later pheasant hunting may be as pure a form of hunting as there is. The hunter then becomes a classic searcher and stalker, shooting less and hunting much, much more. There are still a few ribbon clerks trying to shoot pheasants from cars—but that's a pallid imitation of sport that doesn't really produce much. While the pheasant season is still young, the birds have begun to shrink away from roadsides. The slow ones are dead, and most of the others are likely to be somewhere back in the fields where things are more peaceful. (With exceptions, of course. We know a man who hunts late-season birds in the thick brome of certain I-80 interchanges. He says he does all right. As near as we can figure it, the only law he's breaking is the one prohibiting pedestrians on interstate highways.)

I don't have much late-season cunning, but one practice that's worked out well is simply getting as far as possible from roads. An obvious reason is that most birds have faded away from roadside field edges. Then, too, the very center of a square-mile section of midwestern cornland may be the untidiest part. It's where a farmer tends to sweep stuff under the rug, back where passersby can't see small farm dumps, weed patches, messy fencerows and junk machinery.

I once found a mile-square section whose exact center was low and boggy, and whose owner had never gone to the expense and effort of extending tile lines from there to the nearest road ditch a half-mile away. Since the swale was probably lower than the distant road ditch, drainage wouldn't have been possible, anyway. The result was a little two-acre oasis that was abandoned to wild grasses and forbs. And pheasants, of course. Unless a man stood on the cab of his pickup truck (which I did), this could not be seen from the road.

In contrast is a certain square mile of central Iowa farmland that lies on a terminal moraine. In most of my home country a man can plow all day and not see a stone bigger than a walnut, but this particular township has sprinklings of glacial erratics. Over the years, farmers had removed such debris from their fields to a slight lift of land in the center of my hunting ground, where today a modest boulderfield covers almost an acre—together with several rolls of old fencing and a mantle of goldenrod, lesser ragweed, and sumac. This little niche is a magnet for wildlife, although I never hit it hard nor often. Once a season is enough.

Out here in the corn country—and about everywhere else—a man must exploit two extremes in his late-season pheasant hunting. He must hunt close and far, alternating between dense coverts and wide, naked fields.

There are genuine pheasant hunters who think nothing of reducing new canvas pants to shredded rags in the course of a single hunting season. They churn around in terrible places—deep pockets of raspberry canes undergrown with dense grass, rough weedy creekbanks thick with catbriar tangles, and the steep banks of old bullditches with their overgrowth of ragweed and sumac. You know—the kinds of cover that hurt just to look at. But these are the haunts of late-season roosters, and the men who rout them out of such stuff do so with the premise that the only places worth hunting in late season are in cover that no sane man would ever enter.

Such attention to detail, and willingness to suffer for it, applies to open field gunning as well. It may mean hunting in rough plowing, such as plowed pastures where broken sod is left to mellow over the winter. These are the devil's own fields to walk in; the black surfaces of the upturned sods become as slippery as grease during the midday thaw, and a man can break his bones there. Still, roosters may be sheltering in sun-warmed hollows between and under the big clods, and a hunter must go where the birds may be. If there's any comfort in this, it's knowing that pheasants are as reluctant to run in heavy plowing as men are. Well, almost.

This breed of hunter will turn aside from a comfortable fenceline and stumble across a quarter of plowing to hunt a wisp of grassed waterway only a few yards long, or walk hundreds of yards out of his way to investigate a basket-sized tuft of foxtail in a picked cornfield, or a distant hay bale that the farmer failed to pick up. No cover feature in the barren winter landscape is too minor to overlook. It is hunting based on three articles of faith: 1) that much of the pre-season rooster population is still out there, and although 2) there is no cheap late-season pheasant, 3) the longer you hunt without flushing a bird, the closer you are to flushing one.

Pheasants range more widely in winter than at any other time of year. They are constantly adjusting to impending storms, snow-choked roosts, and deep cold and wind. Vagaries of wind and snow drifting will eliminate certain niches of the birds' range, and bring others into play. Marvelously rugged and adaptable birds, winter pheasants never cease probing and exploring.

Aldo Leopold observed that Wisconsin pheasants were sometimes restless in coverts of less than ten acres. Where small coverts prevailed, pheasants were likely to adopt a winter "circuit-type" movement, traveling from one covert to another in a sequence spreading over a mile of distance and several days' time. Leopold believed that Wisconsin pheasants in good winter range had an average cruising radius of one-eighth to one-half mile, and two or three miles at the most.

Since today's winter coverts in the primary pheasant range are almost always less than ten acres, such fiddle-footed drifting may be a common trait in many regions. Although a particular covert may not hold birds today, it doesn't mean that they might not be there tomorrow or a couple of days from now. On the contrary, it could mean that they probably will be.

Our most successful wild birds and mammals are those that have not been fixed in rigid frames of specialization, but are generalized in design and function. The pheasant is a pretty good example of this, owing much of his success to a rather generalized form and a knack for ready adjustment. We can't really ascribe much intelligence to the pheasant. After all, the chicken tribe wasn't at the head of the line when the brains were passed out. But the ring-neck is certainly "country smart;" he may not know his way to town, but he sure ain't lost. He develops a remarkably shrewd sense of range. Not as well as the red fox or whitetail deer, perhaps, but infinitely better than the men who hunt him there.

We human hunters are likely to regard countrysides in terms of drainage systems and patterns of cultivation and habitation. Or, at best, in terms of entire brushy creeks, dry sloughs and weedy fields. Wild hunted creatures like the pheasant learn their native heath in terms of minute, intimate crannies—little sections of overhung creekbank, the tree stump covered with vines and weeds, that old roll of fencewire smothered with giant foxtail. Our eyes are always about six feet above the ground; the pheasant's are down there among the details, down in the tangled heart of the covert, and an instant later his eyes may be 40 feet in the air. A pheasant is exposed to the major and minor features of his home range in ways that the hunter can never hope to be, and he is highly capable of exploiting that exposure in stress situations.

While trading from one major winter covert to another, a pheasant is about as likely to walk as fly. In the course of such commuting he continually adds to his experience bank. If the obvious winter hangouts are regularly disturbed by hunters, many ringnecks begin to rely on interim coverts—little pockets of sanctuary that they have happened upon along the way. This occurs too often to be a fluke—occasions when certain birds are not to be found in any conventional shelter-belt or weedy slough, but are shut down in the weedy mouth of an old culvert or in a snug form of tented bluegrass in an orchard. The compleat pheasant hunter must learn to think in such terms. This is one of the reasons that I enjoy hunting pheasant on snow. It's all written out there, although I often fail to comprehend what I read.

It's on snow that one can trace daily feeding patterns, some of the winter circuitry between far-flung coverts, and the bewildering and often admirable interactions of winter pheasants and their harsh world. Such tracking is more likely to instruct in natural history than to result in shooting. My lifetime success rate for converting pheasant tracks to Sunday dinners can't be much more than two percent. Something usually goes wrong.

But if I've learned one thing about trailing, it's this: to never think in terms of a pheasant resting placidly at the end of a line of tracks. If those tracks are really fresh, the pheasant is almost certainly aware of being trailed and you will rarely get a shot while the bird is on the move. It's his pausing-place that you must find. If the trail appears to lead across rather open ground to a distant pocket of weedy cover, swing far to the side and come in from behind. I think this may be the only way I've ever trailed and killed pheasants—by leaving the trail and flanking the bird at some point ahead. Several times, on fresh snow, I have found that roosters had entered bits of cover and had hooked around in order to watch their backtrails.

Snow lends certain advantages to the pheasant hunter. Birds can be more easily seen in distant feeder fields and coverts in snowtime, crippled birds can be readily trailed, and dead pheasants are easier to find in heavy cover. Yet, snowtime is hardly a situation in which the calloused gunner exploits a vulnerable population and kills pheasants at will. My success rate at tracking and shooting pheasants on snow is about the same as my fox-trailing with a rifle—reinforcing my long-held conviction that the ring-necked pheasant is nothing less than a feathered fox.

There's something I miss in my late-season hunting these days.

For years I have begun pheasant hunts on wheels instead of legs, leaving home in car or truck, driving as many miles as necessary, and returning in comfort. The day that I began to do this marked the end of my boyhood and pushed back the prairie horizons, but it wasn't necessarily progress.

It will never be like just stepping off the back stoop and loading my gun, walking across the garden, and being in hunting grounds almost at once. Pure hunting, that was, from home den out into the coverts and back to den again, like a young fox. It was never diluted, as now, with synthetic beginnings on highways.

Each cover patch would point to one beyond until I had overextended myself as I always did, and night had found me far from home. There is a keen and poignant quality in being a famished boy far afield with night coming on and miles of crusted snow yet to negotiate, the pheasants hanging over your shoulder with their legs tied with binder twine, and the little Monkey Ward double gun beginning to weigh heavy. (I had bought the gun's mismatched 16-gauge shells at Walsh's Hardware, out of a bin where they were all mixed together and served up like rock candy—three cents apiece and you took what came up in the scoop, with no picking over the shells for preferred shot sizes or other such nonsense.)

Night coming on and glory lost, for there would be no daylight in which to parade past neighbor girls' houses, the bright roosters hung from my shoulder. The girls would never know what they had missed, but I would.

Now, for the first time in ten hours, a weakness beginning in the legs, and that exquisite knifelife stab high between the shoulder blades. Ten hours since oatmeal and coffee, with long crossings over plowed ground, and ranging through horseweed thickets laced with wild plum and raspberry canes, through fallow pastures of heavy tented grass, creekside willow slaps, over the high fields and under the bluffs, and into little cattail sloughs whose icy floors were skeined with pheasant tracks. And once, a half-mile dash along a crusted fenceline trying to flush a running rooster and failing to, gasping in the cold air and coughing for an hour afterward.

My lips and nose would be raw and sore from hours of wiping them with the backs of woolen mittens that were quickly frozen. There was a winter twilight when I stopped and leaned against an old wolf cottonwood to rest, and took off my woolen stocking cap to mop my sore nose. It was the first time since morning that I'd taken off the cap; when I ran my fingers through my matted hair it protested at being disturbed, and I remember thinking it was funny that even my hair should hurt, but not funny enough to laugh about.

The wind freshening, swinging into the northwest and freighted with the smell of more snow. By now my corduroy pants are frozen to the knees, as stiff as stovepipes and rattling against each other and against the shoepacs that I had bought with my first fur check the year before. One foot ahead of the other, breaking through snow crust at each step, the slung birds cutting through old sheepskin coat and into thin shoulder, and a sort of homesickness growing at the sight of each lighted kitchen window in farmhouses across the fields. And finally, up ahead in the gathering darkness, a square of yellow reflecting on snow, strangely warm and vivid after the long hours of unrelieved white and gray. There ahead, a circle of light and warmth for a young hunter come home of a winter evening, late in pheasant season.

At last, up the back steps and out of the wild night into the rich kitchen smell of home, where potroast with whole onions and carrots and potatoes is waiting on the back of the stove, and buttercrusted rolls still hot, with much-loved voices laughing and half-scolding and the close comfort of it wrapping a boy like a grandmother's quilt. I would take off coat and mittens before I began eating—but only because mother forced me to. And soon to sleep, out in the back room with its icy linoleum, mounded over with lamb's-wool comforters and fleecy blankets smelling of cedar, the deep guiltless slumber of a hunter who has spent everything that he had of himself, and hunted as well as he knew how.

Just being young was part of this, of course, and coming home was part of it, too. But there was more—a wild purity of hunting that was wholly free and true. It was hunting with all the fat rendered away, and reduced to the clean white bone. It was a closing of the magic circle of man, animal and land, and once a boy glimpses this he remembers it all of his days.

This is the essence for which I will always hunt, for I often misplace it and seem seldom able to find it in the old full measure that I knew. But when it's found, it will likely be on some iron prairie at the knell of the year, with a cunning old ringneck out ahead and showing me the way.

Tracks to Remember

BY TOM HENNESSEY

THERE MUST BE something in the air up there in Bangor, Maine. Or maybe it's the water. I don't know, but the fact is that two really fine writers live only a few blocks from each other and year after year keep turning out the kind of prose people want to read.

One writer is the mega-bestseller novelist Stephen King, internationally famous. The other is Tom Hennessey, Outdoor Columnist for the *Bangor Daily News,* whose fame will never match Stephen King, of course, but who has been writing memorable pieces appreciated by Maine readers for many years.

"Tracks to Remember" is a little gem of a whitetail hunting story and is one of the pieces collected in Tom's book *Feathers 'n Fins,* published by Amwell Press in 1989.

Tom's talent does not end with his writing. He is an artist whose paintings, prints, and drawings are eagerly sought by collectors. By the time you read this, Tom will have out a new book of stories and paintings, *Handy to Home,* published by Down East Books. And no doubt at the same time Stephen King will have something new on the bestseller lists.

Steeple-like spruces were silhouetted against a sky of gunmetal gray as Hank Lyons slipped five 170-grain cartridges into the magazine of his .30-30 carbine. Fully loaded, the magazine held six of the flat-nosed .30s. Somewhere long ago—probably because he liked the lines, angles, and curve of its configuration—Hank had decided that five was his lucky number.

With a flip of the lever action he chambered a round, then eased the cocked hammer onto the safety position. At a brisk pace, he began hiking the grown-up tote road that would cross a brook about a mile into the woods. You'd have thought it was springtime. Two days earlier, Ol' Man Winter had thrown one of his white-with-rage tantrums. Shortly thereafter, he began running a temperature and now the woods were shrouded with ground fog. Every bough and branch wore beads of moisture.

Arriving at the brook, Hank wasn't surprised to see that the log bridge had partially collapsed under the constant weight of time. The makeshift span had been old when, years before, he first crossed it while bird hunting. A short distance beyond the brook, several sets of deer tracks crisscrossed the road. "Does," Hank allowed. "At least a couple. Maybe a fawn with 'em—got to be a buck around somewhere." The tracks indicated that deer were using the mixed growth to the left of the road, and a fir thicket to the right.

The mixed growth climbed a knoll whose top was crowned with apple trees glowing with "golden nuggets." Quietly, Hank worked his way up the slope until he had a commanding view of the area. "As good as any and better than most," he said as he brushed the snow from a wind-toppled spruce. Sitting among the boughs, he checked the hammer of the carbine.

Hank Lyons could sit all day in a duck blind, but he found it difficult to stay anchored for more than an hour on a deer stand. For that reason he had waited until afternoon to enter the woods. Within an hour and a half at the most, dusk would demand his departure. Along the ice-rimmed brook, the ground fog was more concentrated. Thickening and thinning, it swirled like ghosts rising from snow-covered crypts.

Directly across from where Hank was sitting—about sixty yards away—a leaning birch opened a white gash in the gray-green timber. Slightly to the right of the birch squatted the stub of what was once an immense pine. Now and then, the ground fog became so cottony that those objects were momentarily obscured from Hank's view. The wind must have been weary—it never so much as sighed in the tops of the spruces.

"There ain't no sense in sittin' out a deer," Hank had been told early on, "if you can't sit still." That much he had learned. Any movement he made was slower than a Southern drawl. The carbine was cradled across his lap. Slush slid off a bough and stabbed coldly down his neck. Hurry up and wait.

A drizzle that came close to rain began falling and watercolored the woods a shade darker. It seemed that Hank watched the second-hand of his watch sweep the next half hour away. He had about convinced himself that he was wasting his time when he saw a flicker of movement. Near the tote road, the tip of a fir bough nodded. An instant later a dark-furred animal made a swift crossing and disappeared into the fir thicket. "Fisher," Hank observed. "Probably squirrel hunting. He'll do a hell of a lot better than I will."

Again he glanced at his watch. Again he slowly scanned the steamy surroundings. When his eyeballs locked up, he felt it all the way down to his toes.

Squarely in front of the pine stub stood a deer—wearing horns. Just like that. No sight. No sound. Just there. When it comes to quiet, they'd put a shadow to shame. In a situation like that, it takes a second or so to sort things out. From its coiled-tight posture, Hank knew this was no young buck blinded by doe scent, and there was no mistaking that the eight-pointer sensed his presence.

Statue-still, and with a tautness almost tangible, hunter and hunted stared. "If I make a wrong move," Hank thought, "his mainspring will unwind all at once." Directly the buck eased his nose forward, slowly lowered his head and turned it to one side—like a bird dog sifting scent. Hank's thumb cocked the hammer of the carbine. To him, the muffled click sounded like a rock being dropped through shell ice. Taking a step backward, the buck blew. "Please, God."

So slowly it was painful, Hank began lifting the carbine from his lap. To his left—thicker than smoke from a smudge—a bank of fog was following the brook. Like a curtain of white being drawn across a dimly lit stage, it drifted between them, obliterating the buck from Hank's view. Seizing the opportunity, he snapped the carbine to his shoulder, snugged his cheek onto the stock, and squinted through the drizzle-fuzzed sights. Long moments later, the birch leaned. "Right . . . about . . ." The pine stub squatted. Shocked, Hank lifted his head and stared into the dripping, dusky woods. No antlers. No ears. No rut-swollen neck. Not to be outdone, the woods-wise buck also had taken advantage of the well-timed "smoke screen."

Springing to his feet, Hank searched for movement. Not a sign. Hoping for a last-chance shot, he hurried down the slope and crossed the brook. Locating the buck's tracks, he followed them. The wary whitetail had exited through the same door he used for his entrance. In the woods, dusk means darkness. Disappointed as he was, Hank, with a steamy expulsion of breath, conceded, "Just as well. If I wounded him I wouldn't have had time to trail him, and it's a pretty good bet the coyotes would catch up with him during the night—just as well."

If you've never been in the woods on a wet November night, then you don't know the meaning of darkness. Hank's spirits were brightened, however, and his strides lengthened as he recalled the words of a now-departed deer hunter: "You'll soon forget the ones you drag out," his grandfather had said, "but the ones that outfox you will leave tracks on your mind."

Remembering Shooting-Flying:
A Key West Letter

BY ERNEST HEMINGWAY

A MONG SEVERAL EXCELLENT pieces Ernest Hemingway wrote for *Esquire* magazine, including the short story *The Snows of Kiliman-jaro,* "Remembering Shooting-Flying" is a classic example of bonded "Papa Hemingway" prose of the Key West years, the 1930s. The piece appeared in *Esquire* in February, 1935, as one of the series of "Key West Letters" Hemingway had been encouraged to write by his friend, *Esquire* founder and editor Arnold Gingrich. While Hemingway's safari classic, *The Green Hills of Africa,* and the short story "The Short, Happy Life of Francis Macomber," are well known, many readers may not have seen "Shooting-Flying." If so, they will be struck by the vitality and freshness of the prose, both Hemingway trademarks when Papa was "going good" and getting it all on paper "the way it was."

Among the most memorable moments in the "Key West Letters" is the "Letter" called "Marlin Off Morro," in which Hemingway mentions, almost casually, an old commercial fisherman's epic struggle to land a huge marlin, then having it eaten by sharks. In the early '50s, of course, that incident had gestated in Hemingway's mind long enough and emerged on paper as *The Old Man and the Sea.*

There is a heavy norther blowing; the gulf is too rough to fish and there is no shooting now. When you are through work it is nearly dark and you can ride out on the boulevard by the sea and throw clay targets with a hand trap against this gale and they will dip and jump and rise into strange angles like a jacksnipe in the wind. Or you can throw them out with the gale behind them and they will go like a teal over the water. Or you can get down below the sea wall and have some one throw them out high over your head riding the wind, but if you puff one into black dust you can not pretend it was an old cock pheasant unless you are a better pretender than I am. The trouble is there isn't any thud, nor is there the line of bare trees, nor are you standing on a wet, leaf-strewn road, nor do you hear the beaters, nor the racket when a cock gets up and, as he tops the trees, you are on him, then ahead of him, and at the shot he turns over and there is that thump when he lands. Shooting driven pheasants is worth whatever you pay for it.

But when you cannot shoot you can remember shooting and I would rather stay home, now, this afternoon and write about it than go out and sail clay saucers in the wind, trying to break them and wishing they were what they're not.

When you have been lucky in your life you find that just about the time the best of the books run out (and I would rather read again for the first time *Anna Karenina, Far Away and Long Ago, Buddenbrooks, Wuthering Heights, Madame Bovary, War and Peace, A Sportsman's Sketches, The Brothers Karamazov, Hail and Farewell, Huckleberry Finn, Winesburg, Ohio, La Reine Margot, La Maison Tellier, Le Rouge et le Noire, La Chartreuse de Parme, Dubliners,* Yeats's *Autobiographies* and a few others than have an assured income of a million dollars a year) you have a lot of damned fine things that you can remember. Then when the time is over in which you have done the things that you can now remember, and while you are doing other things, you find that you can read the books again and, always, there are a few, a very few, good new ones. Last year there was *La Condition Humaine* by André Malraux. It was translated, I do not know how well, as *Man's Fate,* and sometimes it is as good as Stendhal and that is something no prose writer has been in France for over fifty years.

But this is supposed to be about shooting, not about books, although some of the best shooting I remember was in Tolstoi and I have often wondered how the snipe fly in Russia now and whether shooting pheasants is counter-revolutionary. When you have loved three things all your life, from the earliest you can remember; to fish, to shoot and, later, to read; and when, all your life, the necessity to write has been your master, you learn to remember and, when you think back you remember more fishing and shooting and reading than anything else and that is a pleasure.

You can remember the first snipe you ever hit walking on the prairie with your father. How the jacksnipe rose with a jump and you hit him on the second swerve and had to wade out into a slough after him and brought him in wet, holding him by the bill, as proud as a bird dog, and you can remember all the snipe since in many places. You can remember the miracle it seemed when you hit your first pheasant when he roared up from under your feet to top a sweet briar thicket and fell with his wings pounding and you had to wait till after dark to bring him into town because they were protected, and you can feel the bulk of him still inside your shirt with his long tail up under your armpit, walking in to town in the dark along the dirt road that is now North Avenue where the gypsy wagons used to camp when there was prairie out to the Des Plaines river where Wallace Evans had a game farm and the big woods ran along the river where the Indian mounds were.

I came by there five years ago and where I shot that pheasant there was a hot dog place and filling station and the north prairie, where we hunted snipe in the spring and skated on the sloughs when they froze in the winter, was all a subdivision of mean houses, and in the town, the house where I was born was gone and they had cut down the oak trees and built an apartment house close out against the street. So I was glad I went away from there as soon as I did. Because when you like to shoot and fish you have to move often and always further out and it doesn't make any difference what they do when you are gone.

The first covey of partridges I ever saw, they were ruffed grouse but we called them partridges up there, was with my father and an Indian named Simon Green and we came on them dusting and feeding in the sun beside the grist mill on Horton's Creek in Michigan. They looked as big as turkeys to me and I was so excited with the whirr of the wings that I missed both shots I had, while my father, shooting an old lever action Winchester pump, killed five out of the covey and I can remember the Indian picking them up and laughing. He was an old fat Indian, a great admirer of my father, and when I look back at that shooting I am a great admirer of my father too. He was a beautiful shot, one of the fastest I have ever seen; but he was too nervous to be a great money shot.

Then I remember shooting quail with him when I do not think I could have been more than ten years old, and he was showing me off, having me shoot pigeons that were flying around a barn, and some way I broke the hammer spring in my single barrel 20 gauge, and the only gun down there at my Uncle's place in Southern Illinois that no one was shooting was a big old L. C. Smith double that weighed, probably, about nine pounds. I could not hit anything with it and it kicked me so it made my nose bleed. I was afraid to shoot it and I got awfully tired carrying it and my father had left me standing in a thickety patch of timber while he was working out the singles from a covey we had scattered. There was a red bird up in a tree and then I looked down and under the tree was a quail, freshly dead. I picked it up and it was still warm. My father had evidently hit it when the covey went up with a stray pellet and it had flown this far and dropped. I looked around to see nobody was in sight and then, laying the quail down by my feet, shut both my eyes and pulled the trigger on that old double barrel. It kicked me against the tree and when I opened it up I found it had doubled and fired both barrels at once and my ears were ringing and my nose was bleeding. But I picked the quail up, reloaded the gun, wiped my nose and set out to find my father. I was sick of not hitting any.

"Did you get one, Ernie?"

I held it up.

"It's a cock," he said. "See his white throat? It's a beauty."

But I had a lump in my stomach that felt like a baseball from lying to him and that night I remember crying with my head under the patchwork quilt after he was asleep because I had lied to him. If he would have waked up, I would have told him, I think. But he was tired and sleeping heavily. I never told him.

So I won't think any more about that but I remember now how I broke the spring in the 20 gauge. It was from snapping the hammer on an empty chamber practicing swinging on the pigeons after they wouldn't let me shoot any more. And some older boys came along the road when I was carrying the pigeons from the barn to the house and one of them said I didn't shoot those pigeons. I called him a liar and the smaller of the two whipped hell out of me. That was an unlucky trip.

On a day as cold as this you can remember duck shooting in the blind, hearing their wings go whichy-chu-chu-chu in the dark before daylight. That is the first thing I remember of ducks; the whistly, silk tearing sound the fast wingbeats make; just as what you remember first of geese is how slow they seem to go when they are traveling, and yet they are moving so fast that the first one you ever killed was two behind the one you shot at, and all that night you kept waking up and remembering how he folded up and fell. While the woodcock is an easy bird to hit, with a soft flight like an owl, and if you do miss him he will probably pitch down and give you another shot. But what a bird to eat flambé with armagnac cooked in his own juice and butter, a little mustard added to make a sauce, with two strips of bacon and pommes soufflé and Corton, Pommard, Beaune, or Chambertin to drink.

Now it is colder still and we found ptarmigan in the rocks on a high plain above and to the left of the glacier by the Madelener-haus in the Vorarlberg with it blowing a blizzard and the next day we followed a fox track all day on skis and saw where he had caught a ptarmigan underneath the snow. We never saw the fox.

There were chamois up in that country too and black cock in the woods below the timber-line and big hares that you found sometimes at night when we were coming home along the road. We ate them jugged and drank Tyroler wine. And why, today, remember misses?

There were lots of partridges outside of Constantinople and we used to have them roasted and start the meal with a bowl of caviar, the kind you never will be able to afford again, pale grey, the grains as big as buck shot and a little vodka with it, and then the partridges, not overdone, so that when you cut them there was the juice, drinking Caucasus burgundy, and serving French fried potatoes with them and then a salad with roquefort dressing and another bottle of what was the number of that wine? They all had numbers. Sixty-one I think it was.

And did you ever see the quick, smooth-lifting, reaching flight the lesser bustard has, or make a double on them, right and left, or shoot at flighting sand grouse coming to water early in the morning and see the great variety of shots they give and hear the cackling sound they make when flighting, a little like the noise of prairie chickens on the plains when they go off, fast beat of wings and soar, fast beat of wings and soar stiff-winged, and see a coyote watching you a long way out of range and see an antelope turn and stare and lift his head when he hears the shotgun thud? Sand grouse, of course, fly nothing like a prairie chicken. They have a cutting, swooping flight like pigeons but they make that grouse-like cackle, and with the lesser bustard and the teal, there is no bird to beat them for pan, the griddle or the oven.

So you recall a curlew that came in along the beach one time in a storm when you were shooting plover, and jumping teal along a water course that cut a plain on a different continent, and having a hyena come out of the grass when you were trying to stalk up on a pool and see him turn and look at ten yards and let him have it with the shotgun in his ugly face, and standing, to your waist in water, whistling a flock of golden plover back, and then, back in the winter woods, shooting ruffed grouse along a trout stream where only an otter fished now, and all the places and the different flights of birds, jumping three mallards now, down where the beavers cut away the cottonwoods, and seeing the drake tower, white-breasted, green-headed, climbing and get above him and splash him in the old Clark's Fork, walking along the bank watching him until he floated onto a pebbly bar.

Then there are sage hens, wild as hawks that time, the biggest grouse of all, getting up out of range, and out of range, until you came around an alfalfa stack and four whirred up one after the other at your feet almost and, later walking home, in your hunting coat they seemed to weigh a ton.

I think they all were made to shoot because if they were not why did they give them that whirr of wings that moves you suddenly more than any love of country? Why did they make them all so good to eat and why did they make the ones with silent flight like wood-cock, snipe, and lesser bustard, better eating even than the rest?

Why does the curlew have that voice, and who thought up the plover's call, which takes the place of noise of wings, to give us that catharsis wing shooting has given to men since they stopped flying hawks and took to fowling pieces? I think that they were made to shoot and some of us were made to shoot them and if that is not so well, never say we did not tell you that we liked it.

A Bearded Legend:
My Best All-Time Trophy

BY CHARLES ELLIOTT

IN MY CAREER of working in the outdoor magazine field, particularly with *Sports Afield* and *Outdoor Life,* one of the things I have treasured most has been my association with Charlie Elliott. A fellow Georgian whom I never dreamed of meeting when I first began devouring his stories as a teenager, Charlie Elliott is not only one of the most important writers in *Outdoor Life*'s history, he is a sportsman and gentleman in the ultimate measure of those words. Here, from the book *Turkey Hunting with Charlie Elliott,* is the story of his greatest hunt. I don't think you'll ever find a finer story or a finer man.

From the time of man's creation until he steps beyond the shadows, his life is not so much a matter of years, or seasons, or days as it is of moments. A vast majority of these are so vapid and humdrum that the mind makes no attempt to file them away in its incredible storehouse. Many others remain as memories or facts available to our mental computers. A few of the latter stand out bright and vivid and, in spite of the years, never lose one sparkle of their original brilliance or beauty.

One of those highlights in my life had to do with a wild turkey gobbler. I have avoided saying *the* highlight for fear of domestic or other repercussions, but my moment of grandeur with that magnificent bird stands close to the top of the list. There's not a sound or movement or spot of color in that high drama that I've forgotten, or will ever forget.

When I first met the Cohutta gobbler, I had no faint suspicion that he and I were embarking on such a splendid outdoor adventure. The woods were dressed in pastel shades of greens and golds and splotched with chalky clumps of dogwood, making them seem almost unreal. This was spring gobbling season in the mountains, and I was hunting alone in the Cohutta Range on the Georgia-Tennessee line.

For me, this is one of the most stimulating hunt seasons of the year. The forest floor is bright with flowers, tree buds are bursting with new life, and the vitality of the woods and its creatures make it seem on the verge of erupting into some unbelievable fantasy of sound and color.

At dawn I'd walked out the backbone of an isolated ridge and paused to listen for resonant notes that might indicate a big buck turkey on its roost or on the prowl. For an hour I stood there with my back against an oak tree, while the dawn woods came to life and the sun touched a distant mountain with burnished copper.

About flying-down time, when there's light enough for a turkey to distinguish the bushes from the bobcats, I yelped the cedar box in my hand, making notes like those of an amorous hen. This sound will sometimes set a silent old tom's genes to percolating and motivate him to reply with a lusty gobble to tell his intended that he's in the mood to solve her problem—and his.

When, after fifteen minutes, my yelps brought no response, I strolled another quarter-mile along the ridgetop to try again.

There I first heard him, somewhere beyond the wild jumble of ridges and valleys sprawled out below me. His notes, high-pitched and vibrant, denoted an old gobbler. From long experience I knew that the closer I could get without spooking him, the better my chances would be to put him in the bag. So I struck out in a beeline across the ragged series of ridges, navigating the rough valleys and pausing on each ridge to call and get an answer.

On the fourth ridge I sensed that he was somewhere near. When I clucked my yelper and didn't get an answer, I considered that the bird and I were at close range. I stood motionless, straining my ears, and after a few minutes heard some creature working in the dry leaves that blanketed the shallow cove just beyond the hilltop. The crest of the summit was thinly clad in laurel, and the ground around the thickets was reasonably bare of leaves. In a half-crouch to keep my head below the narrow backbone of the ridge, I circled to a point directly above where I could hear the parched leaves rattling.

After listening for a moment, I concluded definitely that the sound was made by turkeys scratching for sustenance in the brown carpet, though they hadn't made a note of any kind to verify their presence. I stood perfectly still, trying to determine what my next move should be.

I have little doubt that I'd have concocted some scheme to get a look at those birds over my gunsights, if a gray squirrel hadn't chosen that exact moment to make a trip through the scrubby timber. When I heard him rattle the bark on a tree above me, I instinctively glanced up. The squirrel was so close I could have touched him with the tip of my gun barrel. I had my camouflage clothing on but had neglected to smear my face that morning with bowhunter's paint, preferring instead to use a gauze mask when the time came to sit in a blind and call up a gobbler.

When the squirrel saw my white face and identified me, he seemed to go berserk. He made a flying arc to the next tree, another long leap, and then in his third jump he either misjudged distance or broke a limb in his headlong flight. I got a glimpse of him in midair, then heard him hit the leaves on the slope below.

If those startled turkeys had taken to the sky, I could have killed one. They were scratching within 40 feet of where I stood. When I heard them running in the leaves, I charged through the laurel, hoping for a shot. But by the time I spotted the birds, they were sprinting up the far slope, out of shotgun range. One was the tallest gobbler I'd ever seen in the woods. He simply dwarfed the two jakes with him.

The season was running out, but I spent m last eight days on the trail of that big turkey. I still feel that if all those slopes were piled on top of one another, I must have climbed a hundred miles high. Joel Biggs, a local wildlife officer, told me that turkeys often range as far as 4 or 5 miles, and I must have looked in every cove and on top of every ridge in those 20 square miles.

I hunted through the open seasons in Georgia and Tennessee and on the Ocoee Wildlife Management Area. On five different occasions I could have put a young gobbler in the bag, but I passed up each one. One had a raspy voice I thought belonged to my old bird. He gave me a few hair-raising moments. Yet when he walked around the end of a log, 50 feet away, I saw that his head was no longer than my index finger.

I was stricken with big-turkey fever. That huge gobbler had my tag on him and I wanted him more than any big-game trophy I'd ever brought home—and that included sheep, bears, elk, and caribou.

Before the hunt was over that spring, I met one other mountain man who was on the trail of this same bird. Gobbler hunters have a special feeling of camaraderie. If they happen to meet on a high ridge or isolated woodland trail, it's like two Daniel Boones bumping into one another. They exchange cordialities either by sign language or in whispers, briefly swap plans so they won't conflict in choice of territory, and trade bits of information on fresh scratchings or other sign. They might even take a few minutes off to compare the tones of their turkey calls. Then, for the remainder of the day, each man will listen for the sound of the other's gun—hoping all the while he won't hear it.

This grizzled mountaineer I met came down the trail as softly as a forest cat. After the usual ritual of greetings, he showed me his call and I yelped my box for him. The old fellow listened with a slightly cocked ear to the notes, then nodded.

"Gobblers around here shore oughta like that Southern accent," he commented. Since he seemed a very affable and gracious fellow, I took his words with a grain of saltpeter.

During the three seasons that I devoted my full attention to this long-bearded old patriarch of the forest, I learned all over again that killing a large wild gobbler presents perhaps the greatest challenge in hunting. It doesn't take the courage needed to coldly face a charging grizzly or the stamina necessary to climb for a mountain goat or trophy ram. But nothing else requires more in woodsmanship, patience, and ingenuity.

As I said, I stayed on the trail of the Cohutta gobbler for three seasons. I filed my license in my home state of Georgia and took birds in Alabama, Mississippi, Oklahoma, and New Mexico, and could have added Tennessee to the list with a lesser gobbler, had there not been only this one I was truly interested in.

To make the cheese more binding, as they say in Crackerese, I learned that my old gobbler had already acquired a reputation in both the Cohutta Mountains and around Ocoee. Several of the local sportsmen had an eye on him, and more than a few had devoted most of their spring gunning to the bird. So I approached each April season with the growing apprehension that one of those mountain men might get to the gobbler before I had another chance at it.

I saw the bird a number of times. It seemed to lead a charmed life. Only once could I have blown the whistle on him. He walked across the road in front of my car. He was only a few yards away when I stopped, jumped from behind the steering wheel, and threw a shell into the chamber of my gun. The huge gobbler walked unhurriedly and almost majestically up the slope, as though he knew just as well as I that I wouldn't shoot. To bushwhack that old patriarch would have been as heinous a crime as ambushing my best friend.

Once I called him to within 75 yards of my blind. For thirty minutes he stayed in one spot, strutting and gobbling. Then he vanished as suddenly and completely as if he had been erased. It made me wonder if I'd seen him at all and should seek psychiatric help.

On another occasion I ran into him at least a couple of miles from where we'd first met. He was on the Georgia side of the line, on the last day of the Georgia open season. I was traveling a long "lead" (which is the local term for a main ridge) just after daylight. When I paused on the brow of a slope to call, he answered. At least, I was almost certain I recognized his voice.

I made a breathless detour of more than a mile to the ridge above him. But before I could get into position, half a dozen crows spotted the tom. Ganging up on and harassing a lone wild turkey is a favorite crow pastime, and from their language I knew they were really working this one over.

I crept downhill as close as I dared to get to the melee and set up my stand for business. For more than an hour we maneuvered around on that point of the ridge. Finally the crows, or an unknown intruder, or something I said on my wingbone call or cedar box spooked him. Or maybe he just got tired of playing games. He turned away and crossed a shallow cove to the thick laurel on the next ridge. The crows apparently lost him in the laurel, but when he hit the open ridgetop they found him again. Finally the whole side show continued out of hearing over the crest.

The foreboding that someone else would get to that gobbler before me grew acute when, on the third season of our acquaintance, I had to miss the first three open days. My only consolation was that spring came later than usual that year and those first legal days were rainy and cold, which might somewhat dampen the ardor between toms and hens, normally in full blossom by then. As for the dedicated gobbler hunters, I knew they'd be in the woods even if we were in the middle of a second ice age.

On the morning of the fourth day, I was on the mountain half an hour before daylight. The brown carpet of leaves was white with frost, and a cold blanket of air lay across the hills.

I wasn't exactly pleased with the way my plans had been disrupted on this particular morning. Phil Stone (an old hunting partner) and I had decided to hunt together through the gobbling hours, then separate and scout out a tremendous territory for signs. My wife Kayte refused to stay in camp alone and insisted on coming with us.

Three's a crowd, even at turkey hunting, so when we parked in a little gap, Phil took off down a dim logging road that skirted a narrow valley. I'd have sent Kayte in the other direction, but she gets lost even in our backyard, and I knew we'd then have to spend the rest of the season looking for her. So she stayed with me, which meant confining my hunting to the more gentle terrain around the car.

As the first dawn light turned the woods from black to gray, a ruffed grouse flashed across the road. Farther down the valley we flushed two more of these colorful birds out of a branch bottom. The dawn was bright and cold as we climbed the point of a low ridge overlooking the valley. From this spot I knew we were high enough to hear turkeys on any of the half-dozen ridges sloping away from that massive range around Big Frog Mountain. Kayte and I got settled and waited until the noise we'd made in the frozen leaves was forgotten by the forest creatures around us and they began to move about once more.

On my box I gave the low, plaintive notes of a hen. After a few minutes without an answer, I called much louder. A quarter of an hour later, I rattled the box with the throaty call of a gobbler. All this activity produced exactly no results, except for the raucous notes of a crow across the valley and the loud drumming of a woodpecker on a hollow stub nearby.

Kayte and I climbed over the crest of the ridge into the next valley to repeat our performance. The sun spotlighted the tops of the highest hills and the line of light gradually crept down the mountains until it touched and warmed our half-numb hands and cheeks.

We moved from one ridge to another and heard nothing that resembled the notes of a turkey. At 8:30 A.M. we made our way back over the trail to where we met Phil Stone, who'd also gone through an unproductive session.

The three of us discussed the situation and decided that, with the season so retarded, the birds were not yet courting and probably not even speaking to one another. This evaluation gave me a vast sense of relief, along with some assurance that my big gobbler had not yet been disturbed and that I'd see him again somewhere in these mountain woods.

Kayte and Phil were already in the car, impatiently waiting for me while licking their chops in anticipation over the Bloody Marys they would be soon having at breakfast. I don't know whether it was impulse, instinct, or some strange intuition that suddenly impelled me to step away from the car to the edge of the road with the turkey call in my hand.

I clucked a couple of times, gave the low, breathless notes of a hen, and then listened. No response. I'd expected none. Still, merely to complete the routine, I half-heartedly rattled my box to simulate the call of a gobbler.

There was nothing half-hearted in the challenge that bounced back from the next ridge, almost quickly enough to pass for an echo.

I have no idea how my two partners got out of the car and beside me so fast and so noiselessly, but they now appeared to have lost all interest in breakfast or Bloody Marys. I touched my finger to my lips.

"Stand here a few minutes," I whispered, "and let's see which direction he's headed."

When the buck turkey gobbled again, he was 100 yards farther down the ridge. That was enough for me. My partners agreed that I could travel faster and get ahead of the gobbler if I went alone, and that I also might have a better chance of seeing and definitely identifying him as the one bird I wanted. As for myself, I already knew.

I climbed the slope and circled the side of the hill in a half-run. At the spot where I hoped to intercept the gobbler, I zipped up my camouflage suit and sat down at the base of a big tree with emerald vegetation growing before it.

I wasn't sure yet who it was the tom answered, but he gobbled again shortly after I'd given him the soft, gentle notes of a hen on my slate-type call. Minutes later a second gobbler, this one with a younger voice, set the woods to ringing off to my left.

The smaller tom definitely was coming to me, but the turkey I had planned to intercept walked off his ridge, crossed a rivulet in the hollow, and climbed to a cove that angled away from where I'd taken my stand.

I left the young buck turkey decoying to my squeal and took off across the slope. I didn't even try to convince myself I was acting foolishly in giving up a bird in the hand for a try at that old boy with the rusty pipes. The big tom had already cost me at least five gobblers since I'd first met him. I figured he should be worth at least one more.

By midmorning the leaves had lost their frosty coating. The drying forest floor became much noisier underfoot. I had to pause every few minutes to get another fix on the gobbler, who continued to answer my calls. We were walking at about the same speed. By the time I reached the road that separated Georgia's Cohutta Range from Tennessee's Ocoee, the tom had crossed the road and climbed the side of a massive mountain into the forbidden area.

This appeared to be the end of the trail. The Ocoee area was closed except for five two-day periods in April, and I wouldn't have another chance at him until then. It looked like old long-beard had once again given me the shaft.

By all sane criteria, I knew it was hardly possible to entice that cagey gobbler to backtrack so late in the day over the route he'd just taken. Especially since he had been intent on going the other way from the moment we'd first heard him.

One thing for sure. I had nothing to lose by trying. I whacked my cedar box with a couple of lusty yelps. Almost instantly, he came back with a high-pitched gobble. I settled down in a little clump of pines in legal territory to wait. At least ten minutes went by before his resonant tones again rolled down the mountain—and this time they seemed to come from farther off. I waited. His next call came from near the top of the mountain. There wasn't any doubt in my mind now that he was walking out of the picture. In desperation I gobbled my box as loud as I could make it quaver.

For a full twenty minutes, complete silence. Then he sounded off again from approximately the same spot where I'd last heard him. My heart gave an extra thump or two. At least I'd stopped his flight . . . momentarily.

I waited. And waited. And waited. I have no idea how long I sat in that one spot, trying to convince myself he'd already gone on and over the mountain. I suppose the only thing that kept the seat of my pants pressed against the unfriendly rocks and roots was the knowledge that many times when a tom stops gobbling, but hasn't been spooked, he's coming to investigate. If so, there wasn't any harm in giving him my exact location. Stealthily I reached for the slate and cedar stick, touched them softly together for a few dainty clucks, then dropped them beside me on the ground. Most novice hunters are likely to call much too much.

To wait—and keep on waiting—requires an enormous amount of patience. Even more so, when there's no hint of any kind whether you are on the verge of success.

At last I gave up. The rocks and roots now seemed to be actively attacking my hindquarters. My legs felt numb from sitting in one position. Phil and Kayte—and beyond them the Bloody Marys, country sausage, eggs, and biscuits—were waiting. I hadn't heard a peep out of my gobbler for three-quarters of an hour. By now he could be in the next county. With disappointment welling through me, I shifted my position to reach for the slate and cedar stick I had dropped to the ground.

Suddenly somewhere a limb or twig cracked; the sound a deer makes as it tiptoes through the woods. I came to full attention again, straining my eyes for a glimpse of feet or head or brown deerhide. For a dozen minutes I sat motionless. At last I decided that the animal or whatever that had cracked that stick must have drifted on by.

Once more I relaxed and prepared to gather up my gear and call it a day. I was on the verge of standing up to give my numb muscles some relief when I heard footsteps in the leaves. The cadence was exactly that of a man who slips stealthily along, stalking unseen quarry.

Again I froze. I couldn't see a man or make out movement of any kind, but at the moment there wasn't anything I needed less than a load of high brass No. 4 or 6 pellets smack in my face.

I had been straining so hard to see some deer or human form that my first glimpse of the gobbler now came as a distinct shock. He was beyond and walking parallel to a contour that dropped off like a terrace about 20 yards in front of my blind. The contour hid all but the meaty, wrinkled top of his head above the wattles. I couldn't see enough yet to definitely identify him as the old patriarch who had led me on a merry three-year chase, but that one glimpse still had me all shook up inside.

He took two more steps, bringing his head higher up above the contour, but I still couldn't see his beard or judge his size. He put his head down to peck at something on the forest floor, and while his eye was out of sight I quickly raised my gun. On its way up, the gun dislodged a dead Y-shaped stem. It straddled and lodged on the gun barrel in such a way that I couldn't see the sights. The bird continued to walk, growing taller and taller as it came up the shoulder of the hill, and I moved the barrel slowly to keep it in line with his head.

It was purely a matter of luck that at the same moment my gobbler walked behind a large tree trunk, a protruding twig suddenly flipped the Y-stem from my barrel. When the tom stepped past the tree, my sights were directly on his head.

My 12-gauge Winchester pump gun was loaded with shells holding No. 6 shot. Some hunters like large shot—No. 4 or No. 2—but I know I have a better chance of hitting the vital parts of a bird's head and neck with a denser pattern. Most shots in this type of hunting are at a bird's head and neck while he's still on the ground. I often back up my first round of No. 6 with a No. 4 and then a No. 2 load, which gives me a reserve of progressively larger pellets to break down a turkey that flies or runs after the first shot.

There he stood for all of five seconds with his head up in a patch of sunlight, as tall and majestic as I remembered him from two springs before. He was so close it seemed I could reach out and touch him with my gun. The sunlight on his feathers made them ripple in a display of copper, green, and gold so resplendent that I caught my breath. What a beauty. Then I saw his heavy beard and knew beyond any doubt that he was indeed the old patriarch I'd dreamed about for so long.

It was almost sacrilegious to shatter that magnificent moment with a shot—but the powerful impulses developed in a lifetime of hunting triggered the gun. It was a clean, one-shot kill.

That's when all the excitement of the past two hours finally hit me. My hands shook as I tried to unstrap the camera from my shoulder. When I hefted the bird for weight and saw how far I had to lift his feet so that his head would clear the ground, I got the shakes all over again.

He pulled the hand on the corroded old camp scales up to 25$\frac{1}{2}$ pounds—the largest mountain gobbler I've seen, and one of the biggest turkeys I had ever killed, including the heavier breeds from some of the Southern plantations.

Phil peered wonderingly over his glasses at the scales.

"There just ain't no telling," he said, "what this critter might have weighed, if these scales weren't so rusty." (We checked them later on and found that the scales did, in fact, read almost $1^1/_2$ pounds too low.)

At that moment, though, the gobbler's weight didn't make too much difference. He had given me my finest hunt in turkey woods, and he still remains my most highly prized big-game trophy.

The Wings of Dawn

BY GEORGE REIGER

A S CONSERVATION EDITOR of *Field & Stream* magazine, George Reiger strives every month to sustain and protect the outdoor resources we all cherish. But Reiger's considerable talents as a writer are not confined to prose that lashes out at bureaucratic fools and greedy politicians. George Reiger also produces articles and books that plumb the depths of the hunting and fishing experience, from misty mornings of ducks and geese to moonlit nights when the stripers are running. George is an inveterate countryman, living on the Eastern Shore of Virginia. Among his books are the hugely engaging *Heron Hill Chronicle* about his lifestyle on his salt marsh farm, and the widely heralded waterfowling magnum opus, *The Wings of Dawn*, both published by Nick Lyons. This piece is the closing chapter of *The Wings of Dawn* and takes you, quite literally, to the marsh with George Reiger.

Outsiders call us sadists or masochists; sometimes both. Others— mostly ourselves—describe our activities in romantic, even heroic, terms. We take ourselves very seriously and tend to forget that much of duck and goose hunting is fun and sometimes ridiculous.

For two days last season, I scouted a piece of salt marsh where several black ducks and mallards appeared to be in residence. I decided to go in the next day at dawn with my layout boat to try to decoy a limit. All night long, a northeast wind pushed the ocean through the inlets and over sod islands so that by first light, with my retriever tucked between my knees and myself tucked horizontally into the 9-foot punt, the tide began to float the boat off the point where I had hidden her.

I worried lest the boat's rocking would alarm ducks and wondered whether the brisk breeze wouldn't blow the punt completely clear of the reeds. I sat up, took one of the oars, shoved it hard down into the mud, and tied the painter to it. Now let her blow!

A half hour passed with no ducks to the decoys. Geese were flying high overhead, and ducks were trading in the distance. But the storm tide had lifted the boat well above the grass, and little white-capped waves slapped the hull and rocked my half-dozen decoys.

I was on the verge of packing it in when a pair of black ducks appeared low over the marsh obviously looking for company. I squiggled lower, hissed at my dog to stay down, and watched the birds approach from under the brim of my cap. My face was blackened, my pale hands were gloved, and only the stark bar of blued metal and wood resting across my camouflaged chest would spark the birds' suspicions.

Ordinarily they should have come straight in. But with all the marsh under water, they were wary of the curious "log" bumping near their rock-and-rolling buddies. Something wasn't right. They decided to swing by, look the situation over, and think about it.

"Just one," I pleaded. "Just one would make a perfect day. But, Lord, wouldn't a double be sweet!"

The ducks were gone half a minute. Then I noticed them to my right, flying wide of the decoys, but lower. When they turned upwind, no more than ten feet off the water, I knew they were coming—100 yards, 90, 80, 70 . . .

When the birds were less than 60 yards away, the oar suddenly pulled from the mud, surged into the air, slammed down on my head, startled the dog into jumping overboard, and the boat shipped a barrel of icy water that poured in like electricity around my crotch. I watched the black ducks blow away: 150 yards, 200, 300 . . . Then the sky broke loose and sleet obliterated the scene.

With the punt drifting away from the decoys, the dog paddling and whimpering in circles around me, and freezing water sloshing around my hips every time I made the slightest move, I did what any sane man would do: I laughed. I laughed and cussed and laughed again at all the follies of our magnificent recreation.

Halfway through the season, I left a dozen decoys out overnight in a pond. When I returned at dawn, I found two teal missing from the rig. Considerable searching turned up only one where an otter had pulled the bird—dragging the line and weight behind it—30 yards from the edge of the water. Somehow this otter, or a companion—the busy, back-and-forth tracks of otter never make such things clear—had contrived to carry off the other decoy to do with it what only an otter can tell.

I was fascinated; I was charmed. What a bizarre fate for a teal drake facsimile: that it becomes an otter's plaything. When I told one of my neighbors about the experience, he snorted and asked if I had shot enough ducks that day to make up the loss. But then, this man doesn't pretend to be a sportsman.

Two Washington, D.C., friends came down to share a seaside outing with me. An hour after dawn I was looking behind the blind and out to the ocean when I spotted a pair of puddle ducks coming down the coast. I provided the following, over-the-shoulder commentary for my companions:

"They're not too high—They should see the decoys—They have seen the decoys!—They're coming lower—They're going to circle—You should see them by now—They should be right over you—Why doesn't somebody shoot?!"

I turned and found both my companions peering around their end of the blind trying to see where I had been looking. No one was minding the store out front.

"Where are the ducks?" they whispered.

I looked up and saw a pair of gadwall hovering and staring down at me with something approaching bemusement.

"There!"

Guns began blazing and seven shots later we had one of the two birds.

"All right, guys, no more Gong Shows. Each person watches a different direction, and we'll use compass points to indicate where the birds are."

"Good idea," said Paul. "That's south."

"No, that's east."

"South."

"Paul, I live here; that's east."

"You're both wrong," announced Mel, uncapping a tiny compass he had tucked among his spare shells. "That's eastsoutheast."

Debating the fine points of the compass kept us busy until a goldeneye buzzed over the decoys without a shot being fired. We then decided to wrap up the compass conversation and concentrate on duck hunting. We compromised by calling "south" and "eastsoutheast," east and boxed the rest of the imaginary compass card accordingly. Going through the drill made us feel better. It was as though we had actually learned something—as though this time we were prepared for any and all contingencies, even though experience indicates that each fiasco in waterfowling is somehow unique and unforeseeable.

Suddenly we heard the distant murmur of geese.

"North," said Mel, "and coming this way!"

"More like northwest," said Paul, "and the wind will carry them wide."

"Start calling," I ordered. "And stay back in the blind. We don't want to spook them while trying to get a look."

The sound of Canada geese carries a long distance under most any atmospheric condition. Biologists suspect the birds may use their calling to echolocate their way through fog. When Canadas are flying downwind toward a trio of expectant hunters, the honking seems to come from a public address system mounted on the roof of the blind—even when the birds are still half a mile away.

But this time there was no rubber-necking. This time we were ready. My companions and I scrunched into the corners of the blind and matched yelp for yelp the calling of the geese behind us. We didn't go into action until we saw a wingtip flash about 30 yards above the edge of the plywood roof.

"NOW!"

Mel and Paul leaped up and did an audition for a movie called "Abbott and Costello Go Hunting." Paul stepped on Mel's foot, and Mel recovered his balance by knocking Paul back into the corner. Then swinging on the nearest bird, which look as large as a bomber, Mel squeezed the trigger of his empty gun. He had forgotten to reload after the gadwall farce.

Meanwhile I had somehow contrived to insert the thumb tang on the bolt of my semi-automatic shotgun through a hole in my right glove and couldn't get my hand free. My frantic gyrations and furious oaths brought the dog around to the entrance of the blind where he peered in to see what was going on.

A dozen geese flew by unscathed, but our imprecations quickly turned into such uproarious laughter it took still another missed opportunity to sober us up. No, we hadn't been drinking. And we did quite well when we finally got organized. Funny though: I don't remember those details half as well as the foolish way we began.

How do you explain waterfowling to anyone who does not share your faith? How can you even describe events to those who care but were not there?

With my final shot last season, I killed a black duck. That is a simple statement of fact. But those few words mask a range of sensations which could not be duplicated with a sound-and-light replica of the outing.

This is because you'd have to know my dog is old and that day lame, and I wanted to get his mind off his hurt by doing something he loves and does well: jump shooting. You'd also have to know that I had watched half a hundred black ducks angle down in the afternoon mist toward a series of meanders in two drains of the high marsh, and despite a following wind which blew every crunch of spartina grass underfoot ahead of us to spook the wary birds, I was confident that eventually Rocky and I would find an elbow of water to which we could turn upwind and find an unsuspecting duck.

You'd have to hear the whispering wings of birds in the air, and see how I'd periodically squat, less with the hope of having a shot, than to pause and watch the panorama of waterfowl returning to the evening marsh. You'd have to see the pair of mallards pitch to a pond several hundred yards away, and know that because I'd rather kill one of these interlopers of the salt lands than a native black duck, I made a special effort to reach the alert drake and his oblivious hen. You'd see the mallards sitting close by the opposite shore and then noisily flushing out of range. You'd watch Rocky and me turn back to our original course, and when we were 75 yards away, you'd glance back in time to see a solitary black duck take to the air a few feet from where we'd stood while contemplating the fleeing mallards. You'd hear me chuckle and tell my dog that I hoped the crafty bird lived another decade, and you'd see Rocky look up as if he understood every word.

Other ducks were getting up in the mist, but only a few were at extreme range, and you'd know that once the gun was fired, every bird in the marsh would be up and gone. So you wait with me for the shot that can't be missed.

You'd watch me come to a deep, unwadable creek, and while I look for a possible ford, two black ducks leap up from the other side. Despite the fact you are hunting them, the sudden rise of a pair of ducks is always a strangely unexpected event.

You are behind my eyes as I fire at the furthest bird in an attempt to score a double, miss, swing on the nearest, and kill it with a charge of steel 2s. While Rocky swims the channel to retrieve the fallen bird, you let the sight and sound of dozens of ducks rising from all parts of the darkening marsh and the cold mist on your cheek saturate your senses.

My watch tells me there are still seven minutes left in the season. But my day, my year, is done. I turn back toward the distant blind and calculate that in a narrow, ten-square-mile band of salt marsh, I am the only human being, and the proud, head-high sashaying dog striding before me with a black duck in his mouth is all the human companionship a waterfowler needs.

An oar, an otter, a tangled glove, and a last-chance duck. These are the memories of waterfowling. These are the words and experiences we seek to recover or revise each time we return to the marsh. If we weren't dedicated, we would not suffer the small tribulations surrounding our recreation. And it is this dedication—call it "obsession" if you like—that provides hope for the future.

Thousands of years ago, men crouched at the edge of ponds to fling their stones and arrows at ducks and geese lured by crude facsimiles of themselves. So long as waterfowl and men exist, we will hunt the wings of dawn.

Susitna Moose Hunt

BY RUSSELL ANNABEL

WHEN I ARRIVED at *Sports Afield* magazine as an associate editor in 1967, longtime editor-in-chief Ted Kesting told me that Russell Annabel's stories were arguably the most popular hunting features in the magazine, with the legendary Jason Lucas ("the man who fished 365 days a year") leading the fishing readership. Set mostly in Alaska, Annabel's tales were so numerous and so exuberant that readers sometimes wondered if they were really true, or indeed if the man actually existed at all.

"Rusty," as Ted called him, was in fact very real and did spend a large part of his life hunting, fishing, and guiding in Alaska after migrating there from the Upper Midwest. His earlier—and best in my opinion—stories were published in *Sports Afield, Field & Stream,* and *True,* and many of them have been collected in various anthologies. Annabel's strongest book is *Hunting and Fishing in Alaska,* from which this selection is taken. It was published by Knopf and edited by Annabel's friend Angus Cameron. Long out of print, that particular volume can be hard to come by.

Annabel passed away in 1979 while living in Mexico, his home for the last thirty years of his life. Many of the tales he wrote during the final years are an obvious blend of fact and fiction but remain imminently readable.

It was the day Doc and I found out how to hunt the brush country of the great new Susitna moose range. It was a violent day. It was the day Doc got his second chance at the marceled bull. The train of events began while we were sitting in a wild-rose thicket rattling a bone knife-handle across the tines of a shed moose antler, in the hope a bull would hear us and think we were another bull and try to pick a fight with us. A gale of wind had come up with the sunrise and was screaming off the tall Talkeetna peaks, filling the air with a chromatic blizzard of autumn leaves. Doc touched my arm and pointed to a snag a couple of hundred yards distant.

"What in blazes is the matter with that snag?" he inquired. "How come it's bending against the wind?"

I looked at it, and it was bending against the wind all right. The top of it was weaving and jerking erratically, but the wind wasn't doing it. It was lurching against the gusts, not with them. Something was pushing it—something concealed from us by the incredibly dense thickets that covered this area from stream bars to the cliffs. I think we both realized at the same instant that the snag's unusual gyrations were being caused by a bull moose. The animal was polishing his antlers against it. Doc stood up and, with a this-is-it-boys look in his eye, eased a shell into the chamber of his Springfield.

We headed out through the rose brush, guided by the swaying snag, and we came to a knoll with a big rough-barked fallen cottonwood lying across it. Doc was in the lead. I hated to see him do it, but he climbed onto the windfall and began making his way, teetering under the rowdy slaps of the gale, up the tilted, lichen-slippery trunk. He wanted altitude. He wanted to get high enough to see over the brush. I followed close behind him, and felt the splintered tree settle ominously under us as we neared the top of the knoll. I had my fingers crossed. Doc is a man with many admirable qualities in the woods, but cleverness on his feet is not one of them. We were a good ten feet above the ground when he halted abruptly, stared ahead a moment, then glanced back at me. His eyes were rounded in utter astonishment. As I tried to see past his percheron shoulders, he said:

"Now, there is a sight to write home about—and it's the answer to all the doggoned troubles we've had trying to hunt this piece of country. Take a look. Ain't that something?"

I crowded up even with him. The scene in the timber ahead was something out of a sportsman's dreams. To explain it and give it due emphasis, I had better interrupt here to tell you the background of the Susitna moose range and to describe what had been happening to us since our arrival there.

In the first place, we knew there were plenty of heavy antlered bulls in the vicinity, for we had seen them. Our charter pilot, before landing on a blue rock-rimmed lake near the head of the narrow, lovely Montana Creek Valley, thirty miles east of Talkeetna, had given us a low-altitude look at the place, power-dragging both sides of the valley at treetop level. Moose were standing about wherever you looked, peaceful as cattle in a pasture. They hadn't been hunted for years, and their unconcern as the plane roared over them showed it. The bulls' antlers, fresh out of the velvet and polished to the last tine and pothook, flashed handsomely in the morning sunlight. In their dark autumn pelage the animals looked enormous against the silvery sea of grass. With so many moose gathered in an area of about four square miles, you would have thought it would be a simple matter to get in among them and take a head. It seemed doubly easy to Doc and me because, since the rut was not yet in full swing, a number of the bulls still were banded together.

We decided at once to take our time, sizing up the old bulls at slingshot range, until we found one that suited us. We were going to be particular. We intended to look long and critically at a lot of heads. This, however, was our first trophy hunt in this extremely tricky game range. We had much to learn about taking heads here, and we were fated to learn it the hard way.

This Susitna country is probably America's newest and least-known major big-game area. Few trophy-hunters have discovered it. The majority of Alaskans living outside the region do not know about it. Doc, who has spent twenty years in the territory, had heard only vague reports of the swiftly increasing moose herds here. His reaction, when we had flown in a straight line over the district for an hour with moose in sight almost every minute of the time, was typical. "For gosh sake, how long has this been going on?" he wanted to know. Actually, it has been going on for about six years. It is the direct result of vast forest fires, which, when the Alaska Railroad was being constructed in 1920, denuded thousands of acres of heavily forested country on both sides of the Susitna River. When a nurse-crop of aspen and birch had covered the burned area and grown tall enough to reach above the deep snows and provide winter browse, the moose began drifting in. They multiplied amazingly and spread into the tributary valleys—the Kahiltna, Yentna, Skwentna, Chulitna, and Talkeetna forks. Nobody knows how many moose now are in the district, but estimates run from ten thousand up.

It is significant that this moose range is getting its start almost exactly as the world-famous Kenai range did. According to the Indians, moose appeared on the Kenai in numbers only after fires had raged over the peninsula from Lake Tustumena to Turnagain Arm and a deciduous nurse-crop had covered the burn. There are indications now that the Kenai is nearing the completion of its cycle—the heavy growth of browse is growing old and the tender terminal shoots on which the moose feed are lifting out of reach. But the Susitna range is on its way up. My belief, and the belief of many other woodsmen, is that the Susitna country soon will provide moose hunting second to none in the world; that sportsmen of the coming generation will speak of it as affectionately as their rifle-toting, trophy-covetous fathers today speak of the Kenai.

But for the next few years, until the nurse-crop grows tall and thins out somewhat, the moose-hunters faring into this wilderness will have to contend with such incredible brush thickets as couldn't be equaled this side of the tropical jungles.

Doc and I had our initiation within an hour after the plane landed us. We found out about the brush, and we briefly encountered the moose that Doc named the Marceled Bull. We were sweating through a matted, lovingly intertwined, fantastically dense series of thickets, looking for a camp site. From the air this unholy mess of vegetation had the appearance of multi-colored plush, but when you got into it, it was something quite different. You couldn't see farther than the length of a fly-rod in any direction. It diabolically grew to a height exactly three inches above my head. I think a man living here would acquire a permanent habit of walking on tiptoe, trying to see over the stuff.

We came to the travel rim of an old creek channel and started to climb it. The bank was fifteen feet high and lay on a pitch of sixty degrees. With our toes dug into the loose pea-size gravel, precariously balancing our heavy packs, we paused at the brink looking for something without thorns to catch hold of and pull ourselves up to level ground. At this embarrassing juncture the bull made his appearance.

The animal stepped into view on a little rise of ground and posed under the golden branches of a towering schoolmarm cottonwood, like a Lynn Bogue Hunt illustration. He was an uncommonly fine bull and seemed to know it. He stood so close to us that I could have hit him in the ribs with a rock. I could see how his rut-swollen neck barreled out from jaw to shoulder. I could see the wicked flare of green in his deep-set little eyes, and the coarse ruck of his mane as it started to lift. At his throat he had a muff but no bell, which classified him as an old-timer. His antler spread was considerably greater than half the length of his body; so if you figured his length was average—110 inches—he had better than a sixty-inch spread. The head had plenty of points, the palms were wide, and the brow tines were sufficiently long and massive to be interesting. But the thing that gave him special distinction was the fact that each antler had a wave in it about eight inches from the tip, a sort of dip and flare that made him look very jaunty and rakish. I had seen single antlers that were waved, but this was the first time I had seen a pair of them.

"That's for me," Doc said. "That marceled baby is my moose, mister."

Now, Doc was poised by sheer balance on the side of the gravel bank, with nothing to cling to. In his great haste to shoot, he tried to shrug free of his pack and drop it without taking his gaze off the moose. It was a mistake. Doc weighs two hundred and fifty pounds, and while he is as powerful as a professional weight-lifter, you couldn't reasonably say he is agile or light-footed. In the woods he just plows through things, brown bear fashion, and trips over logs, and starts rocks rolling at awkward moments. He can't help it. When he is working at his trade—surgery—he is the personification of deftness and precision, but the knack of it just never got down to his feet, I guess. Anyhow, he dropped his ninety-pound pack, and as it fell, one of the straps caught on the handle of his belt knife. The result was like a jujitsu trick. He executed a back somersault and, amid a clatter of rocks and pots and pans, landed with a despairing groan in a clump of devil's club. The bull snorted—a sound like a yard of sailcloth ripping—and slammed out through the timber. His antlers were so wide that I saw him bank them to pass among the cottonwood boles. When he had vanished from my sight, I went down the bank to see how Doc had fared. He was sitting on the pack, picking out thorns and talking to himself. The subject he was developing, with gestures, was clumsiness, with himself as horrible example.

"Don't feel so bad about it," I said. "It could have happened to anybody."

"Nope," he said with conviction. "Only to me. I am the only guy in the world who can absolutely be counted on to do something like that. Once I fell over a camp stove in the dark and burned up a cabin. Another time I stepped off a dock right through the bottom of a row-boat filled with people. I can't understand why anybody associates with me in the woods. I'm a menace. I ain't safe to be with."

We made camp in a thicket of brilliant wolf willows beside an icy streamlet that spilled into a beaver pond, and spent the following week trying for another chance at the bull with marceled antlers. We had no luck. We were surrounded by moose, but we couldn't see them. The undergrowth simply was too dense. They heard us coming and went elsewhere. Or maybe they just stood still and let us pass them. I don't know. So we decided the way to handle this country was to take a stand at a good spot and ambush the moose. We lurked for several days beside sundry trails and at divers creek crossings, shivering in the mountain breeze, forgoing cigarettes, and conversing only in whispers. We saw no moose. I now suspected the animals were just too smart, that they had us located and were craftily bypassing us. I didn't want to return to still hunting because I was afraid we would spook the moose out of the valley. There were at least fifty of the animals in this small area and I wanted them to stay there until we figured out a way to find them.

"I got an idea," Doc said one morning as we were breakfasting on hotcakes and some canned beef that the grocer, on his own initiative, had thoughtfully included in our outfit. "Can you call a moose?"

"Sure, I can call a moose. Why?"

"Then why don't we call some? What are we waiting for?"

No northern woodsman would ever admit he couldn't call moose, but I never knew one who considered this a practical way of taking the animals. The trouble is that, no matter how expert you may be, the moose seem never to co-operate fully. They have the exasperating habit of circling downwind and getting your scent, after which they depart with great dispatch. Or the young bulls—the "mulligan" moose—respond, and snort and rampage about your stand, challenging you to come out and fight like a man, until all the other moose in the vicinity are thoroughly spooked. Or—and too often this is the case—nothing at all happens. You sit there and make uncouth sounds until the whole thing strikes you as ridiculous, and then you throw away your birch-bark horn or your antler and return to more productive methods.

But Doc had me on the spot, so I said all right, we would call some moose. I made a birch-bark horn and set out to demonstrate my virtuosity with it. I don't know why custom requires a moose-caller to employ a birch-bark horn. Maybe it is because it looks good in photographs, or maybe using one is just a petrified tradition like wearing pink pants on a fox hunt. I am pretty certain a horn doesn't improve the quality of a call. Anyway, to my ear it doesn't. I would just as soon use my cupped hands—or better yet, I would rather not try to call moose at all. But, as I said, to do the thing up right I made a horn, a wrap and a half around with the bark, eight inches across the large end, the bark laced with willow root, all strictly according to venerable usage. We essayed the cow call first. This is supposed to be extremely hot stuff. You imitate the moans and squeals of a willing but as yet unattached cow, and any bull that hears you should, according to the theory, come barreling hell-bent through the timber, all set to add a recruit to his harem. The sound is an eerie one, a rising high-pitched moan that trails off in a wail with a yodel in it. Maybe it sounds sexy and impatient to a bull, but to me it always sounded like a whisky-tenored banshee with a touch of bronchial trouble.

We took a stand between a beaver clearing and a little waterfall that was making enough noise, I hoped, to blur the defects in my efforts. I held the horn close to the ground, as you are supposed to, and gave out with my best. Nothing happened, except that a magpie pitched into the clearing and looked me over carefully. I imagine the bird thought I was perishing and presently would contribute my carcass to the wilds. At any rate, it stuck around, keeping a bright eye on me. Doc was fidgeting. I could see he didn't think much of my technique and wanted to try moose-calling himself.

"Put some appeal into it," he whispered. "Imagine you are a cow moose. You're lonely—wandering through the thickets searching for your boy

friend. You're a little jealous, too. You think the boy friend may be out with another lady moose. Give it the old schmalz."

I handed him the horn. "You give it the old schmalz."

Doc really put personality into it. He gave out with what amounted to
a moose version of *Chloe,* with a quaver in it that should have twisted any bull
moose's heartstrings into a Chinese bowline. But still no results. Doc got out a
cigarette, caught himself before he lit it, and put it back in the pack. When five
minutes had passed, he sent another weird blast of sound across the green-gold
valley. This time he was emphasizing impatience. He was being a petulant
young heifer who wasn't going to be stood up much longer, but who was willing to forgive and forget if a bull, any doggoned bull, would get on the ball and
make an appearance. Doc had never before attempted to call moose, and I
don't believe he had ever heard a cow moose sound off, but he was doing all
right. He was working out his own arrangement of my call, putting the frills
and point lace on it.

To my inexpressible surprise, he got action.

A branch cracked somewhere back in the timber. It sounded like a
large branch. Something with weight and a considerable disregard for silence
was approaching. Doc gave me a glance of triumph and exchanged the horn
for his rifle. We now could see the aspen tops waving. The animal was about
sixty yards distant, headed straight toward us. Doc had a big grin on his face. I
knew what he was thinking. The old schmalz, the universal appeal, the elemen-
tal come-hither—with Maestro Doc in the solo box. I could see where I was
going to have to listen for years to his expert opinions on the art of moose-
calling. At this point the moose walked into the beaver clearing. Doc started as
if he had been stabbed. The animal wasn't a bull—it was a trim, sleek little
black cow. She stood looking eagerly at us, big ears semaphoring. I could swear
I saw her eyes sparkling in anticipation. I laughed until I had to roll on the
ground and gasp for breath. I couldn't help it. I thought it was the funniest situation I had ever seen in the game ranges.

"She musta been nuts," Doc insisted later, propping up his injured dignity. "Any moose in its right mind would have known I was moaning like a
cow. She was just a screwball. Balmy as all hell."

"All moose are nuts in the rutting season," I opined.

I really think they are. Take the way they conduct the rut. If it isn't ev-
idence of congenital lightheadedness I don't know what it is. A bull spends the
entire summer putting on fat that should be used to carry him through the
winter. He grows a great spread of antlers admirably suited to protect him
when the snows come and the meat-eaters begin to prowl. So what does he do

when the rut begins? He collects a harem and wears himself to a shadow guarding it. At the conclusion of the rut, along in November, he is skeleton-poor, worn out, lifeless; and in this condition he faces the fierce subarctic winter. Further, as if this weren't handicap enough, he sheds the antlers he has been all summer growing. He is now slick-headed and ribby, a caricature of himself. He has given all for love. He is a magnificent dope, a bad case of over-specialization, and some day because of it he will join those other splendid over-specialized northern animals the Irish elk and the mastodon in biological oblivion. But I suppose he has fun.

We returned to still hunting for a couple of days. By pure luck we blundered upon an ancient bull, early in the rut, who was holding his harem in a meadow under a rimrock. The bull was so old that his antlers were warped and knobby, with dished palms that had a stubble of undeveloped points on their under surfaces—worthless as a trophy. He was rough-coated and gray, and his belly sagged like that of a superannuated draft horse. He stood dozing in the sunlight, with his head in a willow bush, and now and again he would grunt, a deep sound that seemed to come from the bottom of his underslung stomach. He would wake with a start and jerk up his head to glare about the meadow, apparently counting his four cows to make certain all were present, then would go back to his napping or day-dreaming or whatever he was doing. As we watched him from the rim of the meadow, an interesting bit of moose drama took place.

One of the cows, an animal that had been partially concealed from us by a brush clump, tried to escape from the harem. She stepped into view and gazed for a moment at the bull, then began feeding slowly and innocently across the meadow. Doc nudged me. She was small and sleek, quite dark, with a head so small that her ears seemed enormous. It was the young cow that had responded to Doc's efforts on the birch-bark horn, or her double. She continued across the meadow, moving with deceptive inconsequence, until she was even with the bull's position. Here she abruptly made a dash for the timber. But the old bull apparently hadn't been asleep at all. He was after her instantly, covering ground like a quarter horse. When you see a moose gallop, the animal really is in a hurry, and this patriarch was galloping. He caught the cow before she reached the brush, belted her off balance with an antler blade that smacked her across the rump so hard it raked loose a handful of hair, and hazed her pell-mell back into the meadow, prodding her angrily with his brow tines. If I hadn't seen it, I wouldn't have believed the old-timer had it in him.

As the ivory-tipped antlers jabbed at her, the cow squealed, humping her back and flattening her ears. Suddenly she fought back. She bounded sideways, reared, and struck with both front feet. The bull ignored the attack and kept forcing her toward the other cows, who had ceased feeding to witness the incident. Presently he halted, head down, grunting hoarsely, as if satisfied he had taught the cow a lesson in deportment. She faced him again, and gradually her flattened ears lifted, semaphoring. She took a step toward him and, so help me, began licking his shoulder.

Doc shrugged. "I told you," he declared, "that she was balmy. She ain't not a grain of sense in her head."

Before we reached camp, thunder banged among the huge rock angles of the Talkeetnas, and sheets of cold rain lashed out of a wrack of purple storm cloud. We spent the remainder of the day in the tent. The undergrowth was so wet that if we had tried to hunt we would have been soaked before covering a dozen yards. In the morning it was still raining—and Doc located a moose. He had gone down the creek to bring in a spruce snag for firewood. Within five minutes he came crashing back through the willows. A couple of hundred yards downstream, he panted, there was a bull. He had seen only the animal's hind quarters and the flash of an antler, but he had the impression that it was a large antler. I didn't even take time to lace my pacs or tuck in my shirt tail. I just grabbed my rifle and binoculars and loped down the bars.

We waded the stream, and I was so intent on getting a look at the bull that I didn't feel the icy bite of the water until fifteen minutes later when I found myself shivering. We crawled up the bank and moved a cautious foot at a time through the drenched and maddeningly tangled grass and raspberry brush. After a while we came to a moose trail and followed it. There were tracks in the rain-soaked earth—big tracks, a bull's tracks. Doc said the animal was on high ground, which was why he had been able to see it from the creek. When we had progressed a hundred yards, we halted to scan the painted brush clumps and the ranks of gray tree trunks.

"There he is," Doc whispered.

The bull stood in a circle of cottonwoods, about eighty yards distant, pawing the ground. Doc had hoped the animal would prove to be the marceled bull, but it wasn't. The antlers of this bull were fair, but not good enough. I estimated they would go fifty-five inches. In this range, as on the Kenai, a head should go sixty inches to be within trophy standards. We moved to a vantage point on the roots of a windfall and watched the animal. All through the valley head we had found holes pawed by moose, and I wanted to see one of them being made. The bull seemed to be in a state of excitement. He grunted, tearing at the earth, throwing it back over his hips like an angry range bull. Presently he took a mouthful of the gravel and chewed it so enthusiastically that slobber dripped from his lips and I could hear his teeth gritting. Then he knelt and rubbed first his antlers and then his shoulders in the depression he had made. Finally he squatted over the place. This accomplished, he seemed to lose all interest in the project.

To demonstrate to Doc the keenness of a moose's hearing, I picked up a twig no larger than a match and broke it. The bull's ears lifted, then he turned and trotted out through the timber.

"Okay. So we gotta figure some way of making less noise," Doc said. I said: "Amen."

Three days passed before we saw another moose. During this time we worked hard. We found the shed antler and rattled it, we moaned and grunted through a birch-bark horn, as we lay in ambush beside trails, and we tried still hunting again. No luck. When we finally did make contact with a bull it was in a manner almost insulting. It was no tribute to our skill or to the bull's judgment. The animal was within fifty feet of the tent. It was after midnight and he was grunting at us. I heard him in my sleep, but I kept telling myself it couldn't be so and I was dreaming, so why wake up? I probably wouldn't have wakened, either, if Doc hadn't shaken me.

"Do you hear what I hear?" he inquired.

I listened, and it sounded to me as if the bull was about to enter the tent. To forestall such an untoward invasion, I sat up hastily and parted the flaps with my rifle barrel. It was a still, frosty night, with green aurora curtains flapping among the mountain stars. The bull stood silhouetted against the glow, sixty feet distant, in the moose trail that followed the creek bank. He wasn't even looking toward the tent. He was broadside to us, gazing up the valley. As nearly as I could figure it afterward, he had been traveling along the trail, scouting for cows, and had halted here merely to do some grunting. His head was a sad affair; it wouldn't have made a good hat-rack. But he was a superb grunter. Listening to him at this close range, it was clear to me that nobody could ever hope to duplicate the sound with even approximate fidelity. A good attempt might sound all right to a human, but it would certainly register as a forgery in the supersensitive ears of a suspicious moose. The sound started at the bottom of the animal's chest and rumbled forth with a hoarse, hollow tone quite beyond the capacity of any man's throat and lungs.

"I'll take him for meat," I said. "On my ticket. We can fly what's left of the carcass back to town." I was getting tired of bacon and canned beef.

Doc got out of his sleeping-bag and moved over beside me for a better look at the bull. He stepped on the rim of the frying-pan. The handle flipped up and clanged loudly against a leg of the stove. Startled, Doc sidestepped into the woodpile, lost his balance, and pitched headlong into our groceries and cooking gear. The bull turned a grunt into a snort. I had the barrel of my rifle lined on his shoulder and pulled as he headed for the timber. The impact of the soft-nose knocked him off the bank and I heard him hit the gravel. His hoofs slammed the rocks once or twice and then he was still. We had meat in camp.

Doc was separating himself from the culinary gear. "It never fails," he groaned. "Things reach out and trip me. It doesn't happen to anybody else. Maybe I'm hexed."

We dressed the bull by the light of a flashlight. It was a three-year-old in fine condition. His back and rump had two inches of hard fat on them. Doc said he wanted some moose nose. He had read about moose nose for years, he said, and this was his chance to try it. So in the morning we cooked moose nose. Personally, I wouldn't give one good steak for all the moose nose on the planet. I don't know who started the myth that moose nose and beaver tail are epicurean delights, but I suspect he had a warped sense of humor. When I made my living on the fur trails, I used to eat a lot of beaver tail, not because I liked it but because I thought it was a shade better than the other parts of beaver. As for moose nose, I'll bet I have had to cook it for anyhow a dozen sportsmen, all of whom politely asserted it was all right, but never asked for another meal of it. Like beaver tail, it consists of cartilage that, when cooked, looks like a mess of gristle, fat, and gelatin and tastes like nothing in particular.

I pit-roasted the moose nose for Doc, but I took the precaution to broil some tenderloin steaks too. I broiled them over a Dutch oven, which is a good way to do it if you have a Dutch oven with you. You make a fire of aromatic red willow, and when you have a shovelful or so of coals, scoop them into the Dutch oven. Spit the steaks on green twigs sufficiently long to reach across the top of the Dutch oven and hold the meat over the coals. I made a barbecue sauce of worcestershire, salt, pepper, chopped onion, and melted butter and basted the steaks with it several times as they were cooking. When the meal was ready, Doc sat down with his moose nose and made a valiant effort to enjoy it, but presently gave it up with the comment that it seemed to him to be a waste of time and appetite, and reached for a helping of steak.

"Now this," he stated happily, "is more like it. Every mouthful is worth a bucket of the best pills I ever prescribed."

But to return to the opening of this chronicle of the joys and sorrows of hunting our newest northern moose range. Doc and I were climbing the uptilted windfall to investigate the peculiar motions of a snag when we looked down upon a scene that would have made any sportsman's heart beat fourteen to the dozen.

Under the sheltering trees, rumps to the wind like horses, was a herd of moose. I don't know how many there were—maybe twenty-five, maybe more than that. There were bulls, cows, and calves. For two hundred yards you could see antler blades gleaming among the gray tree trunks. Some of the moose were lying down. One bull was polishing his antlers against the spruce snag, patiently rubbing first one palm and then the other against the hard fire-killed wood. Such a gathering of bulls would have been possible at no other time in the autumn season than the present, the week preceding the full madness of the rut. Moose dislike wind, and it was the wind that had caused them to gather here in the heaviest timber in the valley. Apparently their mating feuds, if they had had any as yet, were temporarily forgotten. I had seen gatherings such as this in the great burns above Tustumena Lake, on the Kenai, but none like it before in the Susitna Range, except, of course, in winter when snow and predators had forced the herds to "yard up."

The really important thing was that we had managed to approach this close without being detected. The wind had drowned out such noise as we had made. I knew now how to hunt moose in the Susitna brush.

I could see at least six fine heads. The characteristics of these Susitna heads, now that we had the opportunity to see a number of them together, were marked. They were not the Kenai type. The palms were as long as those of Kenai heads of comparable spread, but they swept back and tended to flare upward at the tips. It seemed to me they had more symmetry. The points were long and wickedly massive, and they grew out from the palms in orderly, orthodox fashion. I saw none of the freak jumbles of tines that make the Kenai heads so interesting—no double palms, none of the odd pothooks growing out from the under surfaces of the antlers which, in Kenai heads, often give an otherwise ordinary trophy an extraordinary number of inches of spread. I was so busy looking at the heads that for a moment I forgot Doc was here to take a trophy.

"Take a look at that bull lying in the grass, to the right of the mossy log," he whispered. "Isn't he my marceled critter?"

The animal was facing away from us, with one antler hidden in the grass and the other cocked up at an angle that foreshortened it, but it did seem to me that there was a wave in the visible antler. Doc took a step forward, trying for an unobstructed view of the animal. The result of this was dramatic. The windfall we were on had been splintered by its fall across the knoll. When Doc moved forward, it placed him on the farther side of the break. The tree settled under us with a loud creak of wood fibers tearing. A cow heard the sound and whirled with a snort to face us. At once the entire herd was alert. The ones that had been bedded down bounded to their feet. A calf blatted and crowded against its mother. The bull we had been trying to see now stood in plain view.

It was the marceled bull.

Doc jerked up his Springfield and fired. The bull turned and walked away. It had seen hair fly from his shoulder, but it could have been from a grazing shot. The other moose were stampeding, crashing through thickets, knocking down snags, a wave of dun bodies flowing through the windy timber. Doc jacked another shell into the chamber and, like most hunters, stepped forward, trying to get closer. This was too much for the windfall. It collapsed with the suddenness of a trap springing. Doc's shot went through the treetops. We landed in a crow's nest of dead branches, and fortunately I was not on the bottom. We could still hear the moose crashing through the timber, but could no longer see them. We were closed in again by the brush.

"Oh, my good gosh almighty!" Doc moaned. "I've lost him again." He got to his feet and charged through the undergrowth. He made as much noise as any of the moose. He didn't turn aside for anything, he just plowed ahead. I don't know what would have happened if one of the big cottonwoods had been in his path. We had about sixty yards to cover and he made a swell trail for me. When we reached the trampled spot where the near side of the herd had been, we halted to look for blood. There wasn't any. I swung up on the low limb of a tree for a look around. Something moved less than a dozen yards from where Doc stood. It was the hind leg of a moose. The bull had fallen into a hole and lay on its back, with only the one leg visible above the downtrodden grass. I went over to him and found he was shot through the lungs.

The head went sixty-four inches. I have seen some happy hunters, but I think Doc was the happiest. He had a right to be. He was a pioneer trophy-hunter in a new game range, and he had accomplished the thing that sets the head-hunter apart—he had held his fire and waited, withstanding the temptation of lesser heads, undismayed by difficulties, until he got the animal he wanted.

Moreover, he had the secret of hunting the brushlands of the Susitna country, which is: wait for a wind. Have your moose approximately located, and when the wind blows, close in on them. They won't be able to hear you coming. It works. I have since seen it tried many times, and it produces trophies. It is one way to beat the Susitna brush.

Great Morning

BY GENE HILL

D URING THE YEARS he wrote the "Parting Shot," "Tailfeathers,"
and "Hill Country" columns for *Guns & Ammo, Sports Afield,* and
Field & Stream, Gene Hill produced so many wonderful stories
that trying to say any particular one is "the best" seems to me to be
a fool's errand if there ever was one. Ten readers would probably pick ten different stories by this wonderful writer, who passed away in 1997.

"Great Morning" was written by Gene for his "Tailfeathers" column
in *Sports Afield* when I was Editor there. Before he started the piece, Hilly told
me about the emotions he hoped to capture in the story—the very special
thrill of bagging a buck in the presence of his granddad and his dad, "Pop" as
he always called him. "Back then, before World War Two," Gene said, "getting
your buck around Newton, New Jersey, where I grew up, would practically get
your name in the paper. We didn't have the huge deer herds that roam the
countryside today."

Wherever they are hunting now, I can only hope there are other
"Great Mornings" for Gene, his granddad, and his beloved "Pop."

I guess I've been deer hunting for something over thirty years, and I suppose I've killed my fair share of deer. I can look back on many moments when
everything seemed to come alive at the fleeting footfall of a buck—his very
awareness made the forest ring with silence. These times are everlasting in the
memory—but even more memorable are the times when I've been really warm.

Deer hunting and subzero weather seem to go hand in hand in my
part of the East. And I doubt it has ever been colder on an opening day than
the year I got my very first buck.

I woke up that morning about four and crept downstairs to start the
fire in the kitchen stove. About the time the fire got going good, the men began

to drift in from early-morning chores. The kitchen smelled wonderful once all the men had gotten warm. The air was heavy with woodsmoke, tobacco, odors of dog and barnyard. And the not-so-secret source of most of these damp smells was the long-lost and wonderfully warm felt boots. Felt boots were a standard item in every farmer's wardrobe. If you remember, they were made in two parts. A long, thick, felt, socklike affair that came to the knee was covered by a separate heavy rubber shoe that came just above the ankle and fastened by two or three metal buckles. They were heavy as hell—but they were warm! Naturally I had a pair. I also had on a heavy woolen union suit (over a pair of regular underwear), two pair of heavy bib overalls, I forget how many shirts, and topping all this was a blanket-lined denim coat we called an "overall jacket."

My grandfather put me on the first stand, behind a giant fallen chestnut log. I was told to stay put.

"What if I shoot a deer?" I asked, positive that I would.

"Stay put," was the answer.

And stay put I did. I really didn't have too much choice. Wrapped all around me was a giant horse blanket, the kind with a raft of buckles and straps on it. Nestled between my legs was a kerosene hand lantern. I sat there like a human tent with my own personal furnace going. In those days we didn't worry too much about a deer smelling any of us. I guess because we all smelled like so many horses and cows ourselves. If I didn't smell like a horse, it wasn't the fault of the blanket and the kerosene lamp forcing the odor out for a couple of country miles. I probably would have smelled like a horse anyway—and the outfit was plenty of insurance. The real point of all this is the absolute fact that I was deliciously warm. I was more than warm—I was downright cozy. By the time the sun had risen completely over the horizon I had, of course, eaten all my lunch.

Grandpa came by about ten o'clock and asked me how I was. I was just fine and told him so, adding that I was getting a little hungry. He gave me a couple of sandwiches and a handful of cookies that must have weighed a quarter of a pound apiece, and told me again to stay put. I don't think I could have gotten out of that rig if I'd wanted to, but I promised him, and off he went again.

Under the blanket I held my most cherished possession—an old 1897 Winchester pump gun. It wasn't really mine. Pop had borrowed it for me to use. The thirty-inch full-choke barrel stuck up out of the blanket like a chimney, and I kept swiveling it around as best I could without disturbing the oven arrangement. I can tell you, I was mighty eager to use it.

Along about noon I was about half asleep from so much food and the warmth from the old lantern when a sharp crack of a broken twig brought my eyes open. Against the snow, about a quarter-mile off through the woods, I could see the four legs of a deer cautiously working its way down toward my stand. Buck or doe, I couldn't be sure because of the hazel and birch thickets between us. As slowly as I could I eased the old '97 up out of the blanket and across the chestnut log and began following the legs of that deer closer toward me through the woods.

About fifty yards directly in front of me was a tiny brook with a clearing or two on the other side, along the bank. With absolute certainty, the deer—whatever it was—was heading down toward one of those clearings. I eased the hammer back on the Winchester with a very shaky thumb; buck fever was coming on a little faster than the deer. But if I had seen this sight once in my dreams and my imagination, I'd seen it a thousand times.

I couldn't take my eyes off those four legs . . . three or four more steps, and he'd be in the clearing by the brook. And suddenly there he was! A buck—a big curving Y. Somehow as the barrel swung back and forth over the clearing I managed to shoot. Just one shot. I don't believe I could have pumped that gun if my life depended on it. At the shot the buck twitched, stepped carefully back from the brook and just as cautiously as he had come down began to walk away as I helplessly watched him. I really never thought of the second shell (I was only allowed to have two buckshot). With a feeling of abject shame, I saw him disappear into the woods. I had missed him. How would I ever tell Grandpa and Pop?

Well, I sat there feeling lower than a cricket's knee. If I hadn't been eleven, I might have cried. Sooner or later, I knew, the hard part had to come—in the form of my father, and it wasn't fifteen minutes until he showed up. He was kind of smiling, as I remember it.

"You shoot?" he asked.

I nodded.

"Where's the dead deer?"

I said there wasn't any dead deer; that he had just walked away.

"Which way did he walk?"

"Around behind that big beech tree was the last I saw," I told him, fearful that I'd be dealt with pretty harshly for wasting a shell.

"Well, you'd better come along and show me," Pop said, and uncovered me, blew out the lantern and started off toward the beech tree. He made me unload the gun, and I felt pretty small as I shucked out the empty shell that had sat in the chamber, forgotten. I put the other shell in my pocket and trudged along behind him.

I should have suspected something when he quickened his pace as we passed the spot where I had last seen the buck, but deep in misery and head down I just tried to walk in his tracks and keep up. I almost fell over the deer.

"This is him, isn't it?" he said, standing by a fallen fork horn, about fifty yards beyond the big beech.

"Yep," I said, trying to indicate by my tone of voice that I wasn't the most surprised person in the world.

"Well, boy, you'd better drug him down by the brook so's we can clean him out."

I guess I could have dragged a bull moose right then, and drag I did, right into the flowing water where we cleaned and washed him out.

By the time the other men had gathered, and I told how I had shot my first deer, the carcass had frozen solid. Grandpa had come along and gathered up my blanket and lantern and asked me if I'd been warm enough. I said I had, but that I was getting mighty cold again.

"Here, boy," he said, handing me a two-foot loop of rope, "warmest thing in the world."

"How's that going to keep me warm?" I asked.

"Simple," he said, "just wrap one end around the deer's neck and the other around your hand and start walking toward the wagon."

Well, I miss the old felt boots, and I still think the blanket—provided it smells like a dapple-gray—and the lantern are pretty comforting. But to really keep a deer hunter warm, there's nothing like a two-foot rope around a man's hand, with a sleek December buck on the other end.

Dog Upon the Waters

BY JOHN TAINTOR FOOTE

I F YOU HAVE never had the opportunity to follow a good pointing dog in the pursuit of upland birds, your life's book of hunting experiences is missing a vital section. To watch a pointer, setter, or shorthair work the fields and cover, lock up on point, then fetch the bird you down is at the pinnacle of hunting exhilaration. If the dog happens to be yours, then the rush of excitement is positively breathtaking.

Finding, training, and caring for great gun dogs takes some doing. You don't pluck them off bushes like berries. That's why gun dog people are constantly running down news and even rumors of superstar dogs, and will go to the ends of the earth to find or breed that "dog of a lifetime."

Few have ever enjoyed gun dogs more and written about them more eloquently than John Taintor Foote. A short story writer, playwright, and screenwriter, Foote's great dog stories are collected in the book, *Dumb-Bell and Others, The Great Dog Stories of John Taintor Foote.* His other sporting classic is *A Wedding Gift and Other Angling Stories,* published by Lyons & Burford.

Most of Foote's stories were written during the 1920s and '30s, a period during which he was a close friend and field companion of Ray P. Holland, the legendary editor responsible for many of the most classic years of *Field & Stream*'s growth.

"Dog Upon the Waters" is the story of a very special setter named Myrtle, and how a lucky hunter learned she was "the one."

Myrtle is dead. Poor funny little snipe-nosed Myrtle. I left her, bored to extinction, at a gun club in Maryland. Between shooting seasons, life to her was a void. It consisted of yawns, the languid pursuit of an occasional flea, the indifferent toying with bones and dog biscuits and a mournful, lackluster gazing at fields and thickets near by.

During these dreary months she was never chained or confined in any way. Self hunting, which spoils so many gun dogs, did not affect Myrtle. Occasionally, when the dragging days became more than she could bear, she would betake herself listlessly to quail cover, find a covey, point it for a moment, flush it and watch the birds whir off into the pines. She would then return, sighing heavily, to a twitching nap somewhat around the clubhouse.

She must have perished during one of these efforts to break the monotony of existence in a gunless world, because a letter from the club steward tells me that she was caught in a muskrat trap in the big marsh and drowned. The big marsh is perhaps a half mile from the clubhouse.

Drowned! Except for Chesapeake and a spaniel or two, I never saw a better swimmer. And yet, in preventing a similar tragedy, she became my dog, body and soul. Also I learned to sniff audibly when scientific fellows announce in my presence that animals cannot reason.

And now, I fear me, I shall have to divulge a secret that has been closely kept for many a day. I am about to spread reluctantly on the printed page the one formula for securing the kind of quail dog that fills an owner with unspeakable joy from dawn to dark, year in, year out, come heat or cold, or drought or rain.

It has nothing to do with sending a check to a professional breeder and then waiting, all expectant, for a shipping crate to be delivered at one's door. It has nothing to do with raising endless litters of distemper-ridden puppies. If you want the rarest, the most perfect instrument for sport in all the world, and not the average plodder and flusher of commerce or home industry, stick to my formula. I set it down exactly as it was given to me by a wise man of the South many years ago.

Here it is: "A Georgia cracker will sell anything—his land, his mule, his house, his wife. By God, he'll sell a bird dog—a real one, I mean. Just show him cash money and he'll reach for it."

These words—after I had learned their true significance—accounted, some years ago, for my spending a winter in Atlanta. My string of gun dogs, so my handler told me, had petered out. I was looking for another string, and Atlanta is the clearing house for information about noteworthy setters and pointers located in various counties of south and central Georgia where the most quail and, ipso facto, the most good gun dogs are found. Working out from Atlanta by motorcar, as rumors of dogs that knew their business drifted into town, I had secured four pointers. I had shot over perhaps fifty dogs in selecting them. The four were all fast, wide-going, covey finders. Class dogs are good for about three hours at top speed. I, therefore, had a pair for mornings and a pair for afternoons, but I needed something that would stay in closer and go slower and find singles—an all-day dog—to back up my four whirlwinds.

One evening a voice spoke over the telephone—a voice that I knew well. The voice said: "Listen. The foreman of our bottling plant was down below Macon last week. He got plenty birds. He's been telling me about a little setter bitch he saw work that sounds like what you're after. He says he can fix it for us to go down and shoot over her next Saturday. What say?"

"How far is it?"

" 'Bout a hundred and twenty miles."

"Does your foreman know a good dog when he sees one?"

"Yep!"

"What does he say she's like?"

"He says she's a ball of fire."

"Doing what?"

"Finding singles—coveys too."

"All right, have him fix it."

Thanks to that telephone conversation, my glance rested upon Myrtle for the first time about eight o'clock the following Saturday morning. She came cat-footing from somewhere behind a paintless shack, set in three or four acres of cotton stalks, at her master's whistle.

I took one look at her. Then my eyes swung reproachfully to the bottling-plant foreman who was responsible for, and had accompanied us on, a one-hundred-and-twenty-mile drive to see her.

"Never you mind," said he stoutly. "You want a bird dog, don't you?"

I did want a bird dog. I have ever been contemptuous of him who goes gunning with a silky-coated, bench-show type of setter calculated to drive a sportsman to undreamed-of heights of profanity with one hour's work in the field. But this specimen before me was—well, I felt that I could never bring myself to admitting the ownership of such a dog.

I had been told she was little. She was. She did not weigh much more than twenty pounds. She had a wavy black-white-and-ticked coat that gave her a claim on the setter family. Her muzzle was so pointed that her head suggested the head of a fox—a black fox—except for a pair of drooping bird-dog ears. Her tail was short, clubby and without any flag. She carried it drooping and a bit to one side. Her eyes were the yellow fox eyes that belonged in such a head. Her gait, as she had come loping to us, seemed more cat than fox, but it reminded me of both.

Delicacy made me omit the opening of the ritual expected at such a time. "How's she bred?" was never spoken. I inquired without interest about her age.

"Comin' three. Reck'n me an' you better stay together, an' yoh friends hunt their dogs."

"All right," I agreed feebly. I was in for it! A-hunting we must go!

And a-hunting we did go. My friend and the bottling-plant man with two of the former's dogs in one direction; my hapless self, with the unspeakable little setter and her lanky owner, in another. She had been named Myrtle, he told me, after his old woman. I had caught a glimpse of the "old woman" through the door of the shack ere we set forth. She was all of sixteen.

We walked in silence up a lane, and so came to fields and promising cover. "Get along, Myrt," said my companion, in a conversational tone, and Myrt drifted to our left into some high grass and disappeared. We found her presently, perfectly still, looking without particular interest straight before her. "She's got birds," I heard. And this, indeed, was true, if our finding a covey twenty yards ahead of her proved it. Accustomed to the tense rigidity on point of more orthodox shooting dogs, Myrt's method was disconcerting.

I shall not attempt to describe that day—my first day afield with Myrtle. She found, in her cat-fox fashion, twelve coveys, as I remember. After each covey find, she proceeded to point and promptly retrieve, when killed, every scattered bird of every covey—or so it seemed to me. And the day was hot, and the day was dry. Incidentally her master shot rings around me.

Her final exhibition that evening would have settled my desire to call her mine if she had not already won me completely hours before. We had joined my friend and the bottling-plant foreman. They had found two coveys and a few singles, had killed four birds, and my friend's pair of pointers were the apple of his eye.

"There just weren't birds in the country we worked over," my friend explained.

I saw the owner of Myrtle open his mouth to speak, then close it resolutely. We started down the lane to the house, my friend, with his dogs at heel, in the lead; Myrtle, cat-footing behind her master, in the rear.

The dusk had closed in softly about us. It was already too dark for decent shooting. The lane down which we plodded had a high wire fence on either side, with pine woods to the left and a flat, close-cropped field to the right.

Suddenly I heard a whine behind me. I stopped and turned. Myrtle was trying to squeeze through the right-hand wire fence to get into the field beyond.

"Birds out yonder," said Myrtle's owner.

I called to my friend and explained.

Now his dogs had just passed that way without a sign. Also, the field was almost as bare of cover as a billiard table.

"Out there!" he snorted. "Wait till we get back to Atlanta. Maybe we'll find a covey in the middle of Five Points."

Perhaps I should say here that Five Points is to Atlanta what Trafalgar Square is to London.

Myrtle's owner met the insult by picking her up and dropping her over the fence. She went straight out into the field and stopped. There followed an exhibition of fence climbing against the watch by my friend and the bottling-plant foreman. They managed to scratch down two birds from the covey that roared up in the gloom somewhere out ahead of Myrtle.

Thirty minutes later she was stretched out on the back seat of the car on her way to Atlanta, too tired to wonder where she was going or with whom.

She cost me—steady, gentlemen, don't throw anything; just observe the workings of the formula—forty dollars. The amount was simply spread carefully before her owner. The result was inevitable.

And so I became the owner of Myrtle. But that was all. I made a point of feeding her myself. I brought her into the house and begged her to accept my favorite overstuffed chair. I petted her fondly. She accepted food and chair without enthusiasm. She barely submitted to the caresses. She was not interested in a mere owner. She wanted a master. She wanted the lanky cracker— that was clear. As to the matter of forty dollars changing hands, she completely ignored the transaction.

Having endured a few days of this, I accepted an invitation to go down with one of the best quail shots in the South to shoot with friends of his near Americus. I wanted birds smacked right and left over Myrtle. I wanted her to see shooting that was shooting, with the lanky cracker far, far away. This, I felt, might aid her perception of property rights. I loaded her into the car then, among a reassuring welter of gun cases, shell boxes and shooting coats, and, lest she be distracted while learning that forty dollars is forty dollars, I left the four whirlwinds straining at their chains, yelping prayers and curses after me, as we drove off.

Eventually we reached a plantation house and its broad acres, over which we were to shoot, to be greeted by two tall brothers who owned it all. A mincing, high-tailed pointer, who seemed to be walking on eggs, and a deep-muzzled, well-feathered setter helped to welcome us. They were a fine-looking pair of dogs. I opened the rear door of the car and Myrtle came forth.

Now our hosts were true gentlemen of the South. After a look at Myrtle, they spoke earnestly of the weather and the crops and of how hard it was to get hold of good corn liquor. The crack shot from Atlanta became absorbed in assembling his gun. All in all, the moment passed off well.

In due time we marched out over the fields, four guns in line. We had planned to separate into pairs when we reached wider country. This we never did. I do not like to shoot with more than one other gun. I wanted the crack shot to help me kill birds instantly and stone dead when Myrtle found them; but, in a surprisingly short time, the brothers showed little desire to leave us, despite their pair of dogs ranging splendidly through the cover.

Myrtle, as we started, had run whining from one man to another for some moments. At last she stopped to stand and watch the other dogs quartering out ahead. She turned and looked deliberately at, or rather through, each of the gunners, myself included. Then with a last small whimper, she got to work. It became clearer and clearer from then on that the place to kill birds that day was in the vicinity of Myrtle.

That miniature, misbegotten what-not found covey after covey and heaven knows how many singles. Her work was marred, however. When a bird fell, she would find it at once and pick it up. She would stand uncertain for a moment and whimper, then start with the bird in her mouth for the nearest man. Having visited all four of us, she would begin to move in a vague circle, whining and looking about. Once she dashed for a high black stump in a field, to return dejectedly with the bird still in her mouth.

I blew my whistle at such times. She never seemed to hear it. I would go toward her, calling her name, and ordering her to "Bring it here!" She only retreated from me, whimpering as I advanced. Getting to her at last, I would take hold of the bird and persuade her to let go of it. All this took time. It was also, to me, her legal owner, somewhat mortifying.

I shared my lunch with Myrtle. She accepted a sandwich, then withdrew a little from the rest of us, to stand looking off into the distance. Suddenly she was away like a shot. I looked in the direction she was going and saw a Negro field hand working along the bottoms, gun in hand, looking for rabbits. I blew and blew my whistle. She rushed on. When close to the Negro, she stopped, looked at him, and came slowly back to where we sat. I rubbed her behind the ears and along the back. She submitted, gazing off into space.

Later that afternoon a covey scattered in a narrow thicket along the bank of the river. The river was in flood—a wide, tawny plain with hummocks of fast water in the middle and still reaches of backwater at its edges.

Myrtle pointed a single within inches of the water. The bird, when flushed, swung out over the river. The deadly gun from Atlanta cracked. The bird came down in the backwater just at the edge of the current. Myrtle was in the river swimming for the bird the moment it fell. She got to it quickly, but an eddy or the wind had carried it out into the current. As she turned to come back with the bird in her mouth, the force of the river took her, and downstream she went.

There was a bend just there, curving away from our side. We four stood helpless on its outer rim and watched her work slowly shoreward, going downstream ten feet for every foot she gained toward the backwater and safety. I remember yelling, "Drop it, Myrt—drop it!" knowing that she could make a better fight without that wretched bird. She did not obey. She struggled on until she came at last to the backwater with the bird still in her mouth.

We all breathed sighs of relief and watched her swim swiftly toward us when free from the drag of the current. "Good girl! Bring it here!" I called, and got out a cigarette with shaking fingers. I began to bask in exclamations I heard along the bank: "Hot damn! That's the baby!" And "Come on home with the bacon, gal!" At least I was her owner.

But trouble swiftly met that small swimmer. There were cat briers growing below her in the flooded ground. One of the longer of these through which she swam fastened in her collar—the new collar I had bought her only the day before. Swim as she might, it held her fast. Her stroke became less smooth. She began to paw the water with her front feet—splashing as she did so.

My shooting coat, filled with shells, came off and in I went. No swimming, I found, was required. I was no more than up to my armpits in icy water when I reached Myrtle. For this I was duly thankful.

Myrtle was showing fright and exhaustion by now. She was no longer swimming. She was dog-paddling frantically to keep her head above water. The quail was still in her mouth.

I disengaged the brier from her collar and carried her to shore. Then I sat down to empty my hunting boots. I thought I felt the rasp of a pink tongue on the back of my hand as I did so. I can't be sure, for I was pretty cold.

The day was well along and my bedraggled state demanded the plantation house and a fire. We started toward both, hunting as we went.

I was at the left end of the line. Myrtle stopped on point, out in front and to the right. It was evidently a single, since flushed birds had gone that way. I called, "Go in and kill it!" And stood to watch the shot.

The bird fell at the report of the gun. Myrtle went into some brambles to retrieve. She emerged with the bird in her mouth. "Bring it here!" I heard from the man to whom it rightfully belonged. If Myrtle heard him, she gave no sign. Nor did she give that whimper of uncertainty that I had heard throughout the day, as she had stood with a recovered bird in her mouth. She came to me on a straight line, running eagerly, to lay the dead quail in my extended palm.

Her eyes had that look—half pride in work well done, half love and faith and companionship—which is characteristic of a shooting dog as a bird is brought to the master's hand. "Here it is, boss!" that look seemed to say. "It's yours. And I am yours—to slave for you, to adore you, as long as I shall live."

Although my teeth were chattering, I was warmed suddenly from within.

Myrtle rode back to Atlanta that night, curled in my lap, a weary but contented little dog.

The Game of the High Peaks: The White Goat

BY THEODORE ROOSEVELT

I N HIS LOVE of the strenuous, outdoor life as a hunter and naturalist, the twenty-sixth President of the United States was a man unlike any other at his level of influence and authority. And the man could write—and did! This old world is not likely to ever see another Theodore Roosevelt.

Of Roosevelt's many volumes of hunting and exploration, my personal favorite is *Ranch Life and the Hunting-Trail*. Roosevelt based the book on his experiences after he moved to the West for three years to live the life of an ordinary rancher following the death of his young wife and his mother within 12 hours of each other in 1884. Roosevelt's ranch was in the Dakota Territory on the Little Missouri River. From there, he ranged far and wide in his hunting adventures.

Despite his political achievements and his courage in battle, as exemplified by San Juan Hill, I'll always hold in my head an image of this remarkable man sitting by the campfire, the light playing off those thick eyeglasses, as he relives the day's experiences with his cowboy companions.

In the fall of 1886 I went far west to the Rockies and took a fortnight's hunting trip among the northern spurs of the Cœur d'Alêne, between the towns of Heron and Horseplains in Montana. There are many kinds of game to be found in the least known or still untrodden parts of this wooded mountain wilderness—caribou, elk, ungainly moose with great shovel horns, cougars, and bears. But I did not have time to go deeply into the heart of the forest-clad ranges, and devoted my entire energies to the chase of but one animal, the white antelope-goat, then the least known and rarest of all American game.

172

We started from one of those most dismal and forlorn of all places, a dead mining town, on the line of the Northern Pacific Railroad. My foreman, Merrifield, was with me, and for guide I took a tall, lithe, happy-go-lucky mountaineer, who, like so many of the restless frontier race, was born in Missouri. Our outfit was simple, as we carried only blankets, a light wagon sheet, the ever-present camera, flour, bacon, salt, sugar, and coffee: canned goods are very unhandy to pack about on horseback. Our rifles and ammunition, with the few cooking-utensils and a book or two, completed the list. Four solemn ponies and a ridiculous little mule named Walla Walla bore us and our belongings. The Missourian was an expert packer, versed in the mysteries of the "diamond hitch," the only arrangement of the ropes that will insure a load staying in its place. Driving a pack train through the wooded paths and up the mountain passes that we had to traverse is hard work anyhow, as there are sure to be accidents happening to the animals all the time, while their packs receive rough treatment from jutting rocks and overhanging branches, or from the half-fallen tree-trunks under which the animals wriggle; and if the loads are continually coming loose, or slipping so as to gall the horses' backs and make them sore, the labor and anxiety are increased tenfold.

In a day or two we were in the heart of the vast wooded wilderness. A broad, lonely river ran through its midst, cleaving asunder the mountain chains. Range after range, peak upon peak, the mountains towered on every side, the lower timbered to the top, the higher with bare crests of gray crags, or else hooded with fields of shining snow. The deep valleys lay half in darkness, hemmed in by steep, timbered slopes and straight rock walls. The torrents, broken into glittering foam masses, sprang down through the chasms that they had rent in the sides of the high hills, lingered in black pools under the shadows of the scarred cliffs, and reaching the rank, tree-choked valleys, gathered into rapid streams of clear brown water, that drenched the drooping limbs of the tangled alders. Over the whole land lay like a shroud the mighty growth of the unbroken evergreen forest—spruce and hemlock, fir, balsam, tamarack, and lofty pine.

Yet even these vast wastes of shadowy woodland were once penetrated by members of that adventurous and now fast vanishing folk, the American frontiersmen. Once or twice, while walking silently over the spongy moss beneath the somber archways of the pines, we saw on a tree-trunk a dim, faint ax-scar, the bark almost grown over it, showing where, many years before, some fur-trapper had chopped a deeper blaze than usual in making out a "spotted line"—man's first highway in the primeval forest; or on some hill-side we would come to the more recent, but already half-obliterated, traces of a miner's handiwork. The trapper and the miner were the pioneers of the mountains, as the hunter and the cowboy have been the pioneers of the plains; they are all of the same type, these sinewy men of the border, fearless and self-reliant, who are ever driven restlessly onward through the wilderness by the half-formed desires that make their eyes haggard and eager. There is no plain so lonely that their feet have not trodden it; no mountain so far off that their eyes have not scanned its grandeur.

We took nearly a week in going to our hunting-grounds and out from them again. This was tedious work, for the pace was slow, and it was accompanied with some real labor. In places the mountain paths were very steep and the ponies could with difficulty scramble along them; and once or twice they got falls that no animals less tough could have survived, Walla Walla being the unfortunate that suffered most. Often, moreover, we would come to a windfall, where the fallen trees lay heaped crosswise on one another in the wildest confusion, and a road had to be cleared by ax work. It was marvelous to see the philosophy with which the wise little beasts behaved, picking their way gingerly through these rough spots, hopping over fallen tree-trunks, or stepping between them in places where an Eastern horse would have snapped a leg short off, and walking composedly along narrow ledges with steep precipices below. They were tame and friendly, being turned loose at night, and not only staying near by, but also allowing themselves to be caught without difficulty in the morning; industriously gleaning the scant food to be found in the burnt places or along the edges of the brooks, and often in the evening standing in a patient, solemn semicircle round the camp fire, just beyond where we were seated. Walla Walla, the little mule, was always in scrapes. Once we spent a morning of awkward industry in washing our clothes; having finished, we spread the half-cleansed array upon the bushes and departed on a hunt. On returning, to our horror we spied the miserable Walla Walla shamefacedly shambling off from the neighborhood of the wash, having partly chewed up every individual garment and completely undone all our morning's labor.

At first we did not have good weather. The Indians, of whom we met a small band,—said to be Flatheads or their kin, on a visit from the coast region,—had set fire to the woods not far away, and the smoke became so dense as to hurt our eyes, to hide the sun at midday, and to veil all objects from our sight as completely as if there had been a heavy fog. Then we had two days of incessant rain, which rendered our camp none too comfortable; but when this cleared we found that it had put out the fire and settled all the smoke, leaving a brilliant sky overhead.

We first camped in a narrow valley, surrounded by mountains so tall that except at noonday it lay in the shadow; and it was only when we were out late on the higher foot-hills that we saw the sun sink in a flame behind the distant ranges. The trees grew tall and thick, the underbrush choking the ground between their trunks, and their branches interlacing so that the sun's rays hardly came through them. There were very few open glades, and these were not more than a dozen rods or so across. Even on the mountains it was only when we got up very high indeed, or when we struck an occasional bare spur, or shoulder, that we could get a glimpse into the open. Elsewhere we could never see a hundred yards ahead of us, and like all plainsmen or mountaineers we at times felt smothered under the trees, and longed to be where we could look out far and wide on every side; we felt as if our heads were in hoods. A broad brook whirled and eddied past our camp, and a little below us was caught in a deep, narrow gorge, where the strangling rocks churned its swift current into spray and foam, and changed its murmurous humming and splashing into an angry roar. Strange little water wrens—the water-ousel of the books—made this brook their home. They were shaped like thrushes, and sometimes warbled sweetly, yet they lived right in the torrent, not only flitting along the banks and wading in the edges, but plunging boldly into midstream, and half walking, half flying along the bottom, deep under water, and perching on the slippery, spray-covered rocks of the waterfall or skimming over and through the rapids even more often than they ran along the margins of the deep, black pools.

White-tail deer were plentiful, and we kept our camp abundantly supplied with venison, varying it with all the grouse that we wanted, and with quantities of fresh trout. But I myself spent most of my time after the quarry I had come to get—the white goat.

White goats have been known to hunters ever since Lewis and Clarke crossed the continent, but they have always ranked as the very rarest and most difficult to get of all American game. This reputation they owe to the nature of their haunts, rather than to their own wariness, for they have been so little disturbed that they are less shy than either deer or sheep. They are found here and there on the highest, most inaccessible mountain peaks down even to Arizona and New Mexico; but being fitted for cold climates, they are extremely scarce everywhere south of Montana and northern Idaho, and the great majority even of the most experienced hunters have hardly so much as heard of their existence. In Washington Territory, northern Idaho, and north-western Montana they are not uncommon, and are plentiful in parts of the mountain ranges of British America and Alaska. Their preference for the highest peaks is due mainly to their dislike of warmth, and in the north—even south of the Canadian line—they are found much lower down the mountains than is the case farther south. They are very conspicuous animals, with their snow-white coats and polished black horns, but their pursuit necessitates so much toil and hardship that not one in ten of the professional hunters has ever killed one; and I know of but one or two Eastern sportsmen who can boast a goat's head as a trophy. But this will soon cease to be the case; for the Canadian Pacific Railway has opened the haunts where the goats are most plentiful, and any moderately adventurous and hardy rifleman can be sure of getting one by taking a little time, and that, too, whether he is a skilled hunter or not, since at present the game is not difficult to approach. The white goat will be common long after the elk has vanished, and it has already outlasted the buffalo. Few sportsmen henceforth—indeed, hardly any—will ever boast a buffalo head of their own killing; but the number of riflemen who can place to their credit the prized white fleeces and jet-black horns will steadily increase.

The Missourian, during his career as a Rocky Mountain hunter, had killed five white goats. The first he had shot near Canyon City, Colorado, and never having heard of any such animal before had concluded afterward that it was one of a flock of recently imported Angora goats, and accordingly, to avoid trouble, buried it where it lay; and it was not until fourteen years later, when he came up to the Cœur d'Alêne and shot another, that he became aware of what he had killed. He described them as being bold, pugnacious animals, not easily startled, and extremely tenacious of life. Once he had set a large hound at one which he came across while descending an ice-swollen river in early spring. The goat made no attempt to flee or to avoid the hound, but coolly awaited its approach and killed it with one wicked thrust of the horns; for the latter are as sharp as needles, and are used for stabbing, not butting. Another time he caught a goat in a bear trap set on a game trail. Its leg was broken, and he had to pack it out on pony-back, a two-days' journey, to the settlement; yet in spite of such rough treatment it lived a week after it got there, when, unfortunately, the wounded leg mortified. It fought most determinedly, but soon became reconciled to captivity, eating with avidity all the grass it was given, recognizing its keeper, and grunting whenever he brought it food or started to walk away before it had had all it wished. The goats he had shot lived in ground where the walking was tiresome to the last degree, and where it was almost impossible not to make a good deal of noise; and nothing but their boldness and curiosity enabled him ever to kill any. One he shot while waiting at a pass for deer. The goat, an old male, came up, and fairly refused to leave the spot, walking round in the underbrush and finally mounting a great fallen log, where he staid snorting and stamping angrily until the Missourian lost patience and killed him.

For three or four days I hunted steadily and without success, and it was as hard work as any that I had ever undertaken. Both Merrifield and I were accustomed to a life in the saddle, and although we had varied it with an occasional long walk after deer or sheep, yet we were utterly unable to cope with the Missourian when it came to mountaineering. When we had previously hunted, in the Big Horn Mountains, we had found stout moccasins most comfortable, and extremely useful for still-hunting through the great woods and among the open glades; but the multitudinous sharp rocks and sheer, cliff-like slopes of the Cœur d'Alêne rendered our moccasins absolutely useless, for the first day's tramp bruised our feet till they were sore and slit our foot-gear into ribbons, besides tearing our clothes. Merrifield was then crippled, having nothing else but his cowboy boots; fortunately, I had taken in addition a pair of shoes with soles thickly studded with nails.

We would start immediately after breakfast each morning, carrying a light lunch in our pockets, and go straight up the mountain sides for hours at a time, varying it by skirting the broad, terrace-like ledges, or by clambering along the cliff crests. The climbing was very hard. The slope was so steep that it was like going upstairs; now through loose earth, then through a shingle of pebbles or sand, then over rough rocks, and again over a layer of pine needles as smooth and slippery as glass, while brittle, dry sticks that snapped at a touch, and loose stones that rattled down if so much as brushed, strewed the ground everywhere, the climber stumbling and falling over them and finding it almost absolutely impossible to proceed without noise, unless at a rate of progress too slow to admit of getting anywhere. Often, too, we would encounter dense underbrush, perhaps a thicket of little burnt balsams, as prickly and brittle as so much coral; or else a heavy growth of laurel, all the branches pointing downward, and to be gotten through only by main force. Over all grew the vast evergreen forest, except where an occasional cliff jutted out, or where there were great land-slides, each perhaps half a mile long and a couple of hundred yards across, covered with loose slates or granite bowlders.

We always went above the domain of the deer, and indeed saw few evidences of life. Once or twice we came to the round foot-prints of cougars, which are said to be great enemies of the goats, but we never caught a glimpse of the sly beasts themselves. Another time I shot a sable from a spruce, up which the little fox-headed animal had rushed with the agility of a squirrel. There were plenty of old tracks of bear and elk, but no new ones; and occasionally we saw the foot-marks of the great timber wolf.

But the trails at which we looked with the most absorbed interest were those that showed the large, round hoof-marks of the white goats. They had worn deep paths to certain clay licks in the slides, which they must have visited often in the early spring, for the trails were little traveled when we were in the mountains during September. These clay licks were mere holes in the banks, and were in spring-time visited by other animals besides goats; there were old deer trails to them. The clay seemed to contain something that both birds and beasts were fond of, for I frequently saw flocks of cross-bills light in the licks and stay there for many minutes at a time, scratching the smooth surface with their little claws and bills. The goat trails led away in every direction from the licks, but usually went up-hill, zigzagging or in a straight line, and continually growing fainter as they went farther off, where the animals scattered to their feeding-grounds. In the spring-time the goats are clad with a dense coat of long white wool, and there were shreds and tufts of this on all the twigs of the bushes under which the paths passed; in the early fall the coat is shorter and less handsome.

Although these game paths were so deeply worn, they yet showed very little fresh goat sign; in fact, we came across the recent trails of but two of the animals we were after. One of these we came quite close to, but never saw it, for we must have frightened it by the noise we made; it certainly, to judge by its tracks, which we followed for a long time, took itself straight out of the country. The other I finally got, after some heart-breaking work and a complicated series of faults committed and misfortunes endured.

I had been, as usual, walking and clambering over the mountains all day long, and in mid-afternoon reached a great slide, with half-way across it a tree. Under this I sat down to rest, my back to the trunk, and had been there but a few minutes when my companion, the Missourian, suddenly whispered to me that a goat was coming down the slide at its edge, near the woods. I was in a most uncomfortable position for a shot. Twisting my head round, I could see the goat waddling down-hill, looking just like a handsome tame billy, especially when at times he stood upon a stone to glance around, with all four feet close together. I cautiously tried to shift my position, and at once dislodged some pebbles, at the sound of which the goat sprang promptly up on the bank, his whole mien changing into one of alert, alarmed curiosity. He was less than a hundred yards off, so I risked a shot, all cramped and twisted though I was. But my bullet went low; I only broke his left fore-leg, and he disappeared over the bank like a flash. We raced and scrambled after him, and the Missourian, an excellent tracker, took up the bloody trail. It went along the hill-side for nearly a mile, and then turned straight up the mountain, the Missourian leading with his long, free gait, while I toiled after him at a dogged trot. The trail went up the sharpest and steepest places, skirting the cliffs and precipices. At one spot I nearly came to grief for good and all, for in running along a shelving ledge, covered with loose slates, one of these slipped as I stepped on it, throwing me clear over the brink. However, I caught in a pine top, bounced down through it, and brought up in a balsam with my rifle all right, and myself unhurt except for the shaking. I scrambled up at once and raced on after my companion, whose limbs and wind seemed alike incapable of giving out. This work lasted for a couple of hours.

The trail came into a regular game path and grew fresher, the goat having stopped to roll and wallow in the dust now and then. Suddenly, on the top of the mountain, we came upon him close up to us. He had just risen from rolling and stood behind a huge fallen log, his back barely showing above it as he turned his head to look at us. I was completely winded, and had lost my strength as well as my breath, while great bead-like drops of sweat stood in my eyes; but I steadied myself as well as I could and aimed to break the backbone, the only shot open to me, and not a difficult one at such a short distance. However, my bullet went just too high, cutting the skin above the long spinal bones over the shoulders; and the speed with which that three-legged goat went down the precipitous side of the mountain would have done credit to an antelope on the level.

Weary and disgusted, we again took up the trail. It led straight downhill, and we followed it at a smart pace. Down and down it went, into the valley and straight to the edge of the stream, but half a mile above camp. The goat had crossed the water on a fallen tree-trunk, and we took the same path. Once across, it had again gone right up the mountain. We followed it as fast as we could, although pretty nearly done out, until it was too dark to see the blood stains any longer, and then returned to camp, dispirited and so tired that we could hardly drag ourselves along, for we had been going to speed for five hours, up and down the roughest and steepest ground.

But we were confident that the goat would not travel far with such a wound after he had been chased as we had chased him. Next morning at daybreak we again climbed the mountain and took up the trail. Soon it led into others and we lost it, but we kept up the hunt nevertheless for hour after hour, making continually wider and wider circles. At last, about midday, our perseverance was rewarded, for coming silently out on a great bare cliff shoulder, I spied the goat lying on a ledge below me and some seventy yards off. This time I shot true, and he rose only to fall back dead; and a minute afterward we were standing over him, handling the glossy black horns and admiring the snow-white coat.

After this we struck our tent and shifted camp some thirty miles to a wide valley through whose pine-clad bottom flowed a river, hurrying on to the Pacific between unending forests. On one hand the valley was hemmed in by an unbroken line of frowning cliffs, and on the other by chains of lofty mountains in whose sides the ravines cut deep gashes.

The clear weather had grown colder. At night the frost skimmed with thin ice the edges of the ponds and small lakes that at long intervals dotted the vast reaches of woodland. But we were very comfortable, and hardly needed our furs, for as evening fell we kindled huge fires, to give us both light and warmth; and even in very cold weather a man can sleep out comfortably enough with no bedding if he lights two fires and gets in between them, or finds a sheltered nook or corner across the front of which a single great blaze can be made. The long walks and our work as cragsmen hardened our thews, and made us eat and sleep as even our life on the ranch could hardly do: the mountaineer must always be more sinewy than the horseman. The clear, cold water of the swift streams too was a welcome change from the tepid and muddy currents of the rivers of the plains; and we heartily enjoyed the baths, a plunge into one of the icy pools making us gasp for breath and causing the blood to tingle in our veins with the shock.

Our tent was pitched in a little glade, which was but a few yards across, and carpeted thickly with the red kinnikinic berries, in their season beloved of bears, and from the leaves of which bush the Indians make a substitute for to-bacco. Little three-toed woodpeckers with yellow crests scrambled about over the trees near by, while the great log-cocks hammered and rattled on the tall dead trunks. Jays that were dark blue all over came familiarly round camp in company with the ever-present moose-birds or whisky jacks. There were many grouse in the woods, of three kinds,—blue, spruce, and ruffed,—and these varied our diet and also furnished us with some sport with our rifles, as we always shot them in rivalry. That is, each would take a shot in turn, aiming at the head of the bird, as it perched motionless on the limb of a tree or stopped for a second while running along the ground; then if he missed or hit the bird anywhere but in the head, the other scored one and took the shot. The resulting tally was a good test of compar-ative skill; and rivalry always tends to keep a man's shooting up to the mark.

Once or twice, when we had slain deer, we watched by the carcasses, hoping that they would attract a bear, or perhaps one of the huge timber wolves whose mournful, sinister howling we heard each night. But there were no bears in the valley; and the wolves, those cruel, crafty beasts, were far too cunning to come to the bait while we were there. We saw nothing but crowds of ravens, whose hoarse barking and croaking filled the air as they circled around over-head, lighted in the trees, or quarreled over the carcass. Yet although we saw no game it was very pleasant to sit out, on the still evenings, among the tall pines or on the edge of a great gorge, until the afterglow of the sunset was dispelled by the beams of the frosty moon. Now and again the hush would be suddenly broken by the long howling of a wolf, that echoed and rang under the hollow woods and through the deep chasms until they resounded again, while it made our hearts bound and the blood leap in our veins. Then there would be silence once more, broken only by the rush of the river and the low moaning and creaking of the pines; or the strange calling of the owls might be answered by the far-off, unearthly laughter of a loon, its voice carried through the stillness a marvelous distance from the little lake on which it was swimming.

One day, after much toilsome and in places almost dangerous work, we climbed to the very top of the nearest mountain chain, and from it looked out over a limitless, billowy field of snow-capped ranges. Up above the timber line were snow-grouse and huge, hoary-white woodchucks, but no trace of the game we were after; for, rather to our surprise, the few goat signs that we saw were in the timber. I did not catch another glimpse of the animals themselves until my holiday was almost over and we were preparing to break camp. Then I saw two. I had spent a most laborious day on the mountain as usual, following the goat paths, which were well-trodden trails leading up the most inaccessible places; certainly the white goats are marvelous climbers, doing it all by main strength and perfect command over their muscles, for they are heavy, clumsy seeming animals, the reverse of graceful, and utterly without any look of light agility. As usual, towards evening I was pretty well tired out, for it would be difficult to imagine harder work than to clamber unendingly up and down the huge cliffs. I came down along a great jutting spur, broken by a series of precipices, with flat terraces at their feet, the terraces being covered with trees and bushes, and running, with many breaks and interruptions, parallel to each other across the face of the mountains. On one of these terraces was a space of hard clay ground beaten perfectly bare of vegetation by the hoofs of the goats, and, in the middle, a hole, two or three feet in width, that was evidently in the spring used as a lick. Most of the tracks were old, but there was one trail coming diagonally down the side of the mountain on which there were two or three that were very fresh. It was getting late, so I did not stay long, but continued the descent. The terrace on which the lick was situated lay but a few hundred yards above the valley, and then came a level, marshy plain a quarter of a mile broad, between the base of the mountain and the woods. Leading down to this plain was another old goat-trail, which went to a small, boggy pool, which the goats must certainly have often visited in the spring; but it was then unused.

When I reached the farther side of the plain and was about entering the woods, I turned to look over the mountain once more, and my eye was immediately caught by two white objects which were moving along the terrace, about half a mile to one side of the lick. That they were goats was evident at a glance, their white bodies contrasting sharply with the green vegetation. They came along very rapidly, giving me no time to get back over the plain, and stopped for a short time at the lick, right in sight from where I was, although too far off for me to tell anything about their size. I think they smelt my footprints in the soil; at any rate they were very watchful, one of them always jumping up on a rock or fallen log to mount guard when the other halted to browse. The sun had just set; it was impossible to advance across the open plain, which they scanned at every glance; and to skirt it and climb up any other place than the pass down which I had come—itself a goat-trail— would have taken till long after nightfall. All that I could do was to stay where I was and watch them, until in the dark I slipped off unobserved and made the best of my way to camp, resolved to hunt them up on the morrow.

Shortly after noon next day we were at the terrace, having approached with the greatest caution, and only after a minute examination, with the field-glasses, of all the neighboring mountain. I wore moccasins, so as to make no noise. We soon found that one of the trails was evidently regularly traveled, probably every evening, and we determined to lie in wait by it, so as either to catch the animals as they came down to feed, or else to mark them if they got out on some open spot on the terraces where they could be stalked. As an ambush we chose a ledge in the cliff below a terrace, with, in front, a breastwork of the natural rock some five feet high. It was perhaps fifty yards from the trail. I hid myself on this ledge, having arranged on the rock breastwork a few pine branches through which to fire, and waited, hour after hour, continually scanning the mountain carefully with the glasses. There was very little life. Occasionally a chickaree or chipmunk scurried out from among the trunks of the great pines to pick up the cones which he had previously bitten off from the upper branches; a noisy Clarke's crow clung for some time in the top of a hemlock; and occasionally flocks of cross-bill went by, with swift undulating flight and low calls. From time to time I peeped cautiously over the pine branches on the breastwork; and the last time I did this I suddenly saw two goats, that had come noiselessly down, standing motionless directly opposite to me, their suspicions evidently aroused by something. I gently shoved the rifle over one of the boughs; the largest goat turned its head sharply round to look, as it stood quartering to me, and the bullet went fairly through the lungs. Both animals promptly ran off along the terrace, and I raced after them in my moccasins, skirting the edge of the cliff, where there were no trees or bushes. As I made no noise and could run very swiftly on the bare cliff edge, I succeeded in coming out into the first little glade, or break, in the terrace at the same time that the goats did. The first to come out of the bushes was the big one I had shot at, an old she, as it turned out; while the other, a yearling ram, followed. The big one turned to look at me as she mounted a fallen tree that lay across a chasm-like rent in the terrace; the light red frothy blood covered her muzzle, and I paid no further heed to her as she slowly walked along the log, but bent my attention towards the yearling, which was galloping and scrambling up an almost perpendicular path that led across the face of the cliff above. Holding my rifle just over it, I fired, breaking the neck of the goat, and it rolled down some fifty or sixty yards, almost to where I stood. I then went after the old goat, which had lain down; as I approached she feebly tried to rise and show fight, but her strength was spent, her blood had ebbed away, and she fell back lifeless in the effort. They were both good specimens, the old one being unusually large, with fine horns. White goats are squat, heavy beasts; not so tall as black-tail deer, but weighing more.

Early next morning I came back with my two men to where the goats were lying, taking along the camera. Having taken their photographs and skinned them we went back to camp, hunted up the ponies and mules, who had been shifting for themselves during the past few days, packed up our tent, trophies, and other belongings, and set off for the settlements, well pleased with our trip.

All mountain game yields noble sport, because of the nerve, daring, and physical hardihood implied in its successful pursuit. The chase of the white goat involves extraordinary toil and some slight danger on account of the extreme roughness and inaccessibility of its haunts; but the beast itself is less shy than the mountain sheep. How the chase of either compares in difficulty with that of the various Old World mountain game it would be hard to say. Men who have tried both say that, though there is not in Europe the chance to try the adventurous, wandering life of the wilderness so beloved by the American hunter, yet when it comes to comparing the actual chase of the game of the two worlds, it needs greater skill, both as cragsman and still-hunter, to kill ibex and chamois in the Alps or Pyrenees—by fair stalking I mean; for if they are driven to the guns, as is sometimes done, the sport is of a very inferior kind, not rising above the methods of killing white-tail in the Eastern States, or of driving deer in Scotland. I myself have had no experience of Old World mountaineering, beyond two perfectly conventional trips up the Matterhorn and Jungfrau—on the latter, by the way, I saw three chamois a long way off.

My brother has done a good deal of ibex, mountain sheep, and markhoor shooting in Cashmere and Thibet, and I suppose the sport to be had among the tremendous mountain masses of the Himalayas must stand above all other kinds of hill shooting; yet, after all, it is hard to believe that it can yield much more pleasure than that felt by the American hunter when he follows the lordly elk and the grizzly among the timbered slopes of the Rockies, or the big-horn and the white-fleeced, jet-horned antelope-goat over their towering and barren peaks.

Forty-Crook Branch

BY TOM KELLY

W HEN GRITS GRESHAM first told me about Tom Kelly several years ago, he was emphatic. "This guy can write," Grits said, "and *The Tenth Legion* is the best book ever written about turkey hunting."

Now Grits is a man who knows his way around in the turkey woods, and a lot of other places, so I quickly followed up on his tip. And just as I thought it would, *The Tenth Legion* turned out to be an unforgettable book, and the name of Tom Kelly went onto my list of favorite writers.

Tom Kelly has written other books since *The Tenth Legion* (which has been reprinted by Nick Lyons), including *Better on a Rising Tide,* published by Lyons & Burford in 1995 and which is the source of this story-telling gem.

Turkey Call magazine has called Tom Kelly "the poet laureate of modern turkey hunting." You're about to see why.

If you happen to hunt a great deal, or if you spend a lot of time in the woods for any other reason, there always seems to be a half-section of land, somewhere, that fits you better than it fits anybody else.

Any number of things can attract you to a certain place. It may be that you killed a particularly difficult turkey there, or you may find some specific bend in a creek to be unusually attractive. It could be an outcropping of rock, maybe a special view, or perhaps a stand of trees, but it seems that you never go to that place without the distinct feeling that you are coming home, that every tree and rock and fold in the ground is an old friend, and that nothing but good things are ever going to happen to you while you are in there.

Almost invariably, you keep quiet about it.

If, by design, you have hunted with the same man for a number of years, he will be aware of this flaw in your character—though he will never discuss it—and will respect your idiosyncrasy. If you are not a wholly insensitive and barbaric clod, you will very likely detect a similar flaw in him and return the favor.

I know, for example, a man who gets distinctly uneasy whenever the area just north of Whetstone Creek creeps into the discussion. He does not fidget, particularly, or shift his eyes rapidly from side to side, or anything quite so obvious, but his face takes on that carefully expressionless look you use when you are being introduced fulsomely as an after-dinner speaker; or when you fill an inside straight. Anytime we hunt near there, I am as careful to go in the direction he suggests—and stay there—as I am to listen to the location of the guest bathroom in a strange house and to refrain from opening any other doors on my way down the hall.

I open no strange doors whatever along Whetstone Creek. I do it to be polite. But even if I were impolite and opened them, whatever I saw might not strike my fancy particularly. I only know that somewhere in there something strikes his. Somewhere in there is something he considers private and wants to keep for himself. Obviously, he has found a combination of associations that soothe his soul and it would be as inappropriate for me to pry into it as it would be to ask to see the love letters he wrote his wife when they were courting.

Besides, I am not all that interested, anyway, so long as he leaves Forty-Crook Branch alone.

I am not really the sole owner of Forty-Crook Branch. To be perfectly honest about it, I hold no color of title whatsoever. I pay no taxes on it, run no lines, and have no fences. I know that other people go there. I even know that somebody else hunts it. Some bastard killed a hen turkey in there last fall and picked her at the head of the hollow before he smuggled her out. I found her feathers.

But I have never seen anyone there, and if I am lucky, I never will. On those sleepless nights when I prowl around the house, I take a power of comfort in the hope that perhaps the hen murderer has died of leprosy, or maybe some infinitely more loathsome and disgusting disease I never even heard of.

The fact that unknown people may go there doesn't really matter. My lack of proprietorship does not really get into the quick. The core of the matter is that while I am there, I own it; and that is enough.

Now that I have committed the impropriety of discussing the place at all, I cannot tell you exactly what it is that makes it so appealing. God knows I have looked at enough land and timber during my life to be selective, and I have the added advantage of knowing precisely and exactly what my limits are in this respect.

I found this out a good many years ago, when I was assigned to make a critical assessment of the value of a tract of nearly a quarter-million acres that had been purchased and was to be divided into five equal parts.

We had a timber cruise, naturally, and had spent some little time poring over stand types and acres and volumes and all the other things that constitute value. But it was decided that a careful appraisal of the property, section by section, made by a single head that had been relieved of all other duties, could best put together an objective opinion of the relative values of the individual fifths.

I began the job on Thanksgiving Day and finished March 1st. Every morning I was waiting in the woods for daylight, and when it got too dark to see, I quit and drove home. With the exception of Christmas Day, when I rested, I spent the entire time, with no distractions whatsoever, in a careful and conscientious examination of a block of land with an excellent road net. At just about the 200,000-acre mark, I made a discovery.

Until then, I could take the map and put my finger on a section at random, shut my eyes, and picture the area in my head with a high degree of accuracy. After that point, old sections passed out of my mind as fast as new ones were added.

Obviously, then, I have a 200,000-acre head.

I have not offered these senile maunderings in an attempt to be impressive, but rather to establish the fact that there is a basis for judgement, that I do have a head full of timber, and that this is not the opinion of a necktie salesman with Grandmother's eighty acres for comparison.

Forty-Crook Branch and its environs is something special. If you draw the line from the upper end of Mobile Bay to the northeast corner of the state, go partway up the line and a little to the right, you will be able to locate it— and that is as complete a description as you are ever going to get.

The name of the branch itself no longer appears on the map, and I have no idea who named it originally. Most of our place names in this part of the world, except along the very coast itself, are either Indian or Scotch-Irish in origin. Whatever other abilities the Celts may have, they have a marvelous flair for pungent and distinctive place names and have left the mark of this descriptive poetry on natural landmarks all over the southeast. Names like Burnt Corn Creek and Oven Bluff and Gin House Branch and Goat Hobble Bald, the list is almost endless. The Indian names may be even more pungent but I cannot tell since I speak neither Creek nor Choctaw.

I suspect that Forty-Crook Branch was named for the number of curves in it, rather than in any illusion to the companions of Ali Baba, but you never know. At any rate, it is remarkably crooked, and the terrain on both sides of the branch and its tiny feeder streams are as steep as any we have. The most pronounced feature of the area is a single central ridge that runs northwest and has a hollow on either side of it that is distinctly different from its matching hollow on the other side.

The hollow on your left—west—is a mixed stand of pine and hardwood and is almost an even mixture of each. I killed a turkey there one fall, early in the morning, that has the unique distinction of being the only flying bird I ever shot from above. I had missed them on the roost and they were down in the hollow fighting and squalling at one another to work off the ill humors of early morning when I heard the racket. I was able to stay under the crest of the ridge on the east side until I got abreast of all the noise and then run across the top and shoot down into the hole. They were all the way down in the bottom of the hollow, 120 yards away, and as they came up, one of them flew up the hill to my right, turned, and crossed along the slope of the ridge right to left, and thirty yards below me.

The lead is identical and the swing is exactly the same, but the feeling is decidedly peculiar. I suppose shooting downhill is appropriate for hunters of mountain goats and bighorn sheep, but it is not all that common to bird hunters. Bird hunters get awfully used to looking up when they shoot. Every time I go along that ridge now, I stop and go over to the west side, and in my mind's eye, watch him cross below me. I usually take a practice swing or two there in the highly unlikely event that the situation will ever come up again. I hope it never does. I am batting a thousand in such instances, and lightning never strikes twice.

This remarkable event notwithstanding, the west hollow is not my favorite side. My choice is the one on the east, and its choicest point is at the head of the hollow, just as you walk onto the central ridge.

The central ridge begins as a nonentity. It breaks off from a perfectly ordinary looking hill with some scrubby-looking old-field loblolly pine mixed thinly among a stand of ratty-looking post oak and falls gently away to a pile of limestone in a thicket of mountain laurel. There is an abrupt right-hand turn in the gap between two rocks the size of elephants; and an equally abrupt left-hand turn behind them. Then you step beyond the screen of laurel and down into an open area the size of a small room.

The room is ringed with limestone rocks that have been broken by weather and frost. Fossilized clamshells are visible along all of the breaks. The ring is nearly waist high, and the area commands a view of both hollows and looks along the path that follows the crest of the ridge.

Just below the ring, the ridge saddles, and the path beyond the saddle gently rises and passes from sight among the trees. The central ridge then curves gently to the right, beginning at a point just beyond the disappearance of the path, and you have a fine view along the eastern slope.

The first ten chains of the east hollow is an almost-pure stand of beech.

I have never understood why the druids fooled away their time deifying an oak tree when beech was available. Sargent's manual lists nineteen commercial species of oak indigenous to south Alabama and four species of scrub. After you get past cherrybark oak, there is not fourteen cents worth of class in the lot of them.

Live oak has limbs that twist away from a central trunk for as much as twenty yards and is prone to festoons of Spanish moss, which you always associate with funerals and pallbearers.

Overcup has a regrettable tendency to have sucker sprouts all along the trunk which ruin the symmetry of the bole. All of the red oaks produce a staple food for game, and we have to have them, but corn bread and collard greens with side meat are the same kind of staple. You may eat them all the time, but you don't put on your necktie and specifically take your wife out to dinner just to buy them. They may be good, but they do not go with candle-light and damask napkins and brandy and a good cigar afterward.

Beech does.

Not only is a beech tree handsome, but it has a nut that is perfectly delicious. If I were rich and powerful, I would have beechnuts collected by faithful family retainers and put them in my fruitcake rather than pecans. I might even eat them on my cereal for breakfast. A stand of beech, with its smooth blue-gray bark all the way to the stump, is cool and dim and hushed early in the year, when the leaves are on; and light and open and airy in the fall and winter, when the white bark on the thin, naked branches shines in the afternoon sun.

Forty-Crook Branch itself starts in this hollow and makes up from a spring that first appears from under a monstrous limestone rock. The branch runs in a series of abrupt turns almost from its beginning and on the inside of most of the bends is what can only be called a sandbar, even though most of them are less than ten feet long and eighteen inches wide. The sand in these bars is clean and gray and has tiny flecks of mica in it.

Once, years ago, when she was very small, I took the colonel's daughter there—the last half-mile on my back—and cut her name and the date in small, dainty block letters low down on a beech tree. In my pocket, I had brought a little block of wood with a hole through it, and we set up a flutter mill there in the creek made out of forked and split sticks with halves of magnolia leaves for blades. The whole thing was tied together with strips of bearpaw.

She watched the wheel run, with delight, and got both feet wet in the branch, then she ran her fingers over her name cut in the bark and asked me if the shiny flecks of mica were tiny diamonds. I assured her that they were, with the utmost solemnity, and congratulated her upon her perspicacity in finding them.

We swore never to disclose the location of our mine to anybody, but agreed that if, later on, either of us ever needed money, he or she could come back and gather some.

I have never killed a turkey in this hollow, though there is a perfect place to do it. There is a beech there that overlooks an arena exactly one gunshot across. The tree has two buttressed roots which come away from the bole on both sides of your butt exactly the right distance apart and curve down at just the proper height to support each elbow. The ground in front of the tree drops away just gently enough to allow you to dig your heels in properly and not leave your knees propped up too high. It is as comfortable as a rocking chair, and I have done some of my very best sleeping there, in the fall, after I have scattered turkeys in the morning and had come back after lunch, and it made no real difference where I sat.

I have run a couple of turkeys off the roost there in the spring— turkeys which were gobbling fit to choke themselves—by crowding them in the last few yards of my approach in a futile attempt to get to that tree. In both instances, it was one of those pieces of stupidity that you carefully commit while your native good judgment is shrieking at you continuously to stop.

I am going to do exactly the same the next time it happens, too, because just one time, before I die, I am going to kill a turkey out of that rocking chair. It is important. It gets more important every year I don't get to do it.

Below the rocking chair, the hollow begins to widen and you move out of pure beech and begin to run through the mixed stands of upland oak and hickory common to the upper coastal plain. It is at this point that I usually climb the central ridge and walk along it, rather than staying down in my favorite hollow. If you are hunting, you have an opportunity to listen in both hollows simultaneously, and if you are just visiting, you get a marvelous overview of either side. The ridge is so narrow and the sides so steep, that as you walk along, you are level with the tops of eighty-foot trees down in either hollow and it is the next-best thing to flying.

Right out on the point of the ridge, nearly a mile from its beginning and just before it drops off, there is a clump of shortleaf pine; not all that big, but old as hell. You can sit there and listen to the wind in the needles and look out over three-quarters of a county. In cold weather, you don't want to stay too long because the wind gets such a clear shot at you out there. But cold or hot, it is always worth the trip. Even if the sun is not shining and the rain has wet you straight through, it is still worth it, because the woods are always gloomy as hell on rainy days and there is a perverse pleasure, in one sense, at looking out over a quarter-million acres of gloom.

When I leave Forty-Crook Branch, I always try to go out so as to pass by the tree in the curve where we built the mill. I never go in to the site itself. I go close enough to see that the tree is still there, that lightning has not struck it, or a summer windstorm blown it flat since the last visit. But I never go far enough to see over the little hill and look in the bottom of the branch.

Because I have never gone back for my share of the diamonds.

In point of fact, I have not put my eyes on her name since the day I cut it in the tree. The mill cannot still be there. It was hardly built for the ages and could not have survived the first rainstorm. I would rather not go back and look at the scene of the ruin. The tree and the mill belong to the day itself, not to any other.

I will never go back.

So long as I never do, my shares are still there, still held in escrow. So long as I never do, she is still there; always four years old, always under the tree with her name on it, stooped in the sand by her mill with the utter absorption of a little child, enchanted with her diamonds.

I hope she never needs them.

"Pothole Guys, Friz Out"

BY GORDON MACQUARRIE

INVENTED IN GORDON MACQUARRIE'S classic stories, the Old Duck Hunters Association, Inc., was never in better form than in this rousing duck hunting tale originally published in *Outdoorsman*. The "Association" consists of MacQuarrie and "Hizzoner"—also called "Mister President." Their various hunting and fishing adventures were originally published in magazine stories but have now been collected in several books edited by my friend and former *Sports Afield* colleague, Zack Taylor. (They are published by Willow Creek Press in Oshkosh, Wisconsin, and are available through numerous mail-order outlets.)

When Zack put together the very first Gordon MacQuarrie anthology—*Stories of the Old Duck Hunters & Other Drivel,* published by Stackpole in 1967 and subsequently republished by Willow Creek Press—he did the book as a personal labor of love to make sure MacQuarrie's wonderful stories would not become lost over time. Zack relates in his introduction that from the moment he came to work for *Sports Afield* as a young associate editor, he felt that MacQuarrie had something special as a writer. Zack's boss, editor Ted Kesting, agreed. "I had, in fact, come to the field only a short time after he [MacQuarrie] started writing. He was one of the first I reached out for to produce the kind of writing and reporting I wanted in *Sports Afield*."

MacQuarrie was a journalism graduate of the University of Wisconsin, and his career bases of operations were the *Superior Evening Telegram* and the *Milwaukee Journal*. All of MacQuarrie's stories are packed with irresistible flavor, totally capturing both the atmosphere and action in this region where hunting and fishing are at their best in stinging, unruly weather, and the wild backcountry is a place of both reward and challenge.

Born in 1900, Gordon MacQuarrie, the wonderful man and writer, was lost to a sudden heart attack in 1956.

The president of the Old Duck Hunters Association, Inc., hauled up in front of my house in the newest, gaudiest automobile which had to that date, turned west off Lake drive onto East Lexington boulevard.

It seemed that even the gray squirrels among the boulevard beeches were impressed by the streamlined vehicle, if not by the inelegant driver, Hizzoner himself, in a flannel shirt and battered brown hat.

I saw him coming for two blocks for I had been expecting him. The village hall and police station are his landmarks. He made a horseshoe turn around the end of the boulevard, slid into the curb and yelled for all to hear:

"The minute I saw the jail I knew where to find you!"

Leaf raking brethren of the chase leaned on their implements and yipped. The Old Man freed himself from his imposing machine and studied a Schnauzer dog which had arrived with a band of kids to investigate the new automotive device. Anent the dog, Mister President demanded:

"Is that a dog or a bundle of oakum?" He is congenitally allergic to all but the hunting breeds.

In due course he came inside. He'd driven the dealer's model super-duper up from the factory and was stopping on the way by prearrangement to rescue me from the city's toils.

"Going through Chicago," he explained, "every cop on Michigan avenue made the same mental note as I drove by—'roughly dressed man in brand new auto.' If the police come, my identification papers are in the glove compartment."

He had climbed into his old hunting clothes for comfort in the long drive.

Later in the evening we loaded the car with decoys, shell boxes, duffel bags and in the early morning while the household slept the Old Duck Hunters Association crept away.

The elements had descended. Streets were semi-granite with frozen sleet.

"Just what the doctor ordered," Mister President exulted. "If it's freezing down here, it's frozen up there."

Daylight came on the feet of snails but long before then the Old Man bade me halt on the slippery road. With the tire gauge in one hand and a flashlight in the other he let 10 pounds of air out of each tire. After that we got along faster.

At Portage, Wis., the President was happier than ever, for snow was falling. We had breakfast and went on. North of Tomah the sleet was gone from the road and dry snow was whipping across the concrete. We re-inflated the tires and pushed on. At Chippewa Falls, crossing the big bridge, visibility up and down the Chippewa river was 200 yards.

Hizzoner nodded in the seat beside me. He was asleep and snoring at Spooner. The snow and the wind increased. The footing for tires was perfect, thanks to the built-up highway over which dry flakes rolled in sheets. Mister President awoke at Minong while a man by the name of Andy Gorud filled the tank.

"Is that it, Andy?" the Old Man asked. For answer Andy took us to his back porch and exhibited a possession limit of snow-sprinkled redheads. Andy said indeed this was it, but if the weather kept up it might drive every duck out of the country before morning.

"Bosh!" said Mister President. "Only the shallow lakes and potholes will freeze. The ducks'll have to wet their feet in big water tomorrow morning."

Such a man, that Andy. Once he walked two miles in the rain with a heavy jack to hoist us up and put on our chains.

The snow kept up. At Gordon we turned off. The Old Man was wide awake now.

"She's a good un," he said, watching the county trunk. "Come so quick they haven't got all the snow fences up. If you see a drift back up and give 'er tarpaper."

Tarpaper was required in several places. I complimented him on the power under the hood of his newest contraption but he was not enthusiastic— "They're all too low, no good in a two-rut road. They're making them so low pretty soon you can use a gopher hole for a garage."

It grew dark. The driving flakes stabbed at the windshield. By the time I was ready to turn off the county trunk onto the town road the Old Man had demanded the driver's seat. He knew that the in-road would be well filled with snow. I protested but he said I could drive "the day you learn your driving brains are in the seat of your pants."

There were a few spots on that narrow road between the jack pines where we barely got over the rises. The car was pushing snow 12 inches deep when we stopped at the top of the last hill.

We went ahead and got a fire going. When I got to the cabin with the first load the fireplace was roaring and he was coaxing the kitchen range to life. By the time I had hauled in the last of the gear and shoveled the snow off the stoop he had water hot enough for tea. While we ate supper the temperature slid from 28 to 24.

We hauled in wood, broke out blankets and took a hooded motor from the shed down through the snow to the lake. We took a boat off its winter roost and set it handy by the edge of the tossing lake. We brought down guns and decoys, put them in the boat and covered everything with a canvas tarp. Then there was time to size up the night.

It was a daisy. There was snow halfway to the knees on the beach. The flashlight's circle revealed a black, tossing lake. From the hill at our backs the wind screamed down through the pine trees.

"How'd you like to be a field mouse on a night like this?" Hizzoner reflected.

We went back up the hill. The last thing Mister President did was study the thermometer. I heard him say, "She's dropped to 22 and it's only 8 o'clock." After that the fireplace crackled, the wind cried, the blankets felt awfully good . . .

In the morning there wasn't a breath of wind. Of course he was up before me, useful and belligerent. Everything was ready, including the country smoked bacon. I started to open the door to inspect the thermometer and he announced, "Fifteen about half an hour ago."

I studied him jealously as I have often. There he was, 30 years older than I, tough as a goat, alert as a weasel. He'd just finished an exhausting business trip. Forty-eight hours before he had been 600 miles from this place. He ate six eggs to my four, eyeing me with the indulgent authority a bird dog man feels for a new pup.

"The hell with the dishes and put on all the clothes you've got," he directed.

The lake in the darkness held an ominous quiet, like a creature which had threshed itself to exhaustion. We flung off the tarp with one flip to keep snow off gear, slid in the boat, screwed on the motor and roared out.

We were afloat on blackness, rimmed with the faint white of snow on the shores. Mister President huddled in the bow in the copious brown mackinaw, its collar inches above his ears. He fished in pockets and drew on mittens and when his hands were warmed he fished again and presently a match glowed over the bowl of his crooked little pipe. I saw that he was grinning, so throttled the motor and yelled, "What's the joke?"

"No joke," he came back. "Just a morning for the books."

The run to this place requires about 30 minutes. Dim landmarks on shore were illuminated just enough by the snow. We cut wide around the shallow point bar and went south for the shallow end of the lake. The Old Man has bet that he can, blindfold, land an outboard within 100 yards of the shallow bay point from our beach. There are no takers.

A little daylight was making as I cut the speed and turned toward the shore. The President said, "Go back down the shore further from the blind. The boat'll stand out against the snow like a silo." We beached 200 yards from the point.

There was plenty of time. When the Old Man is master of ceremonies you get up early enough to savor the taste of morning. And what a morning! Just once in a coon's age do the elements conspire with latitude to douse North Wisconsin with snow of mid-winter depth in October. It is a very lovely thing. We toted up the gear to the blind. I was impatient to get out in the shallows in my waders and spread decoys. The Old Man detained me.

"I suppose," he said. "that when a man quits liking this it's time to bury him."

He was determined to size up the morning, and he did size it up. Between hauls on the blackened brier he continued, "Once before I saw this point just as pretty. Back in 1919. Just about the same depth of snow, same old lake black as ink, trees ag'in the sky . . ."

I had paused to honor his rhapsody, so he snorted, "Get them boosters out there, dang yuh, while I rebuild the blind!"

Rebuild it he did, pausing now and then in the growing light to tell me where to place the next decoy. In the blind I found he had the rough bench swept off, the blind repaired and a thermos of coffee at hand. He sat on the right side of the bench and both our guns, his automatic and my double, were held away from the snowy wall of the blind by forked sticks. It was unmercifully cold for sitting. He explained his thesis for the day—

"The potholes chilled over in the night. The ice crep' out from shore. The ducks huddled up, getting closer and closer as the ice reached for 'em. First good daylight they'll look around at each other and say, 'Let's go. This place is getting too crowded'."

"You don't suppose they've all left the country?" I ventured. There was scorn in his reply.

"The best ducks stay 'til the last dog's hung."

A burst of bluebills went over and planed into the lake, far out.

"They were up awfully high for cold weather ducks," I said. "I'm afraid if they move they'll go a long ways today—if there are any left around."

"They'll be lower," he said.

A pair dropped in from in back of us. It was apparent they'd come in from any quarter in the absence of wind. I reached for the gun and slid out a toe to kick my shellbox. The Old Man put a mittened hand on my right knee. I could feel his fingers squeeze through leather and wool. Following his eyes I saw what he saw.

They were at the left, about a hundred ducks, an embroidery of ducks, skeined out in a long line with a knot at the head. We crouched down and the Old Man whispered:

"Pothole guys, friz out. Might be from Minnesota. Maybe Ontario. They'll swing and size 'er up and the whole dang bundle will——."

Swi-i-i-ish!

While we had watched the mid-lake flock fifty or so had slid into the decoys, bluebills everyone. The President from his corner eyed me and whispered, "Flyin' high did you say? No, don't shoot! We're gonna have fun."

The mid-lake flock swung in, decoyed by their confident cousins. The President of the Old Duck Hunters grinned like a school boy. He was on his knees in the trampled snow, close against the front wall of the blind. So was I and he was laughing at me. Fifty ducks sat in the decoys, another hundred were coming in, and the Old Man said to me:

"Hold out your hand so I can see if you're steady."

At the moment that the landed birds were flailing out the incomers were tobogganing in with their wing flaps down. The Old Man arose and shouted:

"Hello, kids!"

His deliberateness was maddening. I emptied the double before he brought up his automatic. I reloaded and fired again and he still had a shell to go. He spent it expertly on a drake.

Then the ducks were gone and I was trying to stuff a round brass match safe into the breech and the Old Man was collapsed on the bench, laughing.

"Up high for cold weather ducks!" he howled.

There were seven down, two far out, and as I raced back for the boat Mister President heckled, "Wish I had that East Lexington boulevard Snootzer here and I'd learn him to be a dog!"

As I rowed out for the pick-up he shouted across the water, "Do you get a bottle of turpentine with every Snootzer you buy?"

As he had predicted, it was a day for the books. The clouds pressed down. They leaned against the earth. No snow fell but you knew it might any minute. There were not just clouds but layers of clouds, and ramparts and bastions and lumps of clouds in between the layers.

We sat and drank coffee. We let bluebills sit among the decoys. That was after Hizzoner decreed, "No more 'bills. Pick the redheads if you can. If you miss a mallard I'll kill yuh."

The quick dark day sped by. To have killed a hundred diving ducks apiece would have been child's play. Canvasback, whistlers, mergansers, redheads, and bluebills by the hundreds trouped over the hundred-year old decoys which are the sole property of the Old Duck Hunters Association.

"I'd give a lot for a brace of mallards to color up the bag," he said.

The Lady Who Waits for Mister President likes mallards.

Be assured, mallards were present, as well as those dusky wise men, black ducks. They would swing in high over the open water and look it over. They did not care for any part of our point blind in the snow.

"Wise guys," Mister President said. "They see the point and two dark objects against the snow in the blind, and one of the objects wiggling all over the place. That'll be you."

We went back to the boat and fetched the white tarpaulin. He threw it over the top of the blind and propped up the front of it with cut poles. The tarp erased us from above and seven laboring mallards swung closer. Before throwing off the tarp, Mister President whispered: "Slow down sos'te to nail 'em."

Back went the tarp. I missed a climber, then crumpled him. Hizzoner collected three. He just spattered them. Because these were for the Lady Who Waits.

We picked up and hauled out, raising rafted diving ducks in the long run back.

We hoisted the boat onto its winter trestles, upside down, to let it drain and dry. We put the gear beneath it and slung the tarp over it. We went up the hill and stirred the fires.

I got supper. I worried about the super-duper on the hilltop at the road's end but he said he had drained it. I lugged in more wood and heaped up the fireplace.

He said in the morning we might have to break ice to get out from shore. He said, "We might not see much more than whistlers." He said to steep the tea good. He said not to forget to climb down the well and open the bleeder on the pump "because she's going to really drop tonight." He said he thought he'd "take a little nap 'fore supper." And finally he said:

"Draw them mallards will yuh, son? She likes 'em drawed."

The Forest and the Steppe

BY IVAN TURGENEV

THE STORIES COMPRISING Ivan Turgenev's *A Hunter's Sketches* were written and published in installments between 1847 and 1851. [In some translations, the book is called "A Sportsman's Sketches."] The complete book of 22 sketches was published in 1852, and 20 years later three additional chapters were added. Turgenev's fervent passion toward nature and the Russian countryside are evident throughout the book but reach a peak of atmosphere and beautiful descriptions in this piece, the book's final chapter. Ernest Hemingway was responsible for bringing *A Hunter's Sketches* to the attention of many readers by his occasional mentions of the book as a personal reading favorite.

> And slowly something began to draw him
> Back to the country, to the garden dark,
> Where lime-trees are so huge, so full of shade,
> And lilies of the valley, sweet as maids,
> Where rounded willows o'er the water's edge
> Lean from the dyke in rows, and where the oak
> Sturdily grows above the sturdy field,
> Amid the smell of hemp and nettles rank. . . .
> There, there, in meadows stretching wide,
> Where rich and black as velvet is the earth,
> Where the sweet rye, far as the eye can see,
> Moves noiselessly in tender, billowing waves,
> And where the heavy golden light is shed
> From out of rounded, white, transparent clouds:
> There it is good. . . .
>
> (*From a poem consigned to the flames*)

The reader is, very likely, already weary of my sketches; I hasten to reassure him by promising to confine myself to the fragments already printed; but I cannot refrain from saying a few words at parting about a hunter's life.

Hunting with a dog and a gun is delightful in itself, *für sich,* as they used to say in old days; but let us suppose you were not born a hunter, but are fond of nature and freedom all the same; you cannot then help envying us hunters. . . . Listen.

Do you know, for instance, the delight of settling off before daybreak in spring? You come out on to the steps. . . . In the dark-grey sky stars are twinkling here and there; a damp breeze in faint gusts flies to meet you now and then; there is heard the secret, vague whispering of the night; the trees faintly rustle, wrapt in darkness. And now they put a rug in the cart, and lay a box with the samovar at your feet. The trace-horses move restlessly, snort, and daintily paw the ground; a couple of white geese, only just awake, waddle slowly and silently across the road. On the other side of the hedge, in the garden, the watchman is snoring peacefully; every sound seems to stand still in the frozen air—suspended, not moving. You take your seat; the horses start at once; the cart rolls off with a loud rumble. You ride—ride past the church, downhill to the right, across the dyke. . . . The pond is just beginning to be covered with mist. You are rather chilly; you cover your face with the collar of your fur cloak; you doze. The horses' hoofs splash sonorously through the puddles; the coachman begins to whistle. But by now you have driven over four versts . . . the rim of the sky flushes crimson; the jackdaws are heard, fluttering clumsily in the birch-trees; sparrows are twittering about the dark hayricks. The air is clearer, the road more distinct, the sky brightens, the clouds look whiter, and the fields look greener. In the huts there is the red light of flaming chips; from behind gates comes the sound of sleepy voices. And meanwhile the glow of dawn is beginning; already streaks of gold are stretching across the sky; mists are gathering in clouds over the ravines; the larks are singing musically; the breeze that ushers in the dawn is blowing; and slowly the purple sun floats upward. There is a perfect flood of light; your heart is fluttering like a bird. Everything is fresh, gay, delightful! One can see a long way all round. That way, beyond the copse, a village; there, further, another, with a white church, and there a birch-wood on the hill; behind it the marsh, for which you are bound. . . . Quicker, horses, quicker! Forward at a good trot! . . . There are three versts to go—not more. The sun mounts swiftly higher; the sky is clear. It will be a glorious day. A herd of cattle comes straggling from the village to meet you. You go up the hill. . . . What a view! the river winds for ten versts, dimly blue through the mist; beyond it meadows of watery green; beyond the meadows sloping hills; in the distance the plovers are wheeling with loud cries above the marsh; through the moist brilliance suffused in the air the distance stands out clearly . . . not as in the summer. How freely one drinks in the air, how quickly the limbs move, how strong is the whole man, clasped in the fresh breath of spring! . . .

And a summer morning—a morning in July! Who but the hunter knows how soothing it is to wander at daybreak among the underwoods? The print of your feet lies in a green line on the grass, white with dew. You part the drenched bushes; you are met by a rush of the warm fragrance stored up in the night; the air is saturated with the fresh bitterness of wormwood, the honey sweetness of buckwheat and clover; in the distance an oak wood stands like a wall, and glows and glistens in the sun; it is still fresh, but already the approach of heat is felt. The head is faint and dizzy from the excess of sweet scents. The copse stretches on endlessly. Only in places there are yellow glimpses in the distance of ripening rye, and narrow streaks of red buckwheat. Then there is the creak of cart wheels; a peasant makes his way among the bushes at a walking pace, and sets his horse in the shade before the heat of the day. You greet him, and turn away; the musical swish of the scythe is heard behind you. The sun rises higher and higher. The grass is speedily dry. And now it is quite sultry. One hour passes, another. . . . The sky grows dark over the horizon; the still air is baked with prickly heat. "Where can one get a drink here, brother?" you inquire of the mower. "Yonder, in the ravine's a well." Through the thick hazel bushes, tangled by the clinging grass, you drop down to the bottom of the ravine. Right under the cliff a little spring is hidden; an oak bush greedily spreads out its twigs like great fingers over the water; great silvery bubbles rise trembling from the bottom, covered with fine velvety moss. You fling yourself on the ground, you drink, but you are too lazy to stir. You are in the shade, you drink in the damp fragrance, you take your ease, while the bushes face you, glowing and, as it were, turning yellow in the sun. But what is that? There is a sudden flying gust of wind; the air is astir all about you: was not that thunder? Is it the heat thickening? Is a storm coming on? . . . And now there is a faint flash of lightning. Yes, there will be a storm! The sun is still blazing; you can still go on hunting. But the storm-cloud grows; its front edge, drawn out like a long sleeve, bends over into an arch. Make haste! over there you think you catch sight of a hay-barn . . . make haste! . . . You run there, go in. . . . What rain! What flashes of lightning! The water drips in through some hole in the thatch-roof on to the sweet-smelling hay. But now the sun is shining bright again. The storm is over; you come out. My God, the joyous sparkle of everything! the fresh, limpid air, the scent of raspberries and mushrooms! And then the evening comes on.

There is the blaze of fire glowing and covering half the sky. The sun sets; the air near you has a peculiar transparency as of crystal; over the distance lies a soft, warm-looking haze; with the dew a crimson light is shed on the fields, lately plunged in floods of limpid gold; from trees and bushes and high stacks of hay run long shadows. The sun has set; a star gleams and quivers in the fiery sea of the sunset; and now it pales; the sky grows blue; the separate shadows vanish; the air is plunged in darkness. It is time to turn homewards to the village, to the hut, where you will stay the night. Shouldering your gun, you move briskly, in spite of fatigue. Meanwhile, the night comes on: now you cannot see twenty paces from you; the dogs show faintly white in the dark. Over there, above the black bushes, there is a vague brightness on the horizon. What is it?—a fire? . . . No, it is the moon rising. And away below, to the right, the village lights are twinkling already. And here at last is your hut. Through the tiny window you see a table, with a white cloth, a candle burning, supper. . . .

Another time you order the racing droshky to be got out, and set off to the forest to shoot woodcock. It is pleasant making your way along the narrow path between two high walls of rye. The ears softly strike you in the face; the corn-flowers cling round your legs; the quails call around; the horse moves along at a lazy trot. And here is the forest, all shade and silence. Graceful aspens rustle high above you; the long hanging branches of the birches scarcely stir; a mighty oak stands like a champion beside a lovely lime-tree. You go along the green path, streaked with shade; great yellow flies stay suspended, motionless, in the sunny air, and suddenly dart away; midges hover in a cloud, bright in the shade, dark in the sun; the birds are singing peacefully; the golden little voice of the warbler sings of innocent, babbling joyousness, in sweet accord with the scent of the lilies of the valley. Further, further, deeper into the forest . . . the forest grows more dense. . . . An unutterable stillness falls upon the soul within; without, too, all is still and dreamy. But now a wind has sprung up, and the tree-tops are booming like falling waves. Here and there, through last year's brown leaves, grow tall grasses; mushrooms stand apart under their wide-brimmed hats. All at once a hare skips out; the dog scurries after it with a re-sounding bark. . . .

And how fair is this same forest in late autumn, when the snipe are on the wing! They do not keep in the heart of the forest; one must look for them along the outskirts. There is no wind, and no sun, no light, no shade, no movement, no sound; the autumn perfume, like the perfume of wine, is diffused in the soft air; a delicate haze hangs over the yellow fields in the distance. The still sky is a peacefully untroubled white through the bare brown branches; in parts, on the limes, hang the last golden leaves. The damp earth is elastic under your feet; the high dry blades of grass do not stir; long threads lie shining on the blanched turf, white with dew. You breathe tranquilly; but there is a strange tremor in the soul. You walk along the forest's edge, look after your dog, and meanwhile loved forms, loved faces, dead and living, come to your mind; long, long slumbering impressions unexpectedly awaken; the fancy darts off and soars like a bird; and all moves so clearly and stands out before your eyes. The heart at one time throbs and beats, plunging passionately forward; at another it is drowned beyond recall in memories. Your whole life, as it were, unrolls lightly and rapidly before you; a man at such times possesses all his past, all his feelings and his powers—all his soul; and there is nothing around to hinder him—no sun, no wind, no sound. . . .

And a clear, rather cold autumn day, with a frost in the morning, when the birch, all golden like some tree in a fairy-tale, stands out picturesquely against the pale-blue sky; when the sun, standing low in the sky, does not warm, but shines more brightly than in summer; the small aspen copse is all a-sparkle through and through, as though it were glad and at ease in its nakedness; the hoar-frost is still white at the bottom of the hollows; while a fresh wind softly stirs up and drives before it the falling, crumpled leaves; when blue ripples whisk gladly along the river, lifting rhythmically the scattered geese and ducks; in the distance the mill creaks, half hidden by the willows; and with changing colours in the clear air the pigeons wheel in swift circles above it.

Sweet, too, are dull days in summer, though the hunters do not like them. On such days one can't shoot the bird that flutters up from under your very feet and vanishes at once in the whitish dark of the hanging fog. But how peaceful, how unutterably peaceful it is everywhere! Everything is awake, and everything is hushed. You pass by a tree: it does not stir a leaf; it is musing in repose. Through the thin steamy mist, evenly diffused in the air, there is a long streak of black before you. You take it for a neighbouring copse close at hand; you go up—the copse is transformed into a high row of wormwood in the boundary-ditch. Above you, around you, on all sides—mist. . . . But now a breeze is faintly astir; a patch of pale-blue sky peeps dimly out; through the thinning, as it were, steaming mist, a ray of golden-yellow sunshine breaks out suddenly, flows in a long stream, strikes on the fields and in the copse—and now everything is overcast again. For long this struggle is drawn out, but how unutterably brilliant and magnificent the day becomes when at last light triumphs and the last waves of the warmed mist here unroll and are drawn out over the plains, there wind away and vanish into the deep, softly shining heights.

Again you set off into outlying country, to the steppe. For some ten versts you make your way over cross-roads, and here at last is the highroad. Past endless trains of waggons, past wayside taverns, with the hissing samovar under a shed, wide-open gates and a well, from one hamlet to another; across endless fields, alongside green hempfields, a long, long time you drive. The magpies flutter from willow to willow; peasant women with long rakes in their hands wander in the fields; a man in a threadbare nankin overcoat, with a wicker pannier over his shoulder, trudges along with weary step; a heavy country coach, harnessed with six tall, broken-winded horses, rolls to meet you. The corner of a cushion is sticking out of a window, and on a sack up behind, hanging on to a string, perches a groom in a fur cloak, splashed with mud to his very eyebrows. And here is the little district town with its crooked little wooden houses, its endless fences, its empty stone shops, its old-fashioned bridge over a deep ravine. On, on! . . . The steppe country is reached at last. You look from a hill-top; what a view! Round low hills, tilled and sown to their very tops, are seen in broad undulations; ravines, overgrown with bushes, wind coiling among them; small copses are scattered like oblong islands; from village to village run narrow paths; churches stand out white; between willow bushes glimmers a little river, in four places dammed up by dykes; far off, in a field, in a line, an old manor house, with its outhouses, orchard, and threshing-floor, huddles close up to a small pond. But on, on you go. The hills are smaller and ever smaller; there is scarcely a tree to be seen. Here it is at last—the boundless, untrodden steppe!

And on a winter day to walk over the high snowdrifts after hares; to breathe the keen frosty air, while half-closing the eyes involuntarily at the fine blinding sparkle of the soft snow; to admire the emerald sky above the reddish forest! . . . And the first spring day when everything is shining, and breaking up, when across the heavy streams, from the melting snow, there is already the scent of the thawing earth; when on the bare thawed places, under the slanting sunshine, the larks are singing confidingly, and, with glad splash and roar, the torrents roll from ravine to ravine.

But it is time to end. By the way, I have spoken of spring: in spring it is easy to part; in spring even the happy are drawn away to the distance. . . . Farewell, reader! I wish you unbroken prosperity.

Bob White, Down't Aberdeen

BY NASH BUCKINGHAM

ESPITE THE GREAT number of collections of Nash Buckingham stories, and reprints of those collections, this is a tale many
readers have never seen. At least as it reads here. Published in September, 1913, in *Field & Stream,* this Buckingham account of quail
hunting with his Vermont buddy, Col. Harold P. Sheldon, later formed the basis
of the story "Bobwhite Blue! Bobwhite Gray!" included in *De Shootinest
Gent'man* when that book was first published in 1934. This earlier version
stands on its own as a wonderful read, quite different from the later version and
an engrossing look at quail hunting during the long-ago days of multitudinous
coveys. It was included (with the two-word Bob White spelling) in *The Field &
Stream Treasury,* now out of print and fairly hard to come by.

No writer has ever captured the halcyon days of waterfowling and
quail hunting with the volume of engaging prose written by Nash Buckingham. He saw and wrote about the very best shotgunning ever seen in America,
the first 30 years of the 1900s. I have read Buckingham so much that I can see
him in my mind as if I had been alongside him, watching as he waded the
flooded tall timber with his duck call in one hand and in the other his 10-
pound, 32-inch 12-gauge magnum overbored by the master, Burt Becker. Or
followed a pair of pointers with his best buddy, Hal Bowen Howard, on a ten-
covey afternoon of quail hunting.

One aspect of Buckingham's writing that I have always appreciated,
and never seen discussed in print, was his delight in food and his descriptions
of the grub as it is being laid on the groaning boards. Meals are always a big
part of Mr. Nash's sporting days, and his prose leaves no doubt that he was a
trencherman of the first rank.

Andrew's letter was characteristic. "Entirely all right and welcome to include the Gentleman from Boston. Never mind the Yankee strain in his breeding. If he proves a good shot and able to negotiate a few of Colonel Lauderdale's 75–90 h.p. toddies, the Rebels will stand for his pedigree, and even though it leaks out that he's a Republican, why our game laws will protect him. I know a place where the birds are holding a convention. Down across the river, about eight miles from here, in a sandy-loam and pine-hill country full of sedge, pea patches and sorghum. I have a fine old friend there. He runs a water mill, but the last man he killed was a Prohibitionist. Grinds his own flour and believe me, boy, he is *a* biscuit maker. If you don't choose goggle-eyed hen eggs (from contented hens) about twice the size of fifty-dollar gold pieces, and can't choke down real all-pork sausage and baked hams, why bring along your own sum'p'n t'eat. The plug gets in so late that you all may have to go to the hotel for the night but Johnny'll move your outfit out to the house next day. Couldn't do much with Johnny after dark anyhow. There's a ghost scare on down here. A phantom called Mother Hubbard is working around the streets and Johnny claims that she 'done run sev-ul uv his frens' right on to degradation.' Fat chance to get him to hang around till midnight!"

How pleasant the recollection that drifted back a twelvemonth in prospective enjoyment of another visit! We were sitting again in comfortable cane-bottomed rockers on the wide veranda of the High Private's ancestral home. From crevices of the lofty, iron-capped columns clung villages of nests, in and out of which twittered the sparrows, bent either upon warlike sally against shrill encroaching jays or engaged in piercing squabbles relating to matters of domestic retention. It was Sunday afternoon on the Old Home Place, in the sweet purpling of a brave autumnal day. From down Matubba road the *puffity-pant* of the cotton gin was hushed. No crop wagons creaked past in swirls of Indian summer dust with their sputtering crackle of long blacksnake whips, uncoiling over the sodgerin' back and along sleek ribs of "jug-haids." There was no jocose lingo of the mule curse; no bare-fanged country dogs, entrenched beneath the wagons. It was the time of year when flashing dawns melted away the tinge of frost scrolls from russet woodland; when gaud and arrogance of capricious color gave riotous defiance to the approach of sombrous winter. Black fingers twinkled among the hoary yield of cotton bolls; 'possum and coon throve in the bottoms; darky chants rose to exultant pitch with divers harbingers of peace and plenty. Doomed by ripe fatness and assaults with stick and stone, luscious persimmons plumped to earth and schoolboy stomachs. "Egg-bustin' " puppies raced abroad, causing Brer

Rabbit to hoist subject-to-change-without-notice signs. Canvas-coated hunters rode afield; lithe pointers and setters searched hill and dale for Bob Whites that leaped roaring from embrowning covert. And then—

I glanced mournfully through an office window into the forbidding bleakness of our latest cold snap. Surely, I reflected, it was a fine day for a murder or to set a hen. But, to the Gentleman from Boston, languishing at his hotel, I broke the glad tidings of our invitation, and grouchily set about waiting a squarer deal from the elements. Next day dawned clear as a bell. I had just spread the sporting section when Andrew called over Long Distance. At five that afternoon we cast off, aboard the "Plug," an abused little red-in-the-face train with a seven-hour-or-more-trip staring us straight in the stomach. Fast trains chased us into sidings and burly freights hooted us into submission, leaving the poor Plug to scramble home out of breath, practically discouraged and ready to give up. It was past midnight when we finally boomed across the Tombigbee, did a "gran' right an' left" in the switching line and bumped into the silent and aristocratic town of Aberdeen, Mississippi.

Two night-owl porters for rival hotels quarreled bitterly over our bags, one darky threatening to "part yo' hair, niggah, ef yo' doan turn loose dat grip-sack; don' yo' see dat fine-lookin' white man from Memphis don' want to stop at nobody's house 'cep mine?" This sable and subtle flattery had an effect of quelling the incipient riot, so we hastened uptown, registered at the comfortable Clopton House and dug far into our warm beds.

Morning came with reverse English on the fair weather. Leaden, blowy skies, an icy wind that promised chilly creeps and deeply gashed gumbo roads frozen into treacherous depths. Andrew was on hand early and regretted that it would be practically impossible to reach his selected territory. "But," said he, "we'll take in some ground I shot over last week and find all the birds we're lookin' for."

Breakfast over, the steeds were led up; Andrew whistled for Flash and Jim and we were off. The horse allotted the Gentleman from Boston was of dignified personality and winning ways, but the brute I drew was a "low-life" pure and simple. Scarcely had I a leg up, when, for the edification of a morbidly curious public, the wretch came undone right there on Main street. The idea of a regular, everyday Southern horse trying to sunfish and timberline rather surprised me, to say the least, and for a moment, just a moment, I had a good notion to hang my spurs in him and accompany the scratching with a tremendous beating over the head with my hat and a lot of yelling thrown in or off. But I had no spurs, so kept my hat out of the ring, clung to my weapon and pulled leather until Seldom-Fed quit hogging.

Our trek led through the stately old burg past the huge courthouse, crumbly with its struggle against the years, reminiscent of impassioned oratory and bitter but courtly legal battles. At intervals we glimpsed through spacious boundaries of wintered cedar hedge, oak, and locust, old-fashioned homes of singular and comforting beauty. Some, with their broad porches and superb lines of colonial paneling drooping into an almost sagging dilapidation of wartime impoverishment; others bespeaking an eloquent survival and defiance of time.

Leaving town we struck off into a bottom land of down corn and thicket. Out of the north a freezing, stinging wind wrung tears from our eyes with its biting whip. At the first ditch Andrew broke ice, wet our dogs' feet and applied a coating of tannic acid. A moment later, when cast off, they headed up through a corn field. Almost in the same breath it seemed, they froze on a point at an impenetrable thicket bordering a wide pond. We were more than glad to dismount and hurry toward the find. Approaching, we saw the birds flush wild and sweep across the pond into some briar tangles. We skirted the marsh, and, shooting in turn, managed to start the ball rolling with five singles. Leading our mounts, for walking proved far more preferable than facing the wind, we plugged through a creek bottom. We were joined here by a strange pointer belonging, Andrew said, to a gentleman in Aberdeen. "Flight" had evidently observed the departure of our safari, and being of congenial trend, had taken up the trail. Rounding a thicket clump we discovered Jimmy holding staunchly, with Flash backing as though his very life depended upon it. The new dog celebrated his arrival by pausing a second, as though to contemplate the picture, then dashed in, sending birds in every direction. The Gentleman from Boston accomplished a neat double, Andrew singled, but I was too far away to do much of anything save cuss and watch down a single or two. Andrew had Flash and Jim retrieve, then turned and eyed the guilt-stricken Flight with narrowed lids. Placing his gun against a convenient bush, he ripped a substantial switch from a sapling and grittingly invited the hapless one approach. This he did, in fawning, contrite hesitation, while the other dogs loafed in to enjoy the circus and give him the laugh. A moment later his cries rent the air, but the whaling had its effect—he flushed no more that day and attended strictly to business. At the horses we found Joe Howard, Andrew's cousin, who brought with him his good pointer, Ticket. Joe had ridden from his home two miles beyond town and reported tough sledding.

Fording a slushy bayou, we rode a short distance before seeing Flash, rigid as a poker, pointing in a ravine. Tick and Jim flattened on sight and Flight, with vivid memory of his recent dressing down, sprawled when Andrew's sharp warning reached him. A huge bevy buzzed from the sedge.

"Blam-blam and blooie-blooie" ensued, with the result that each man tucked away a pair of birds in his coat. The singles went "home-free" by winging it across an ice-gorged back water. Farther on, Flight re-established himself somewhat in our good graces by a ripping find. It was ludicrous to see the fellow roll his protruding eyes and warn off the covetous Ticket who wormed a bit too near in an effort to assist. But best of all a glorious sun burned a blazing way through the clouds and cheered up everything.

In higher country, following the direction taken by some split-covey singles we saw Flight and Flash standing perhaps forty feet apart at the edge of a dense timber bottom. Thinking they had spotted some truants we separated; the Boston Boy and I going to Flash while Joe and Andrew pinned their faith to Flight's fancy. To our amazement two clustrous bevies roared from the clover almost simultaneously. Ed and I dropped four from our rise, while Joe and Andrew drew equal toll from theirs. For the next half hour we enjoyed the most magnificent of all shooting—single birds scattered in hedge boundaries and along the leaf-strewn files of the timber. We kicked about here and there, joking, laughing, betting on shots, taking turns as the dogs ranged stealthily ahead, pointing, it seemed, almost every moment. Occasionally, when a bird lay low or flushed wild some smooth chap made a getaway, but we begrudged not one of these his escape. Finally, with bulging pockets we returned to the horses.

At a free-flowing artesian well Joe and Andrew produced capacious saddle pockets and unwound savory bundles. Their contents would have made the weariest Fletcherite drool at the mouth and forget his number of chews. There was cold quail and crisp "beat" biscuit. Then came "hog-haid" sandwiches and meaty spareribs, home-made pickles and hard-boiled eggs. And to top off came a jam cake and a chocolate one, the latter inlaid with marshmallow sauce and studded with walnut and pecan hearts.

Nothing disturbed the noon stillness save grunts of purest satisfaction serene and an occasional yell of "Aw, git away f'um here, dawg." After lunch came a pipe for the others and a "touch" by an old colored mammy who came like Rebekah to the Well, with her pitcher and a hard-luck story of the burned cabin. We each shelled out "two bits," and in addition to this purse a fat cane-cutter rabbit that Joe had bowled over surreptitiously sent her on her way rejoicing.

Climbing into our saddles we rode down through the spongy accretions of the bottoms, across a wide slough and out into a vast section of waste or "ole po' land" as Andrew termed it. A short way on Jim was discovered gazing rapturously into a plum thicket. We saw the birds go up and wing past, settling across a drainage ditch. One of the dogs had evidently come along down wind and frisked Jim out of a point, for he was very much embarrassed. Then, in rapid succession the dogs found birds seemingly right and left. Three big gangs were turned up within a radius of ten acres. It was glorious sport and the afternoon wore away almost without our knowledge. What with a puffy kill here, a miss there and the ever-recurring thrill when some tireless dog whirled into discovery, we were almost glad to gather up our reins and hit off toward the line of greening hills that marked the direction of our circle home.

In a short while we splashed across an expanse of meadow and began climbing through sedge-strewn valleys and steep ridges of pine forest. Shadows were lengthening among the trees and our horses' steps were muffled in the needle bedding underfoot. In an opening we halted and look away across the lowlands of our morning to where Aberdeen lay brooding in the peace and quiet of tranquil, fading sunshine. The piercing blast had softened with the chill of falling night. It seemed a thousand miles to the warmth of indoors and the delight of complete well-fed weariness. The faithful dogs had as yet evinced no signs of fatigue, in fact they were splitting the grass at top speed. Just as we reached the Gillespie place boundary fence Jimmy paused at a dry ditch along the road, sniffed, and then with head in air, walked forward as though treading on eggs.

"He's got his Sunday clothes on ag'in, ain't he?" asked Andrew, his face lighting with pardonable pride and a lean expansive grin. "But I believe we've all got pretty durn near the limit."

"Les' try 'em jus' one mo' fair fall," replied Joe, "it would be a shame to put one over on Jim dog after all his trouble."

"Satisfactory to me," pronounced Andrew. "Light down, gents, and bust a few night caps"—shoving two shells into his stubby Parker. Here Jimmy broke his point and tiptoed gingerly after the running birds. Then, out over the brink boiled a veritable beehive of quail. Ensued a miniature sham battle, followed by shouts of "I got two" and counter claims of "I killed that one" and "Fetch daid, suh." Discipline was forgotten for the nonce, but matters were adjusted when the dogs brought in enough birds to credit each man with a clean, undisputed double. "Better count up here," said Joe, "I've gotta leave you lads at the nex' gate." So the tally began, with low murmurings as each chap pulled bird after bird from his multipocketed coat.

"The limit here," announced Andrew, finishing first.

"For the first time in my young life a limit," chortled the Boston Boy.

"Another victory for the untrammeled Democracy," said Joe.

"Sufficiency here," I confessed.

At a padlocked gate, down the road, Joe took leave of us with a parting shout of "See you in the morning, boys, at the Houston place gate." The sun was glowing faintly behind its borderland of western ridge spires. Our dogs, seeming to realize that their day's work was done, leaped gladly along to keep our pace. Through field and brake we trotted, and at length, swinging into a black buckshot road, straightened out for the home stretch down Life Boat Chapel lane. It was to me a familiar way, past homely daubed shacks and cabins, ashine with the gleam of lowly lamplight, redolent of wood fires, frying bacon and contentment.

And how the dogs did bark when we swung into the grounds of our host! What is there better in life than an evening spent within the domain of Sweet Hospitality? What is more delightful than when, clothed in the refreshened garb of citizenry, one lies at ease in a deep armchair or sits down to such a dinner as only an "Auntie" can dish up and send in to her "white folks"? And surely out upon the sea of night there rides no fairer craft than a towering four-poster.

It was past seven o'clock when we found ourselves at family breakfast. You have, no doubt, often begun the morning meal with a luscious orange. But listen! Have you ever seen a "yard boy" stagger in under a huge platter, wide as the bottom of a boat, piled high with quail, smothered as only Aunt Hannah can turn the trick, with a whole bucket of bird gravy for the hominy and grits? You may suit yourself about the spiced aromatic spirits of little pigs, or slices of float-away omelette, but personally I prefer to rather economize on space until the waffles start flocking in in droves. Did you ever tenderly smear a pair of round, crisp, eat-me-quick-for-the-love-of-Mike members of the waffle family; watching the molten country butter search out the receptive crevices and overflow each hollow? Then slathered the twain with a ruddy coating of home-kettled, right-from-the-heart, ribbon cane molasses? But at length Pud sounded retreat by announcing the horses. Scabbards and saddle pockets were tied on and we were off in the bright sunshine of a perfect day.

At the Houston place gate we found Joe waiting with the ever ready Ticket and Lady, the latter a Marse Ben-Bragg-Gladstone pup. Within two hours we had raised six bevies. Ticket was the first to make birds, stiffening in a clover patch along a railroad cut. Then little Lady raced away across a hill and made a neat find on the cast. Flash and Jim were old stagers on these grounds. Jim nailed a gang for Andrew near a blackjack stretch and Flash, after handling some of the singles, delved far into the interior and fastened upon a covey. For some time we had royal sport trying to make respectable averages in the dense tangle and the dogs tried hard to overlook the messy work their masters were doing when brown bullets would whir from the dead leaves and top the blackjacks in whizzing farewell.

After lunch we rode the hill crests, letting the dogs cut up the sides and valleys. On an opposite ridge we saw Andrew approach the top with Lady and Jim flagging ahead. Down went the pair on a clean-cut point.

"It's a shame to take the money," shouted Andrew, and, sure enough, he whirled two of the crowd into bird paradise. Midafternoon is the ideal time for bird finding and it was a treat to see the Boston Boy's eyes widen in wonderment when the dogs picked up bunch after bunch.

"By the gills of the sacred codfish," he exclaimed, feverishly ripping open a fresh box of shells, "I never knew there were this many birds in existence." But at length it again neared knocking-off time, so we spurred through the fields hoping for just one more find to make the day complete.

"There they are," called Joe, rising in his stirrups, pointing to Flash and Jim. And, sure enough, they were at it again, and such a whopper the covey proved! We were actually too amazed to shoot on the rise, but watched the fugitives settle in a marshy strip of iron weed bordering a willow "dreen." Suffice to say that we gave them our personal attention and when the war was over the result proved a fitting climax to another red-letter day. Twenty or twenty-five birds doesn't sound so many to a game hog, perhaps, but shooting four in a party, turn about or shooting alone, when a man has spent the hours afield with nature and taken from her cherished stores the satisfaction of twenty clean kills and the vagrant clinging pangs of many misses, he has done pretty much all that an unselfish heart could ever crave.

"Well," questioned Andrew, when our horses' heads were set toward home, "how does the Minute Man from ye Boston Towne like an everyday, Down-in-Dixie bird hunt, with a little Rebel Yell stuff on the side?"

The Gentleman from Boston sighed a sigh of rich content and stretched wearily in his saddle.

"You are now speaking," said he, with that methodical diction characteristic of the ultra-grammatical Bostonian, "of the very best thing in the universe."

"D'm'f 'taint," I echoed softly.

And Andrew triple-plated this confirmation in the tongue of our Fatherland.

"Sho' is!"

Rams in the Snow

BY JACK O'CONNOR

PERHAPS NO OTHER writer of either guns or hunting will ever enjoy the popularity of the late Jack O'Connor during his years as Shooting Editor of *Outdoor Life*. In stories now collected in several books, O'Connor became a legendary figure, famed as champion of the .270, mountain hunting for all types of game, and hunting in Africa.

O'Connor was a truly talented storyteller. A successful novelist before he began writing for magazines, Jack O'Connor wrote tales of his hunts that left the reader with the feeling of being personally involved, as if the reader was an absent friend being updated on the events that had taken place. From his home in Idaho, O'Connor roamed the globe in pursuit of game and stories. But always, his favorite destinations were in the high peaks of Canada and Alaska, where the great wild sheep made their homes.

(Good old Field Johnson, my guide and companion on this hunt, was so badly mauled by a grizzly in April 1950 that he never fully recovered and eventually died.)

"Old man he tell me: Go big creek left Generk Glacier. High mountains. Good ram country!" This was the dope which Field Johnson and I followed to get into real Yukon ram country on my first trip to the Yukon in the fall of 1945—and therein lies this tale.

My first white Dall ram had come after only two days of hunting. He was the first one I had spotted, and he was a very good one. He saw us and ran, but I managed to cut him down on the run.

From then on, however, my luck seemed to have deserted me. The next sheep camp brought sight of a good many ewes and lambs, but nothing we could be sure was a ram. We moved to another location where Myles

Brown, my companion, got two big rams. Several days of heartbreaking climbing brought me within shooting distance of only small rams. One afternoon in some of the steepest, roughest sheep country I have ever seen, I lay for two hours watching a bunch of fourteen rams which Field and I had stalked to within 300 yards.

With my 8-X binoculars I could see them as plainly as if they were in my own backyard. They had mock battles. They scratched out beds. They fed. They gazed out over the vast, terrible landscape of canyons, rockslides, glaciers. All this is part of sheep hunting, but though I enjoyed it, it wasn't getting my two big rams.

So finally Field and I started out on a last desperate effort to find trophy rams—started on the strength (if you call it that) of what an Indian had found out forty years before. We had two saddle horses, one pack horse, and a small tent. With care we could make our grub last a week. I was to cook; Field was to wrangle the horses.

Midafternoon brought us to the left side of the Generk Glacier in the Yukon near the Alaskan border. Through the binoculars we saw a few ewes, a couple of lambs, and a small ram or two; but nothing that led us to believe we were in any ram paradise.

We pulled out, riding and leading our horses over a series of high, round ridges above timberline toward the head of a creek which I believe is Count Creek. We saw a couple of dozen caribou, mostly small bulls; but at that time the big fellows were still in the scrubby spruce forest just below timberline.

The sun was down when we pulled up our weary horses beside a little creek where grass and willows grew. While Field hobbled the horses and put up the tent, I fried bacon and sheep meat, made toast, and warmed a can of green beans. It was pitch dark when we hit our sleeping bags.

The next morning we rode up toward where the boulder-strewn creek was born in a series of long, white glaciers that streaked tall, black mountains. When we couldn't go much farther we pulled up on the slope, pitched our little tent, hobbled and belled the horses, and ate a belated lunch washed down with tea.

High above us, on either side of the creek, we could see sheep, snow-white against green lichen slopes or black shale and slide rock. On our side of the creek most of them seemed to be rams, and on the nearest—a fellow feeding by himself near a small glacier a mile away and 1,500 feet above us—we could plainly see horns.

We had no spotting scope, however,—and let me say right here that I will never again hunt sheep without one. When I think of the weary miles I climbed on that Yukon trip because I lacked such a scope it makes my legs ache. Often we could see sheep from camp from one to three miles away, but with 8-X binoculars we could seldom tell what sort of heads they had.

Well, that was the trouble now; so up we went. It took us an hour to get within good glassing distance of the ram. We judged him to be a six-year-old with about a 32-inch curl. Since we had gained all that altitude, we explored the country and saw in all about thirty young rams—not one with a trophy head.

Far across the creek, on the opposite slope, we could see three bunches of sheep—one of about thirty, one of ten, and one of fourteen. All had smaller animals which we took to be lambs. Evidently we were on the boy's side of the creek.

In spite of the fact that we were in fine sheep country, we went to bed that night not too encouraged.

Field said, "Tomorrow we go over ridge into basins other side. We find big rams. We get him O.K., that fella!"

His voice, however, had a hollow sound—as if, far from believing it, he thought we were jinxed. That night when we crawled into our bags once more the stars were shining and the northern lights were playing fantastically in the sky. At least, we thought, we were getting a break in the weather.

But next morning snow was falling. The sky was dull and overcast and with only wet willow for wood, far above timberline as we were, we had a tough time getting the fire going. Coffee, bannock, and bacon made the world look a bit brighter. The sky lightened a little and up we went again. Results were the same: The basins on the other side of the range produced rams—but young ones.

By noon we had worked the country out. Then Field began to scan the mountains across the creek once more. The same bunches of sheep were there, but he soon found that others had moved in during the night.

"Look!" he said, handing me the glasses. "Four rams with that big bunch of ewes!"

I looked. I could see that four of the white dots were indeed larger than the others and perhaps a bit more yellowish, but that was all. Field, however, swore our luck had changed at last, so I said, "O.K., let's go."

Down the mountain we plunged, faster than I had ever before come down a slope so steep. Now and then we stopped to glass the rams, and just before an intervening ridge hid them from view I could tell that at least one of them was a beauty. At more than a mile away I could make out his big curling horns. My blood pressure went up and my weary legs found new strength.

At camp we hastily ate a couple of sandwiches and a chocolate bar. Then we set off on the stalk. The sky was dark and lowering now; a few flakes of snow were falling and mist clung to the peaks.

Ours was to be a race against snow and darkness. The creek was knee-deep in water straight from the glaciers and bitterly cold, but we took off shoes and socks, rolled up our pants, and hobbled across to the other side. My feet were so numb that I could have cut off a toe with a dull pocketknife without feeling it.

By climbing a big, bare canyon strewn with great boulders and then scrambling up a cliff at its head we could get above the place where the rams were last bedded. It was tough going but we went fast; two weeks of climbing had left me in fine condition and Field himself seemed to be half mountain sheep.

When we were about to haul ourselves over the cliff the snow began in earnest—big, wet flakes that fell so fast and thick that visibility was cut at one time to about fifty yards. I fought frantically to keep the scope dry enough so that I could see to shoot. On top we waited for the snow to ease up.

When it did, not a sheep was in sight!

We worked cautiously along the edge of the cliff, thinking they were in a basin below us where we had seen them feeding that morning. Suddenly through a rift in the storm we saw them bedded along a slope far to the right. A look with the glasses showed us big rams, ewes, and lambs, all lying there in the storm together. When the snow let up a little we could see them plainly— white against black rock. Then the wind would howl, the flames would thicken, and the sheep would be blotted out.

By cutting back around the cliff we could get up on a sawtooth out-cropping nearer to the sheep. We did. Once we had to cross a slide so steep that we could make it only by running at top speed—just as sheep themselves cross such places. We started rocks rolling that tumbled into the canyon 1,000 feet below us, but the noise was deadened by the howling wind and the hiss of the falling snow.

At last we were over the terrible slides and cliffs to a jagged escarp-ment, which I recognized as being the spot where we had first seen the rams that morning. Here we peeked over.

Along with the ewes and lambs we saw six big, old rams. They were in sets of three above the ewes on a rockslide. Between snow flurries, I managed to see that the ram farthest to the right in the first set had massive horns, broomed and blunted, that came up well past his nose. His head was like that of a fine Canadian bighorn.

"I like that baby farthest to the right in the first bunch," I whispered to Field.

"Best head is one in middle of second bunch," Field told me after a long look with the binoculars. "He got perfect points. Long, too! All hunters want perfect points."

Again I looked the rams over. Visibility was poor. At best we had to see them through falling snow. At worst we couldn't see them at all. So far as I could tell, the one that looked like a bighorn was my first choice and Field's favorite was my second.

Actually, with luck I wouldn't have to choose; for though the Yukon game laws set a one-ram "limit," a second can be taken out on payment of an extra fee, and in addition I had a special permit from the Yukon authorities to get a study specimen for the University of Arizona. I already had one ram; that left these two to go!

How far away were they? I didn't know then—and I don't know now. The reticule cell in the scope on my pet .270 had become loose a few days before and I couldn't use it. I found that it was off by overshooting a wolf three times at 300 yards, then killing it by holding on its feet and breaking its back. I didn't have time, place, or cartridges to attempt to sight the .270 in again. There was nothing to do but to retire it and use my old .30/06 Springfield, which itself was then in the process of getting wet.

So there I was above those rams and at what looked like something more than 300 yards away from the nearest one. My rifle was sighted to put the 180-gr. factory load on the nose at 225 yards. Not long before, when I had used it on a grizzly, the rifle had made a lucky three-inch group behind the bear's shoulder at around 200 yards.

The snow kept coming down, the wind drifting it at a right angle between us and the sheep. Sometimes I could see the rams plainly, but invariably a sudden swirl of big flakes would blot them out. Suddenly the wind began changing and the flakes whirled down from every direction. I was afraid that the wind would carry our scent to the sheep.

"Field," I whispered, "the wind is changing. I'm going to knock those rams as soon as the snow clears a little."

"O.K.," said Field.

I had kept wiping the lens of the scope as snow fell on it, and when the flakes eased up suddenly I was ready.

The ram with the massive horns was lying broadside. I held about two thirds of the way up his body and eased off the shot. Field, who had his glasses on him, called it just below. The ram jumped up as if someone had given him a hotfoot, ran off about twenty-five yards, and stood there. This time I held what looked to be about six inches above his shoulder and squeezed the trigger.

"Can't see where it hit," said Field in my ear.

Just then the ram rolled over and lay there on his side, all four feet stretched out stiffly.

"Other ram at top of bunch right on ridge," Field coached me as he watched with the binoculars.

I could see the sheep he indicated through the snow, but I had to take his word as to which it was. By this time the ocular lens of the scope was plastered with snow. I wiped it off hastily, put the post in the scope just even with the top of the ram's horns as he stood with his rump toward me, and eased the shot off through the blurry image.

"You broke leg," said Field.

I put the post well over the animal's horns and touched off another shot.

"High!" Field cried.

Just then a snowflake as big as a rose petal sailed into the tube of the Stith mount and plastered itself all over the objective lens. My rifle was out of commission until I had wiped off the lens. When I had done so, the ram was over the hump.

Together we slid down a shale slide about 200 feet high and went on across a basin. We ran past the first ram. And there in the bottom of a little canyon lay the second ram, dead.

The shot which Field said broke the sheep's leg had hit the hip and passed out through the abdomen. The second shot had grazed one horn at the base but had not injured it. His horns were a fine example of the most common white sheep type—wide of spread, well past the nose, and with perfect points.

We skinned out the head and took it and a load of meat with us as we went up to examine the first ram. His horns were more massive, blunted and broomed, and they too made more than a complete spiral. He was about twelve years old, to judge from the annual rings on his battered horns. He was not, however, a particularly large sheep. I would guess his dressed weight at about 170 pounds, whereas the big ram with the wide spread and perfect points would probably have gone not far from 200.

Neither, of course, was in the same league—so far as size went—with the great bighorns farther south. Both, however, were fine rams in the record class, and the larger had a curl of more than thirty-nine inches.

By the time we took a few pictures and skinned out the heads, the snow began to fall in earnest and, instead of melting the moment it touched the ground, it now began to stick. The countryside grew darker and a bitter wind howled down from the glaciers at the head of the river. The brush and grass on the lower slopes of the mountain were heavy with wet snow as we came down.

Camp was a mess. Our willow wood was soaked, some of our grub was wet, and the damp snow blowing into the tent had soaked our beds. Luckily Field and I had rolled up some extra clothes in our beds. We made a quick change. Presently I was hobbling around in the snow in a pair of moccasins while my wet shoes dried.

Field got the fire going and heated water for tea. I cooked bacon and sheep liver, cut thin and fried crisp. By way of celebration, we had a can of peas to go with it and some peaches for dessert. The snow was still falling; but there in that lonely subarctic valley with its rugged peaks masked by the snow, with the roar of the turbulent little river in our ears, and the munching of our three horses eating willow leaves, everything seemed fine.

We had climbed over the comb of one range that day and almost to the top of another, but we had two fine trophies I'd never forget—and which I don't think Field will forget either.

The next day we packed and pulled out for the main camp between thirty and thirty-five miles away. Our horses were tired and ferociously hungry after their diet of willows. We walked most of the way, and just as darkness was closing down we smelled the smoke from the cook tent and heard the horse bells at the camp.

I may never hunt the beautiful snow-white rams of the arctic again—actually I have hunted Dall sheep several times since—in 1949, 1950, and in 1956! For all I know, I may never again hunt sheep. But as long as I live I'll remember the time when I still had enough steel in my legs to race down one mountain and up another, and beat the snow and the darkness to two of the finest trophies I ever hope to get!

Are You Lonesome Tonight?

BY ROBERT F. JONES

WHEN LYONS & BURFORD published Bob Jones' *Dancers in the Sunset Sky* in 1996, I was among the many readers eager to add the book to my shelves. *Dancers* is an anthology of Jones' pieces that have appeared in scattered sites since he left the traces at *Sports Illustrated,* where he was a top writer and editor for many years. "Are You Lonesome Tonight?" is a tale about a man, a dog, and a woodcock hunt in the New England uplands. These ingredients are the kind of stuff that make up Bob Jones' lifestyle, and he writes about them beautifully and passionately. In addition to his several books of nonfiction on outdoor subjects, Jones has written eight novels with story lines of rousing, no-holds-barred adventure. These include two set in the opening of the West, with buffalo hunters and Indians in the leading roles—*Tie My Bones to Her Back* (republished as *The Buffalo Hunters*) and *Deadville.* In my opinion both rank right alongside the best works of the mountain man, hunter-trapper genre of Western novels.

The road ran through yellowing woods and fields up over a hill and then dropped away toward a swale where a stock pond glinted back up at them through a dark beard of alders. He turned off to the right at a break in the stone wall and parked the truck out of sight at the top of the ridge behind a copse of young aspens. The dog danced briefly on the seat beside him, teeth clacking with happy little yips barely suppressed. They'd been here before. He let the dog out, then unzipped the sheep-lined case behind the bench seat and withdrew the gun. The dog sat shivering at his boots. He reached in and pulled out the bell collar, a musical tingle of steel that made the dog's ears twitch. He buckled the collar around the dog's thick, black neck, took two shells from his vest, broke the gun, blew down the barrels for luck, and loaded.

Hunt 'em up, Luke.

The dog lined out fast down the footpath, head up, nostrils flared, into the wind. Let him run it out quick, he thought. I could whistle him back and keep him cool, but he needs the run, let him get it out of his system, and there's nothing this close to the road anyway.

But there was. Luke spun in midstride, tail up, and dove nose first into a thicket of maple whips beside the trail. A woodcock sprang twittering skyward and flicked out, twisting on wide, high wings through the leaftops.

Gone before he got the gun halfway to his shoulder.

That'll learn ye, he thought.

Luke glared back at him balefully.

My mistake, he told the dog. *Too slow. But it's only the first of the season. Cut me some slack, why don't you?*

They worked on down an old logging road flanked by a stone wall, with a brush-grown field to their left and a steep hillside of mature shagbark hickory to the right. Luke worked the wall and the puckerbrush beside it, quartering short and quick, nose up, then down, then up again, into the wind. The logging road bent away to the right just past an old, silt-bottomed stock pond where the man paused to give Luke a chance at a drink. But the Lab wasn't thirsty yet. He was hungry only for birds.

The field dropped away to an alder bottom with a square of old apples and second-growth timber rising behind it. Antique apples, varieties grown no more for profit. A small spring-fed brook thick-edged with alders marked the break from field to covert. He called this patch the Seep Square, and over the years it had been good to them. There were two ways to hunt the Seep Square, depending on the amount of time you wanted to hunt.

If you had time enough, you could hunt it from the alder bottom up. That way any birds you flushed and missed would fly deeper into the country, and you could spend a pleasant couple of hours working the hills for reflushes.

Short of time, you could circle out to the top of the Seep Square and push it back fast toward the alder bottom. Unhit birds would not fly across the open field for fear of hawks. They would break to the left for the complex lobe of covert beyond the hickory ridge. That hunt took less than an hour, and was always good for at least a couple of woodcock. But the longer hunt meant more time behind the dog, more time pounding the woods, and held in the thornapples the promise of grouse. It was a luxury.

To hell with time, he thought.

The seep itself was muck-bottomed and tall with ripening cattails and they waded through to the other side, where he called Luke to heel. He knelt beside the dog on dry ground at the edge of the alders and put his arm around the dog's neck. *Take it slow and easy through here. Work it good. They hold tight this early in the season, most of 'em will. They haven't been hunted yet. All right?*

All right, hunt 'em up.

He dropped down off a weathered boulder into the thick of it, weaving and ducking behind the quartering dog, stepping high over the canted trunks of dying alders, pushing others aside with his gloved fore-end hand. The alders cracked like rotten bones. It was dark in here, fetid, windless, with charlie behind the eyeballs, an RPG at the ready. He held the light 20-gauge double upright with his bare trigger hand, angled forward the better to mount it quickly at a flush, moving fast but with his eyes on the dog, alert to any sudden sound or a sudden brightening of Luke's color. Luke always lit up like black neon when he marked a bird, and his flailing feathered tail always shot upright, beating like a metronome gone mad.

It was a familiar tail, a recognized rhythm.

About twenty steps into the alders, Luke cut quickly up toward the dry ground, lighting up, and a woodcock got up, rising loud as penny-whistles up toward the sunlight, and he caught it square at the top of its rise as it hit the light, a russet flash, unconscious of even mounting the gun, and popped the bird down in a puff of tiny, dark-eyed, slowly falling feathers. The alders ate the sound of the shot.

Luke picked up the woodcock and brought it over. The man took it from his easy jaws. A bead of blood glistened at the tip of the long, odd beak, and the big eyes were closed. Dead before it hit the ground.

Good work, man. First of the year. Nines do the job, don't they? He let Luke sniff the blood and suck in the rich, hot, dry mud scent of woodcock fresh dead. Maybe I shouldn't do that, he thought; some say it floods a dog's nose against the scent of the next bird. But Luke loves it so, and it's a luxury anyway. Why shouldn't a dog have a luxury? Then he had a sniff himself. He pocketed the bird, feeling it warm inside the canvas against the small of his back.

Okay, he said. *Hunt 'em up.*

They pushed on down through the rest of the alder brake with no more flushes and cut right along a tumbling stone wall toward the top of the Seep Square. Luke worked the wall thoroughly and cut back across the track of the gun to frisk the interior thickets. They came to the first of the old apple trees, Luke looking back toward the man to make sure he was close enough before he went in on it. A grouse got up with a roar from under the apple tree, boring out low and straight with the tree trunk obscuring the shot, then soared high out of range toward the top of the thornapple rise, tilting, sunlight gleaming silver-stained across his wings and back.

Luke looked over again, pained at the gun's silence.

Yes, the man said, nodding mock gravely. *They'll do that, you know. All the naive birds in these parts were killed off two centuries ago. Only the smart survive.*

He squinted up at the sun, then checked his watch. Twenty minutes from the truck, three flushes, one woodcock in pocket. One woodcock makes mighty thin soup.

Hunt 'em up.

They crossed the far stone wall that marked the top of the Seep Square and cut left again and began to sinuate their way up through the thornapples. Luke picked his steps carefully from bush to bush with memories of those bitterly hooked thorns of yore buried stem-deep in his pads. The man now carried a tweezers in his game vest against that possibility. The first time it happened, ten years ago when they were new to this country, he pulled the thorn out of Luke's paw with his teeth. Such an experience gets a person close to his dog in a hurry.

Halfway up the slope Luke got birdy. He put his nose up, inhaled, then ran fast to his left up and across while the man jumped clear of the thornapples into the open sunlight and a grouse got up, flushing back downhill like thunder toward the man, just over his head; and he spun on his heel, mounting the gun, and caught the bird going away as it poured downhill. He centered it, *pow,* and watched it spin sideways, corkscrewing ass over tip in a long, hard, crazy fall back down toward the bottom of the thornapples. *Thump,* dead, in a splash of feathers. Luke was past him, disappearing into the brush. No one runs on Luke.

The man waited, confident. He heard scrabbling in the leaves below, then the dog emerged from the brush and came wagging slowly uphill, his whole body wagging, with that shy, self-deprecating look they have when they've done it well, grinning around a mouthful of big, dead, head-lolling grouse body, one wing dangling alop.

He sat on the hillside, the gun broken open by his side in the short, dry grass, and took the grouse from Luke's mouth and spread its fan. A bird of the year by its heft, a hen bird by the mottled break in the center of the glossy blue-black tail bar. He lay the bird in his lap and opened the Buck knife, felt around for its crop, slit the neck, and extracted the crop. It felt full and lumpy. He slit the tough, pawky integument of the crop and squeezed its contents into his palm. Chunks of yellow-fleshed, red-skinned thornapple, a few dark green leaves, a catkin or two, probably birch by their color.

A cooling breeze worked back up the slope and he took off his cap to let his brow dry. He pulled out a pack of cigarettes. Luke lay panting by his side, squinting against the sunlight. He lay his free hand on the dog's wide, silken brow and ran it slowly down the heavy-muscled neck, working his fingers deep into the coarse black hairs of Luke's ruff. There was blood on the back of his hand, his own blood, welling slowly to the previous kiss of the briers. The cuts stung faintly, astringent, no worse than the tingle of aftershave.

The dog looked up and raised an eyebrow. He thumped his tail.

The valley spread out below them, yellow and green and red, the big sugar maples ballooning their crowns to the sky. The town lay strung like a necklace of sugar cubes along the winding dirt road, and to the east a church spire offered its impudent finger to heaven. Next to the spire he could see the graveyard, its moss-blackened stones just visible from this height of land. One of the tombstones, he knew, bore a timeworn legend.

ELIZABETH HARDWEAL
May 26, 1798–December 23, 1822
In the 25th Year of Her Age
"She Come to Town on a Viset"

Beyond the valley rose another range of mountains, Shatterack and Bear and Moffat and Equinox most prominent among them, and on the dim-hazed horizon the blue-black rim of the Greens themselves.

He pictures her coming to town for the Christmas season, to visit relatives, probably from Massachusetts or Connecticut where they all came from in those days. What was it? Diphtheria? Fever? The bloody flux? Was she pretty? He hopes so. Perhaps they had partridge for supper before she fell ill. Maybe she went through the ice one night, skating.

God how he loves her. . . .

Are you lonesome tonight?

Well, we all come to town on a viset.

They breathed the sweet fall air, man and dog, in love now with the whole whistling world. The man stood stiffly and pocketed the grouse. Its weight and warmth felt comfortable against the small of his back, more than balancing that of the cooling woodcock. He stooped and picked up the shotgun, reloaded it, and clicked it shut with that sweet sound of a bank vault closing.

There's two more birds still down there, he told the dog, *a big one and a little one. Or at least that we know of.*

Hunt 'em up.

The Thak Man-Eater

BY JIM CORBETT

FOR A TASTE OF real hunting danger, one true account of hunting strides the field like a colossus. The Englishman Jim Corbett's *Man-Eaters of Kumaon* is an entire book of stories of Corbett's encounters with man-eating tigers in India in the 1930s.

Each tiger Corbett hunted had become a legend of stealth and death in killing and eating natives in the secluded Kumaon Hills. The tiger Corbett called "The Thak Man-Eater" was the most difficult of all, and the most dangerous of all. Stalking the Thak Man-Eater, Corbett the hunter unknowingly becomes the hunted.

After reading this wonderful story, the next time you have the chance to see a huge, power-rippling, beautiful tiger in a zoo, you will get a sense of the danger Corbett faced alone in the darkening forest.

Peace had reigned in the Ladhya valley for many months when in September '38 a report was received in Naini Tal that a girl, twelve years of age, had been killed by a tiger at Kot Kindri village. The report, which reached me through Donald Stewart, of the Forest Department, gave no details, and it was not until I visited the village some weeks later that I was able to get particulars of the tragedy. It appeared that, about noon one day, this girl was picking up windfalls from a mango tree close to and in full view of the village, when a tiger suddenly appeared. Before the men working near by were able to render any assistance, it carried her off. No attempt was made to follow up the tiger, and as all signs of drag and blood trail had been obliterated and washed away long before I arrived on the scene, I was unable to find the place where the tiger had taken the body to.

Kot Kindri is about four miles southwest of Chuka, and three miles due west of Thak. It was in the valley between Kot Kindri and Thak that the Chuka man-eater had been shot the previous April.

My most direct route to Kot Kindri was to go by rail to Tanakpur, and from there by foot via Kaldhunga and Chuka. This route, however, though it would save me a hundred miles of walking, would necessitate my passing through the most deadly malaria belt in northern India, and to avoid it I decided to go through the hills to Mornaula, and from there along the abandoned Sherring road to its termination on the ridge above Kot Kindri.

While my preparations for this long trek were still under way a second report reached Naini Tal of a kill at Sem, a small village on the left bank of the Ladhya and distant about half a mile from Chuka.

The victim on this occasion was an elderly woman, the mother of the Headman of Sem. This unfortunate woman had been killed while cutting brushwood on a steep bank between two terraced fields. She had started work at the further end of the fifty-yard-long bank, and had cut the brushwood to within a yard of her hut when the tiger sprang on her from the field above. So sudden and unexpected was the attack that the woman only had time to scream once before the tiger killed her, and taking her up the twelve-foot-high bank crossed the upper field and disappeared with her into the dense jungle beyond. Her son, a lad some twenty years of age, was at the time working in a paddy field a few yards away and witnessed the whole occurrence, but was too frightened to try to render any assistance. In response to the lad's urgent summons the Patwari arrived at Sem two days later, accompanied by eighty men he had collected. Following up in the direction the tiger had gone, he found the woman's clothes and a few small bits of bone. This kill had taken place at 2 p.m. on a bright sunny day, and the tiger had eaten its victim only sixty yards from the hut where it had killed her.

On receipt of this second report, Ibbotson, Deputy Commissioner of the three Districts of Almora, Naini Tal, and Gathwal, and I held a council of war, the upshot of which was that Ibbotson, who was on the point of setting out to settle a land dispute at Askot on the border of Tibet, changed his tour program and, instead of going via Bagashwar, decided to accompany me to Sem, and from there go on to Askot.

The route I had selected entailed a considerable amount of hill-climbing so we eventually decided to go up the Nandhour valley, cross the watershed between the Nandhour and Ladhya, and follow the latter river down to Sem. The Ibbotsons accordingly left Naini Tal on 12 October, and the following day I joined them at Chaurgallia.

Going up the Nandhour and fishing as we went—our best day's catch on light trout rods was a hundred and twenty fish—we arrived on the fifth day at Durga Pepal. Here we left the river, and after a very stiff climb camped for the night on the watershed. Making an early start next morning we pitched our tents that night on the left bank of the Ladhya, twelve miles from Chalti.

The monsoon had given over early, which was very fortunate for us, for owing to the rock cliffs that run sheer down into the valley, the river has to be crossed every quarter of a mile or so. At one of these fords my cook, who stands five feet in his boots, was washed away and only saved from a watery grave by the prompt assistance of the man who was carrying our lunch basket.

On the tenth day after leaving Chaurgallia we made camp on a deserted field at Sem, two hundred yards from the hut where the woman had been killed, and a hundred yards from the junction of the Ladhya and Sarda Rivers.

Gill Waddell, of the Police, whom we met on our way down the Ladhya, had camped for several days at Sem and had tied out a buffalo that MacDonald of the Forest Department had very kindly placed at our disposal; and though the tiger had visited Sem several times during Waddell's stay, it had not killed the buffalo.

The day following our arrival at Sem, while Ibbotson was interviewing Patwaris, Forest Guards, and Headmen of the surrounding villages, I went out to look for pug marks. Between our camp and the junction, and also on both banks of the Ladhya, there were long stretches of sand. On this sand I found the tracks of a tigress, and of a young male tiger—possibly one of the cubs I had seen in April. The tigress had crossed and recrossed the Ladhya a number of times during the last few days, and the previous night had walked along the strip of sand in front of our tents. It was this tigress the villagers suspected of being the man-eater, and as she had visited Sem repeatedly since the day the Headman's mother had been killed they were probably correct.

An examination of the pug marks of the tigress showed her as being an average-sized animal, in the prime of life. Why she had become a man-eater would have to be determined later, but one of the reasons might have been that she had assisted to eat the victims of the Chuka tiger when they were together the previous mating season, and having acquired a taste for human flesh and no longer having a mate to provide her with it, had now turned a man-eater herself. This was only a surmise, and proved later to be incorrect.

Before leaving Naini Tal I had written to the Tahsildar of Tanakpur and asked him to purchase four young male buffaloes for me, and to send them to Sem. One of these buffaloes died on the road, the other three arrived on the 24th, and we tied them out the same evening together with the one MacDonald had given us. On going out to visit these animals next morning I found the people of Chuka in a great state of excitement. The fields round the village had been recently plowed, and the tigress the previous night had passed close to three families who were sleeping out on the fields with their cattle; fortunately in each case the cattle had seen the tigress and warned the sleepers of her approach. After leaving the cultivated land the tigress had gone up the track in the direction of Kot Kindri, and had passed close to two of our buffaloes without touching either of them.

The Patwari, Forest Guards, and villagers had told us on our arrival at Sem that it would be a waste of time tying out our young buffaloes, as they were convinced the man-eater would not kill them. The reason they gave was that this method of trying to shoot the man-eater had been tried by others without success, and that in any case if the tigress wanted to eat buffaloes there were many grazing in the jungles for her to choose from. In spite of this advice, however, we continued to tie out our buffaloes, and for the next two nights the tigress passed close to one or more of them, without touching them.

On the morning of the 27th, just as we were finishing breakfast, a party of men led by Tewari, the brother of the Headman of Thak, arrived in camp and reported that a man of their village was missing. They stated that this man had left the village at about noon the previous day, telling his wife before leaving that he was going to see that his cattle did not stray beyond the village boundary, and as he had not returned they feared he had been killed by the man-eater.

Our preparations were soon made, and at ten o'clock the Ibbotsons and I set off for Thak, accompanied by Tewari and the men he had brought with him. The distance was only about two miles but the climb was considerable, and as we did not want to lose more time than we could possibly help we arrived at the outskirts of the village out of breath and in a lather of sweat.

As we approached the village over the scrub-covered flat bit of ground which I have reason to refer to later, we heard a woman crying. The wailing of an Indian woman mourning her dead is unmistakable, and on emerging from the jungle we came on the mourner—the wife of the missing man—and some ten or fifteen men, who were waiting for us on the edge of the cultivated land. These people informed us that from their houses above they had seen some white object, which looked like part of the missing man's clothing, in a field overgrown with scrub thirty yards from where we were now standing. Ibbotson, Tewari, and I set off to investigate the white object, while Mrs. Ibbotson took the woman and the rest of the men up to the village.

The field, which had been out of cultivation for some years, was covered with a dense growth of scrub not unlike chrysanthemum, and it was not until we were standing right over the white object that Tewari recognized it as the loincloth of the missing man. Near it was the man's cap. A struggle had taken place at this spot, but there was no blood. The absence of blood where the attack had taken place and for some considerable distance along the drag could be accounted for by the tigress's having retained her first hold, for no blood would flow in such a case until the hold had been changed.

Thirty yards on the hill above us there was a clump of bushes roofed over with creepers. This spot would have to be looked at before following up the drag, for it was not advisable to have the tigress behind us. In the soft earth under the bushes we found the pug marks of the tigress, and where she had lain before going forward to attack the man.

Returning to our starting point we agreed on the following plan of action. Our primary object was to try to stalk the tigress and shoot her on her kill: to achieve this end I was to follow the trail and at the same time keep a lookout in front, with Tewari—who was unarmed—a yard behind me keeping a sharp lookout to right and left, and Ibbotson a yard behind Tewari to safeguard us against an attack from the rear. In the event of either Ibbotson or I seeing so much as a hair of the tigress, we were to risk a shot.

Cattle had grazed over this area the previous day, disturbing the ground, and as there was no blood and the only indication of the tigress's passage was an occasional turned-up leaf or crushed blade of grass, progress was slow. After carrying the man for two hundred yards the tigress had killed and left him, and had returned and carried him off several hours later, when the people of Thak had heard several sambur calling in this direction. The reason for the tigress's not having carried the man away after she had killed him was possibly because his cattle may have witnessed the attack on him, and driven her away.

A big pool of blood had formed where the man had been lying, and as the blood from the wound in his throat had stopped flowing by the time the tigress had picked him up again, and further, as she was now holding him by the small of the back, whereas she had previously held him by the neck, tracking became even more difficult. The tigress kept to the contour of the hill, and as the undergrowth here was very dense and visibility only extended to a few yards, our advance was slowed down. In two hours we covered half a mile, and reached a ridge beyond which lay the valley in which, six months previously, we had tracked down and killed the Chuka man-eater. On this ridge was a great slab of rock, which sloped upwards and away from the direction in which we had come. The tigress's tracks went down to the right of the rock and I felt sure she was lying up under the overhanging portion of it, or in the close vicinity.

Both Ibbotson and I had on light rubber-soled shoes—Tewari was bare-footed—and we had reached the rock without making a sound. Signing to my two companions to stand still and keep a careful watch all round, I got a foothold on the rock, and inch by inch went forward. Beyond the rock was a short stretch of flat ground, and as more of this ground came into view, I felt certain my suspicion that the tigress was lying under the projection was correct. I had still a foot or two to go before I could look over, when I saw a movement to my left front. A goldenrod that had been pressed down had sprung erect, and a second later there was a slight movement in the bushes beyond, and a monkey in a tree on the far side off the bushes started calling.

The tigress had chosen the spot for her after-dinner sleep with great care, but unfortunately for us she was not asleep; and when she saw the top of my head—I had removed my hat—appearing over the rock, she had risen and, taking a step sideways, had disappeared under a tangle of blackberry bushes. Had she been lying anywhere but where she was she could not have got away, no matter how quickly she had moved, without my getting a shot at her. Our so-carefully-carried-out stalk had failed at the very last moment, and there was nothing to be done now but find the kill, and see if there was sufficient of it left for us to sit up over. To have followed her into the blackberry thicket would have been useless, and would also have reduced our chance of getting a shot at her later.

The tigress had eaten her meal close to where she had been lying, and as this spot was open to the sky and to the keen eyes of vultures she had removed the kill to a place of safety where it would not be visible from the air. Tracking now was easy, for there was a blood trail to follow. The trail led over a ridge of great rocks and fifty yards beyond these rocks we found the kill.

I am not going to harrow your feelings by attempting to describe that poor torn and mangled thing; stripped of every stitch of clothing and atom of dignity, which only a few hours previously had been a Man, the father of two children and the breadwinner of that wailing woman who was facing—without any illusions—the fate of a widow of India. I have seen many similar sights, each more terrible than the one preceding it, in the thirty-two years I have been hunting man-eaters, and on each occasion I have felt that it would have been better to have left the victim to the slayer than recover a mangled mass of flesh to be a nightmare ever after to those who saw it. And yet the cry of blood for blood, and the burning desire to rid a countryside of a menace than which there is none more terrible, is irresistible; and then there is always the hope, no matter how absurd one knows it to be, that the victim by some miracle may still be alive and in need of succour.

The chance of shooting—over a kill—an animal that has in all probability become a man-eater through a wound received over a kill, is very remote, and each succeeding failure, no matter what its cause, tends to make the animal more cautious, until it reaches a state when it either abandons its kill after one meal or approaches it as silently and as slowly as a shadow, scanning every leaf and twig with the certainty of discovering its would-be slayer, no matter how carefully he may be concealed or how silent and motionless he may be; a one in a million chance of getting a shot, and yet, who is there among us who would not take it?

The thicket into which the tigress had retired was roughly forty yards square, and she could not leave it without the monkey's seeing her and warning us, so we sat down back to back, to have a smoke and listen if the jungle had anything further to tell us while we considered our next move.

To make a machan it was necessary to return to the village, and during our absence the tigress was almost certain to carry away the kill. It had been difficult to track her when she was carrying a whole human being, but now, when her burden was considerably lighter and she had been disturbed, she would probably go for miles and we might never find her kill again, so it was necessary for one of us to remain on the spot, while the other two went back to the village for ropes.

Ibbotson, with his usual disregard for danger, elected to go back, and while he and Tewari went down the hill to avoid the difficult ground we had recently come over, I stepped up onto a small tree close to the kill. Four feet above ground the tree divided in two, and by leaning on one half and putting my feet against the other, I was able to maintain a precarious seat which was high enough off the ground to enable me to see the tigress if she approached the kill, and also high enough, if she had any designs on me, to see her before she got to within striking distance.

Ibbotson had been gone fifteen or twenty minutes when I heard a rock tilt forward, and then back. The rock was evidently very delicately poised, and when the tigress had put her weight on it and felt it tilt forward she had removed her foot and let the rock fall back into place. The sound had come from about twenty yards to my left front, the only direction in which it would have been possible for me to have fired without being knocked out of the tree.

Minutes passed, each pulling my hopes down a little lower from the heights to which they had soared, and then, when tension on my nerves and the weight of the heavy rifle were becoming unbearable, I heard a stick snap at the upper end of the thicket. Here was an example of how a tiger can move through the jungle. From the sound she had made I knew her exact position, had kept my eyes fixed on the spot, and yet she had come, seen me, stayed some time watching me, and then gone away without my having seen a leaf or a blade of grass move.

When tension on nerves is suddenly relaxed, cramped and aching muscles call loudly for ease, and though in this case it only meant the lowering of the rifle onto my knees to take the strain off my shoulders and arms, the movement, small though it was, sent a comforting feeling through the whole of my body. No further sound came from the tigress, and an hour or two later I heard Ibbotson returning.

Of all the men I have been on shikar with, Ibbotson is by far and away the best, for not only has he the heart of a lion, but he thinks of everything, and with it all is the most unselfish man that carries a gun. He had gone to fetch a rope and he returned with rugs, cushions, more hot tea than even I could drink, and an ample lunch; and while I sat—on the windward side of the kill— to refresh myself, Ibbotson put a man in a tree forty yards away to distract the tigress's attention, and climbed into a tree overlooking the kill to make a rope machan.

When the machan was ready Ibbotson moved the kill a few feet—a very unpleasant job—and tied it securely to the foot of a sapling to prevent the tigress's carrying it away, for the moon was on the wane and the first two hours of the night at this heavily wooded spot would be pitch dark. After a final smoke I climbed onto the machan, and when I had made myself comfortable Ibbotson recovered the man who was making a diversion and set off in the direction of Thak to pick up Mrs. Ibbotson and return to camp at Sem.

The retreating party were out of sight but were not yet out of sound when I heard a heavy body brushing against leaves, and at the same moment the monkey, which had been silent all this time and which I could now see sitting in a tree on the far side of the blackberry thicket, started calling. Here was more luck than I had hoped for, and our ruse of putting a man up a tree to cause a diversion appeared to be working as successfully as it had done on a previous occasion. A tense minute passed, a second, and a third, and then from the ridge where I had climbed onto the big slab of rock a kakar came dashing down towards me, barking hysterically. The tigress was not coming to the kill but had gone off after Ibbotson. I was now in a fever of anxiety, for it was quite evident that she had abandoned her kill and gone to try to secure another victim.

Before leaving, Ibbotson had promised to take every precaution, but on hearing the kakar barking on my side of the ridge he would naturally assume the tigress was moving in the vicinity of the kill, and if he relaxed his precautions the tigress would get her chance. Ten very uneasy minutes for me passed, and then I heard a second kakar barking in the direction of Thak; the tigress was still following, but the ground there was more open, and there was less fear of her attacking the party. The danger to the Ibbotsons was, however, not over by any means for they had to go through two miles of very heavy jungle to reach camp; and if they stayed at Thak until sundown listening for my shot, which I feared they would do and which as a matter of fact they did do, they would run a very grave risk on the way down. Ibbotson fortunately realized the danger and kept his party close together, and though the tigress followed them the whole way—as her pug marks the following morning showed—they got back to camp safely.

The calling of kakar and sambur enabled me to follow the movements of the tigress. An hour after sunset she was down at the bottom of the valley two miles away. She had the whole night before her, and though there was only one chance in a million of her returning to the kill I determined not to lose that chance. Wrapping a rug around me, for it was a bitterly cold night, I made myself comfortable in a position in which I could remain for hours without movement.

I had taken my seat on the machan at 4 p.m., and at 10 p.m. I heard two animals coming down the hill towards me. It was too dark under the trees to see them, but when they got to the lee of the kill I knew they were porcupines. Rattling their quills, and making the peculiar booming noise that only a porcupine can make, they approached the kill and, after walking round it several times, continued on their way. An hour later, and when the moon had been up some time, I heard an animal in the valley below. It was moving from east to west, and when it came into the wind blowing downhill from the kill it made a long pause, and then came cautiously up the hill. While it was still some distance away I heard it snuffing the air, and knew it to be a bear. The smell of blood was attracting him, but mingled with it was the less welcome smell of a human being, and taking no chances he was very carefully stalking the kill. His nose, the keenest of any animal's in the jungle, had apprised him while he was still in the valley that the kill was the property of a tiger. This to a Himalayan bear who fears nothing, and who will, as I have on several occasions seen, drive a tiger away from its kill, was no deterrent, but what was, and what was causing him uneasiness, was the smell of a human being mingled with the smell of blood and tiger.

On reaching the flat ground the bear sat down on his haunches a few yards from the kill, and when he had satisfied himself that the hated human smell held no danger for him he stood erect and turning his head sent a long-drawn-out cry, which I interpreted as a call to a mate, echoing down into the valley. Then without any further hesitation he walked boldly up to the kill, and as he noted it I aligned the sights of my rifle on him. I know of only one instance of a Himalayan bear eating a human being; on that occasion a woman cutting grass had fallen down a cliff and been killed, and a bear finding the mangled body had carried it away and had eaten it. This bear, however, on whose shoulder my sights were aligned, appeared to draw the line at human flesh, and after looking at and smelling the kill continued his interrupted course to the west. When the sounds of his retreat died away in the distance the jungle settled down to silence until interrupted, a little after sunrise, by Ibbotson's very welcome arrival.

With Ibbotson came the brother and other relatives of the dead man, who very reverently wrapped the remains in a clean white cloth and, laying it on a cradle made of two saplings and rope which Ibbotson provided, set off for the burning that on the banks of the Sarda, repeating under their breath as they went the Hindu hymn of praise *'Ram nam sat hai'* with its refrain, *'Satya bol gat hai.'*

Fourteen hours in the cold had not been without its effect on me, but after partaking of the hot drink and food Ibbotson had brought, I felt none the worse for my long vigil.

II.

After following the Ibbotsons down to Chuka on the evening of the 27th, the tigress, sometime during the night, crossed the Ladhya into the scrub jungle at the back of our camp. Through this scrub ran a path that had been regularly used by the villagers of the Ladhya valley until the advent of the man-eater had rendered its passage unsafe. On the 28th the two mail-runners who carried Ibbotson's dak on its first stage to Tanakpur got delayed in camp, and to save time took, or more correctly started to take, a short cut through this scrub. Very fortunately the leading man was on the alert and saw the tigress as she crept through the scrub and lay down near the path ahead of them.

Ibbotson and I had just got back from Thak when these two men dashed into camp, and taking our rifles we hurried off to investigate. We found the pug marks of the tigress where she had come out on the path and followed the men for a short distance, but we did not see her, though in one place where the scrub was very dense we saw a movement and heard an animal moving off.

On the morning of the 29th, a party of men came down from Thak to report that one of their bullocks had not returned to the cattle-shed the previous night, and on a search being made where it had last been seen a little blood had been found. At 2 p.m. the Ibbotsons and I were at this spot, and a glance at the ground satisfied us that the bullock had been killed and carried away by a tiger. After a hasty lunch Ibbotson and I, with two men following carrying ropes for a machan, set out along the drag. It went diagonally across the face of the hill for a hundred yards and then straight down into the ravine in which I had fired at and missed the big tiger in April. A few hundred yards down this ravine the bullock, which was an enormous animal, had got fixed between two rocks and, not being able to move it, the tiger had eaten a meal off its hind quarters and left it.

The pug marks of the tiger, owing to the great weight she was carrying, were splayed out and it was not possible to say whether she was the man-eater or not; but as every tiger in this area was suspect I decided to sit up over the kill. There was only one tree within reasonable distance of the kill, and as the men climbed into it to make a machan the tiger started calling in the valley below. Very hurriedly a few strands of rope were tied between two branches, and while Ibbotson stood on guard with his rifle I climbed the tree and took my seat on what, during the next fourteen hours, proved to be the most uncomfortable as well as the most dangerous machan I have ever sat on. The tree was leaning away from the hill, and from the three uneven strands of rope I was sitting on there was a drop of over a hundred feet into the rocky ravine below.

The tiger called several times as I was getting into the tree and continued to call at longer intervals late into the evening, the last call coming from a ridge half a mile away. It was now quite evident that the tiger had been lying up close to the kill and had seen the men climbing into the tree. Knowing from past experience what this meant, she had duly expressed resentment at being disturbed and then gone away, for though I sat on the three strands of rope until Ibbotson returned next morning, I did not see or hear anything throughout the night.

Vultures were not likely to find the kill, for the ravine was deep and overshadowed by trees, and as the bullock was large enough to provide the tiger with several meals we decided not to sit up over it again where it was now lying, hoping the tiger would remove it to some more convenient place where we should have a better chance of getting a shot. In this, however, we were disappointed, for the tiger did not again return to the kill.

Two nights later the buffalo we had tied out behind our camp at Sem was killed, and through a little want of observation on my part a great opportunity of bagging the man-eater was lost.

The men who brought in the news of this kill reported that the rope securing the animal had been broken, and that the kill had been carried away up the ravine at the lower end of which it had been tied. This was the same ravine in which MacDonald and I had chased a tigress in April, and as on that occasion she had taken her kill some distance up the ravine I now very foolishly concluded she had done the same with this kill.

After breakfast Ibbotson and I went out to find the kill and see what prospect there was for an evening sit-up.

The ravine in which the buffalo had been killed was about fifty yards wide and ran deep into the foothills. For two hundred yards the ravine was straight, and then bent round to the left. Just beyond the bend, and on the left-hand side of it, there was a dense patch of young saplings backed by a hundred-foot ridge on which thick grass was growing. In the ravine, and close to the saplings, there was a small pool of water. I had been up the ravine several times in April and had failed to mark the patch of saplings as being a likely place for a tiger to lie up in, and did not take the precautions I should have taken when rounding the bend, with the result that the tigress, who was drinking at the pool, saw us first. There was only one safe line of retreat for her and she took it. This was straight up the steep hill, over the ridge, and into sal forest beyond.

The hill was too steep for us to climb, so we continued on up the ravine to where a sambur track crossed it, and following this track we gained the ridge. The tigress was now in a triangular patch of jungle bounded by the ridge, the Ladhya, and a cliff down which no animal could go. The area was not large, and there were several deer in it which from time to time advised us of the position of the tigress, but unfortunately the ground was cut up by a number of deep and narrow rain-water channels in which we eventually lost touch with her.

We had not yet seen the kill, so we re-entered the ravine by the sambur track and found the kill hidden among the saplings. These saplings were from six inches to a foot in girth, and were not strong enough to support a machan, so we had to abandon the idea of a machan. With the help of a crowbar, a rock could possibly have been pried from the face of the hill and a place made in which to sit, but this was not advisable when dealing with a man-eater.

Reluctant to give up the chance of a shot, we considered the possibility of concealing ourselves in the grass near the kill, in the hope that the tigress would return before dark and that we should see her before she saw us. There were two objections to this plan: (*a*) if we did not get a shot and the tigress saw us near her kill she might abandon it, as she had done her other two kills; and (*b*) between the kill and camp there was very heavy scrub jungle, and if we tried to go through this jungle in the dark the tigress would have us at her mercy. So very reluctantly we decided to leave the kill to the tigress for that night, and hope for the best on the morrow.

On our return next morning we found that the tigress had carried away the kill. For three hundred yards she had gone up the bed of the ravine, stepping from rock to rock, and leaving no drag marks. At this spot—three hundred yards from where she had picked up the kill—we were at fault, for though there were a number of tracks on a wet patch of ground, none of them had been made while she was carrying the kill. Eventually, after casting round in circles, we found where she had left the ravine and gone up the hill on the left.

This hill up which the tigress had taken her kill was overgrown with ferns and goldenrod and tracking was not difficult, but the going was, for the hill was very steep and in places a detour had to be made and the track picked up further on. After a stiff climb of a thousand feet we came to a small plateau, bordered on the left by a cliff a mile wide. On the side of the plateau nearest the cliff the ground was seamed and cracked, and in these cracks a dense growth of sal, two to six feet in height, had sprung up. The tigress had taken her kill into this dense cover and it was not until we actually trod on it that we were aware of its position.

As we stopped to look at all that remained of the buffalo there was a low growl to our right. With rifles raised we waited for a minute and then, hearing a movement in the undergrowth a little beyond where the growl had come from, we pushed our way through the young sal for ten yards and came on a small clearing, where the tigress had made herself a bed on some soft grass. On the far side of this grass the hill sloped upwards for twenty yards to another plateau, and it was from this slope that the sound we had heard had come. Proceeding up the slope as silently as possible, we had just reached the flat ground, which was about fifty yards wide, when the tigress left the far side and went down into the ravine, disturbing some kaleege pheasants and a kakar as she did so. To have followed her would have been useless, so we went back to the kill and, as there was still a good meal on it, we selected two trees to sit in, and returned to camp.

After an early lunch we went back to the kill and, hampered with our rifles, climbed with some difficulty into the trees we had selected. We sat up for five hours without seeing or hearing anything. At dusk we climbed down from our trees, and stumbling over the cracked and uneven ground eventually reached the ravine when it was quite dark. Both of us had an uneasy feeling that we were being followed, but by keeping close together we reached camp without incident at 9 p.m.

The Ibbotsons had now stayed at Sem as long as it was possible for them to do so, and early next morning they set out on their twelve days' walk to keep their appointment at Askot. Before leaving, Ibbotson extracted a promise from me that I would not follow up any kills alone, or further endanger my life by prolonging my stay at Sem for more than a day or two.

After the departure of the Ibbotsons and their fifty men, the camp, which was surrounded by dense scrub, was reduced to my two servants and myself—my coolies were living in a room in the Headman's house—so throughout the day I set all hands to collecting driftwood, of which there was an inexhaustible supply at the junction, to keep a fire going all night. The fire would not scare away the tigress but it would enable us to see her if she prowled round our tents at night, and anyway the nights were setting in cold and there was ample excuse, if one were needed, for keeping a big fire going all night.

Towards evening, when my men were safely back in camp, I took a rifle and went up the Ladhya to see if he tigress had crossed the river. I found several tracks in the sand, but no fresh ones, and at dusk I returned, convinced that the tigress was still on our side of the river. An hour later, when it was quite dark, a kakar started barking close to our tents and barked persistently for half an hour.

My men had taken over the job of tying out the buffaloes, a task which Ibbotson's men had hitherto performed, and next morning I accompanied them when they went out to bring in the buffaloes. Though we covered several miles I did not find any trace of the tigress. After breakfast I took a rod and went down the junction, and had one of the best day's fishing I have ever had. The junction was full of big fish, and though my light tackle was broken frequently I killed sufficient mahseer to feed the camp.

Again, as on the previous evening, I crossed the Ladhya, with the intention of taking up a position on a rock overlooking the open ground on the right bank of the river and watching for the tigress to cross. As I got away from the roar of the water at the junction I heard a sambur and a monkey calling on the hill to my left, and as I neared the rock I came on the fresh tracks of the tigress. Following them back I found the stones still wet where she had forded the river. A few minutes' delay in camp to dry my fishing line and have a cup of tea cost a man his life, several thousand men weeks of anxiety, and myself many days of strain, for though I stayed at Sem for another three days I did not get another chance of shooting the tigress.

On the morning of the 7th, as I was breaking camp and preparing to start on my twenty-mile walk to Tanakpur, a big contingent of men from all the surrounding villages arrived, and begged me not to leave them to the tender mercies of the man-eater. Giving them what advice it was possible to give people situated as they were, I promised to return as soon as it was possible for me to do so.

I caught the train at Tanakpur next morning and arrived back in Naini Tal on 9 November, having been away nearly a month.

III.

I left Sem on the 7th of November and on the 12th the tigress killed a man at Thak. I received news of this kill through the Divisional Forest Officer, Haldwani, shortly after we had moved down to our winter home at the foot of the hills, and by doing forced marches I arrived at Chuka a little after sunrise on the 14th.

It had been my intention to breakfast at Chuka and then go on to Thak and make that village my headquarters, but the Headman of Thak, whom I found installed at Chuka, informed me that every man, woman, and child had left Thak immediately after the man had been killed on the 12th, and added that if I carried out my intention of camping at Thak I might be able to safeguard my own life, but it would not be possible to safeguard the lives of my men. This was quite reasonable, and while waiting for my men to arrive, the Headman helped me to select a site for my camp at Chuka, where my men would be reasonably safe and I should have some privacy from the thousands of men who were now arriving to fell the forest.

On receipt of the Divisional Forest Officer's telegram acquainting me of the kill, I had telegraphed to the Tahsildar at Tanakpur to send three young male buffaloes to Chuka. My request had been promptly complied with and the three animals had arrived the previous evening.

After breakfast I took one of the buffaloes and set out for Thak, intending to tie it up on the spot where the man had been killed on the 12th. The Headman had given me a very graphic account of the events of that date, for he himself had nearly fallen a victim to the tigress. It appeared that towards the afternoon, accompanied by his granddaughter, a girl ten years of age, he had gone to dig up ginger tubers in a field some sixty yards from his house. This field is about half an acre in extent and is surrounded on three sides by jungle, and being on the slope of a fairly step hill it is visible from the Headman's house. After the old man and his granddaughter had been at work for some time, his wife, who was husking rice in the courtyard of the house, called out in a very agitated voice and asked him if he was deaf that he could not hear the pheasants and other birds that were chattering in the jungle above him. Fortunately for him, he acted promptly. Dropping his hoe, he grabbed the child's hand and together they ran back to the house, urged on by the woman who said she could now see a red animal in the bushes at the upper end of the field. Half an hour later the tigress killed a man who was lopping branches off a tree in a field three hundred yards from the Headman's house.

From the description I had received from the Headman I had no difficulty in locating the tree. It was a small gnarled tree growing out of a three-foot-high bank between two terraced fields, and had been lopped year after year for cattle fodder. The man who had been killed was standing on the trunk holding one branch and cutting another, when the tigress came up from behind, tore his hold from the branch and, after killing him, carried him away into the dense brushwood bordering the fields.

Thak village was a gift from the Chand Rajas, who ruled Kumaon for many hundreds of years before the Gurkha occupation, to the forefathers of the present owners in return for their services at the Punagiri temples. (The promise made by the Chand Rajas that the lands of Thak and two other villages would remain rent-free for all time has been honored by the British Government for a hundred years.) From a collection of grass huts the village has in the course of time grown into a very prosperous settlement with masonry houses roofed with slate tiles, for not only is the land very fertile, but the revenue from the temples is considerable.

Like all other villages in Kumaon, Thak during its hundreds of years of existence has passed through many vicissitudes, but never before in its long history had it been deserted as it now was. On my previous visits I had found it a hive of industry, but when I went up to it on this afternoon, taking the young buffalo with me, silence reigned over it. Every one of the hundred or more inhabitants had fled, taking their livestock with them—the only animal I saw in the village was a cat, which gave me a warm welcome; so hurried had the evacuation been that many of the doors of the houses had been left wide open. On every path in the village, in the courtyard of the houses, and in the dust before all the doors I found the tigress's pug marks. The open doorways were a menace, for the path as it wound through the village passed close to them, and in any of the houses the tigress may have been lurking.

On the hill thirty yards above the village were several cattle shelters, and in the vicinity of these shelters I saw more kaleege pheasants, red jungle fowl, and white-capped babblers than I have ever before seen, and from the confiding way in which they permitted me to walk among them it is quite evident that the people of Thak have a religious prejudice against the taking of life.

From the terraced fields above the cattle shelters a bird's-eye view of the village is obtained, and it was not difficult, from the description the Headman had given me, to locate the tree where the tigress had secured her last victim. In the soft earth under the tree there were signs of a struggle and a few clots of dried blood. From here the tigress had carried her kill a hundred yards over a plowed field, through a stout hedge, and into the dense brushwood beyond. The foot-prints from the village and back the way they had come showed that the entire population of the village had visited the scene of the kill, but from the tree to the hedge there was only one track, the track the tigress had made when carrying away her victim. No attempt had been made to follow her up and recover the body.

Scraping away a little earth from under the tree I exposed a root and to this root I tied my buffalo, bedding it down with a liberal supply of straw taken from a near-by haystack.

The village, which is on the north face of the hill, was now in shadow, and if I was to get back to camp before dark it was time for me to make a start. Skirting round the village to avoid the menace of the open doorways, I joined the path below the houses.

This path after it leaves the village passes under a giant mango tree from the roots of which issues a cold spring of clear water. After running along a groove cut in a massive slab of rock, this water falls into a rough masonry trough, from where it spreads onto the surrounding ground, rendering it soft and slushy. I had drunk at the spring on my way up, leaving my foot-prints in this slushy ground, and on approaching the spring now for a second drink, I found the tigress's pug marks superimposed on my foot-prints. After quenching her thirst the tigress had avoided the path and had gained the village by climbing a steep bank overgrown with strobilanthes and nettles, and taking up a position in the shelter of one of the houses had possibly watched me while I was tying up the buffalo, expecting me to return the way I had gone; it was fortunate for me that I had noted the danger of passing those open doorways a second time, and had taken the longer way round.

When coming up from Chuka I had taken every precaution to guard against a sudden attack, and it was well that I had done so, for I now found from her pug marks that the tigress had followed me all the way up from my camp, and next morning when I went back to Thak I found she had followed me from where I had joined the path below the houses, right down to the cultivated land at Chuka.

Reading with the illumination I had brought with me was not possible, so after dinner that night, while sitting near a fire which was as welcome for its warmth as it was for the feeling of security it gave me, I reviewed the whole situation and tried to think out some plan by which it would be possible to circumvent the tigress.

When leaving home on the 22nd I had promised that I would return in ten days, and that this would be my last expedition after man-eaters. Years of exposure and strain and long absences from home—extending as in the case of the Chowgarh tigress and the Rudraprayag leopard to several months on end—were beginning to tell as much on my constitution as on the nerves of those at home, and if by the 30th of November I had not succeeded in killing this man-eater, others would have to be found who were willing to take on the task.

It was now the night of the 24th, so I had six clear days before me. Judging from the behavior of the tigress that evening she appeared to be anxious to secure another human victim, and it should not therefore be difficult for me, in the time at my disposal, to get in touch with her. There were several methods by which this could be accomplished, and each would be tried in turn. The method that offers the greatest chance of success of shooting a tiger in the hills is to sit up in a tree over a kill, and if during that night the tigress did not kill the buffalo I had tied up at Thak, I would the following night, and every night thereafter, tie up the other two buffaloes in places I had already selected, and failing to secure a human kill it was just possible that the tigress might kill one of my buffaloes, as she had done on a previous occasion when the Ibbotsons and I were camped at Sem in April. After making up the fire with logs that would burn all night I turned in, and went to sleep listening to a kakar barking in the scrub jungle behind my tent.

While breakfast was being prepared the following morning I picked up a rifle and went out to look for tracks on the stretch of sand on the right bank of the river, between Chuka and Sem. The path, after leaving the cultivated land, runs for a short distance through scrub jungle, and here I found the tracks of a big male leopard, possibly the same animal that had alarmed the kakar the previous night. A small male tiger had crossed and recrossed the Ladhya many times during the past week, and in the same period the man-eater had crossed only once, coming from the direction of Sem. A big bear had traversed the sand a little before my arrival, and when I got back to camp the timber contractors complained that while distributing work that morning they had run into a bear which had taken up a very threatening attitude, in consequence of which their labor had refused to work in the area in which the bear had been seen.

Several thousand men—the contractors put the figure at five thousand—had now concentrated at Chuka and Kumaya Chak to fell and saw up the timber and carry it down to the motor road that was being constructed, and all the time this considerable labor force was working they shouted at the tops of their voices to keep up their courage. The noise in the valley resulting

from axe and saw, the crashing of giant trees down the steep hillside, the breaking of rocks with sledge hammers, and combined with it all the shouting of
thousands of men, can better be imagined than described. That there were
many and frequent alarms in this nervous community was only natural, and
during the next few days I covered much ground and lost much valuable time
in investigating false rumors of attacks and kills by the man-eater, for the dread
of the tigress was not confined to the Ladhya valley but extended right down
the Sarda through Kaldhunga to the gorge, an area of roughly fifty square miles
in which an additional ten thousand men were working.

That a single animal should terrorize a labor force of these dimensions
in addition to the residents of the surrounding villages and the hundreds of
men who were bringing foodstuffs for the laborers or passing through the valley with hill produce in the way of oranges (purchasable at twelve annas a hundred), walnuts, and chilies to the market at Tanakpur is incredible, and would
be unbelievable were it not for the historical, and nearly parallel, case of the
man-eaters of Tsavo, where a pair of lions, operating only at night, held up
work for long periods on the Uganda Railway.

To return to my story. Breakfast disposed of on the morning of the
25th, I took a second buffalo and set out for Thak. The path, after leaving the
cultivated land at Chuka, skirts along the foot of the hill for about half a mile
before it divides. One arm goes straight up a ridge to Thak and the other, after
continuing along the foot of the hill for another half-mile, zigzags up through
Kumaya Chak to Kot Kindri.

At the divide I found the pug marks of the tigress and followed them
all the way back to Thak. The fact that she had come down the hill after me the
previous evening was proof that she had not killed the buffalo. This, though
very disappointing, was not at all unusual; for tigers will on occasions visit an
animal that is tied up for several nights in succession before they finally kill it,
for tigers do not kill unless they are hungry.

Leaving the second buffalo at the mango tree, where there was an
abundance of green grass, I skirted round the houses and found No. 1 buffalo
sleeping peacefully after a big feed and a disturbed night. The tigress, coming
from the direction of the village as her pug marks showed, had approached to
within a few feet of the buffalo, and had then gone back the way she had
come. Taking the buffalo down to the spring I let it graze for an hour or two,
and then took it back and tied it up at the same spot where it had been the
previous night.

The second buffalo I tied up fifty yards from the mango tree and at the
spot where the wailing woman and villagers had met us the day the Ibbotsons

and I had gone up to investigate the human kill. Here a ravine a few feet deep crossed the path, on one side of which there was a dry stump, and on the other an almond tree in which a machan could be made. I tied No. 2 buffalo to the stump, and bedded it down with sufficient hay to keep it going for several days. There was nothing more to be done at Thak, so I returned to camp and, taking the third buffalo, crossed the Ladhya and tied it up behind Sem, in the ravine where the tigress had killed one of our buffaloes in April.

At my request the Tahsildar of Tanakpur had selected three of the fastest young male buffaloes he could find. All three were now tied up in places frequented by the tigress, and as I set out to visit them on the morning of the 26th I had great hopes that one of them had been killed and that I should get an opportunity of shooting the tigress over it. Starting with the one across the Ladhya, I visited all in turn and found that the tigress had not touched any of them. Again, as on the previous morning, I found her tracks on the path leading to Thak, but on this occasion there was a double set of pug marks, one coming down and the other going back. On both her journeys the tigress had kept to the path and had passed within a few feet of the buffalo that was tied to the stump, fifty yards from the mango tree.

On my return to Chuka a deputation of Thak villagers led by the Headman came to my tent and requested me to accompany them to the village to enable them to replenish their supply of foodstuffs, so at midday, followed by the Headman and his tenants, and by four of my own men carrying ropes for a machan and food for me, I returned to Thak and mounted guard while the men hurriedly collected the provisions they needed.

After watering and feeding the two buffaloes I retied No. 2 to the stump and took No. 1 half a mile down the hill and tied it to a sapling on the side of the path. I then took the villagers back to Chuka and returned a few hundred yards up the hill for a scratch meal while my men were making the machan.

It was now quite evident that the tigress had no fancy for my fat buffaloes, and as in three days I had seen her tracks five times on the path leading to Thak, I decided to sit up over the path and try to get a shot at her that way. To give me warning of the tigress's approach I tied a goat with a bell round its neck on the path, and at 4 p.m. I climbed into the tree. I told my men to return at 8 a.m. the following morning, and began my watch.

At sunset a cold wind started blowing and while I was attempting to pull a coat over my shoulders the ropes on one side of the machan slipped, rendering my seat very uncomfortable. An hour later a storm came on, and though it did not rain for long it wet me to the skin, greatly adding to my discomfort. During the sixteen hours I sat in the tree I did not see or hear anything. The men turned up at 8 a.m. I returned to camp for a hot bath and a good meal, and then, accompanied by six of my men, set out for Thak.

The overnight rain had washed all the old tracks off the path, and two hundred yards above the tree I had sat in I found the fresh pug marks of the tigress, where she had come out of the jungle and gone up the path in the direction of Thak. Very cautiously I stalked the first buffalo, only to find it lying asleep on the path; the tigress had skirted round it, rejoined the path a few yards further on and continued up the hill. Following on her tracks I approached the second buffalo, and as I got near the place where it had been tied two blue Himalayan magpies rose off the ground and went screaming down the hill.

The presence of these birds indicated (*a*) that the buffalo was dead, (*b*) that it had been partly eaten and not carried away, and (*c*) that the tigress was not in the close vicinity.

On arrival at the stump to which it had been tied I saw that the buffalo had been dragged off the path and partly eaten, and on examining the animal I found it had not been killed by the tigress but that it had in all probability died of snake-bite (there were many hamadryads in the surrounding jungles), and that, finding it lying dead on the path, the tigress had eaten a meal off it and had then tried to drag it away. When she found she could not break the rope, she had partly covered it over with dry leaves and brushwood and continued on her way up to Thak.

Tigers as a rule are not carrion eaters but they do on occasions eat animals they themselves have not killed. For instance, on one occasion I left the carcass of a leopard on a fire track and, when I returned next morning to recover a knife I had forgotten, I found that a tiger had removed the carcass to a distance of a hundred yards and eaten two-thirds of it.

On my way up from Chuka I had dismantled the machan I had sat on the previous night, and while two of my men climbed into the almond tree to make a seat for me—the tree was not big enough for a machan—the other four went to the spring to fill a kettle and boil some water for tea. By 4 p.m. I had partaken of a light meal of biscuits and tea, which would have to keep me going until next day, and refusing the men's request to be permitted to stay the night in one of the houses in Thak, I sent them back to camp. There was a certain amount of risk in doing this, but it was nothing compared to the risk they would run if they spent the night in Thak.

My seat on the tree consisted of several strands of rope tied between two upright branches, with a couple of strands lower down for my feet to rest on. When I had settled down comfortably I pulled the branches round me and secured them in position with a thin cord, leaving a small opening to see and fire through. My 'hide' was soon tested, for shortly after the men had gone the two magpies returned, and attracted others, and nine of them fed on the kill until dusk. The presence of the birds enabled me to get some sleep, for they would have given me warning of the tigress's approach, and with their departure my all-night vigil started.

There was still sufficient daylight to shoot by when the moon, a day off the full, rose over the Nepal hills behind me and flooded the hillside with brilliant light. The rain of the previous night had cleared the atmosphere of dust and smoke and, after the moon had been up a few minutes, the light was so good that I was able to see a sambur and her young one feeding in a field of wheat a hundred and fifty yards away.

The dead buffalo was directly in front and about twenty yards away, and the path along which I expected the tigress to come was two or three yards nearer, so I should have an easy shot at a range at which it would be impossible to miss the tigress—provided she came; and there was no reason why she should not do so.

The moon had been up two hours, and the sambur had approached to within fifty yards of my tree, when a kakar started barking on the hill just above the village. The kakar had been barking for some minutes when suddenly a scream which I can only, very inadequately, describe as 'Ar-Ar-Arr' dying away on a long-drawn-out note, came from the direction of the village. So sudden and so unexpected had the scream been that I involuntarily stood up with the intention of slipping down from the tree and dashing up to the village, for the thought flashed through my mind that the man-eater was killing one of my men. Then in a second flash of thought I remembered I had counted them one by one as they had passed my tree, and that I had watched them out of sight on their way back to camp to see if they were obeying my instructions to keep close together.

The scream had been the despairing cry of a human being in mortal agony, and reason questioned how such a sound could have come from a deserted village. It was not a thing of my imagination for the kakar had heard it and had abruptly stopped barking, and the sambur had dashed away across the fields closely followed by her young one. Two days previously, when I had escorted the men to the village, I had remarked that they appeared to be very confiding to leave their property behind doors that were not even shut or latched, and the Headman had answered that even if their village remained untenanted for years their property would be quite safe, for they were priests of

Punagiri and no one would dream of robbing them; he added that as long as the tigress lived she was a better guard of their property—if guard were needed—than any hundred men could be, for no one in all that countryside would dare to approach the village, for any purpose, through the dense forests that surrounded it, unless escorted by me as they had been.

The screams were not repeated, and as there appeared to be nothing that I could do I settled down again on my rope seat. At 10 p.m. a kakar that was feeding on the young wheat crop at the lower end of the fields dashed away barking, and a minute later the tigress called twice. She had now left the village and was on the move, and even if she did not fancy having another meal off the buffalo there was every hope of her coming along the path which she had used twice every day for the past few days. With finger on trigger and eyes straining on the path I sat hour after hour until daylight succeeded moonlight, and when the sun had been up an hour, my men returned. Very thoughtfully they had brought a bundle of dry wood with them, and in a surprisingly short time I was sitting down to a hot cup of tea. The tigress may have been lurking in the bushes close to us, or she may have been miles away, for after she had called at 10 p.m. the jungles had been silent.

When I got back to camp I found a number of men sitting near my tent. Some of these men had come to inquire what luck I had had the previous night, and others had come to tell me that the tigress had called from midnight to a little before sunrise at the foot of the hill, and that all the laborers engaged in the forests and on the new export road were too frightened to go to work. I had already heard about the tigress from my men, who had informed me that, together with the thousands of men who were camped round Chuka, they had sat up all night to keep big fires going.

Among the men collected near my tent was the Headman of Thak, and when the others had gone I questioned him about the kill at Thak on the 12th of the month, when he so narrowly escaped falling a victim to the man-eater.

Once again the Headman told me in great detail how he had gone to his fields to dig ginger, taking his grandchild with him, and how on hearing his wife calling he had caught the child's hand and run back to the house—where his wife had said a word or two to him about not keeping his ears open and thereby endangering his own and the child's life—and how a few minutes later the tigress had killed a man while he was cutting leaves off a tree in a field above his house.

All this part of the story I had heard before, and I now asked him if he had actually seen the tigress killing the man. His answer was no; and he added that the tree was not visible from where he had been standing. I then asked him how he knew that the man had been killed, and he said, because he had heard him. In reply to further questions he said the man had not called for help but had cried out; and when asked if he had cried out once he said, 'No, three times,' and then at my request he gave an imitation of the man's cry. It was the same—but a very modified rendering—as the screams I had heard the previous night.

I then told him what I had heard and asked him if it was possible for anyone to have arrived at the village accidentally, and his answer was an emphatic negative. There were only two paths leading to Thak, and every man, woman, and child in the villages through which these two paths passed knew that Thak was deserted and the reason for its being so. It was known throughout the district that it was dangerous to go near Thak in daylight, and it was therefore quite impossible for anyone to have been in the village at eight o'clock the previous night.

When asked if he could give any explanation for screams having come from a village in which there could not—according to him—have been any human beings, his answer was that he could not. And as I can do no better than the Headman, it were best to assume that neither the kakar, the sambur, nor I heard those very real screams—the screams of a human being in mortal agony.

IV.

When all my visitors, including the Headman, had gone, and I was having breakfast, my servant informed me that the Headman of Sem had come to the camp the previous evening and had left word for me that his wife, while cutting grass near the hut where his mother had been killed, had come on a blood trail, and that he would wait for me near the ford over the Ladhya in the morning. So after breakfast I set out to investigate this trail.

While I was fording the river I saw four men hurrying towards me, and as soon as I was on dry land they told me that when they were coming down the hill above Sem they had heard a tiger falling across the valley on the hill between Chuka and Thak. The noise of the water had prevented my hearing the call. I told the men that I was on my way to Sem and would return to Chuka shortly and left them.

The Headman was waiting for me near his house, and his wife took me to where she had seen the blood trail the previous day. The trail, after continuing along a field for a short distance, crossed some big rocks, on one of which I found the hairs of a kakar. A little further on I found the pug marks of a big male leopard, and while I was looking at them I heard a tiger call. Telling my companions to sit down and remain quiet, I listened, in order to locate the tiger. Presently I heard the call again, and thereafter it was repeated at intervals of about two minutes.

It was the tigress calling and I located her as being five hundred yards below Thak and in the deep ravine which, starting from the spring under the mango tree, runs parallel to the path and crosses it at its junction with the Kumaya Chak path.

Telling the Headman that the leopard would have to wait to be shot at a more convenient time, I set off as hard as I could go for camp, picking up at the ford the four men who were waiting for my company to Chuka.

On reaching camp I found a crowd of men round my tent, most of them sawyers from Delhi, but including the petty contractors, agents, clerks, timekeepers, and gangmen of the financier who had taken up the timber and road construction contracts in the Ladhya valley. These men had come to see me in connection with my stay at Chuka. They informed me that many of the hillmen carrying timber and working on the road had left for their homes that morning and that if I left Chuka on 1 December, as they had heard I intended doing, the entire labor force, including themselves, would leave on the same day; for already they were too frightened to eat or sleep, and no one would dare to remain in the valley after I had gone. It was then the morning of 29 November and I told the men that I still had two days and two nights and that much could happen in that time, but that in any case it would not be possible for me to prolong my stay beyond the morning of the first.

The tigress had by now stopped calling, and when my servant had put up something for me to eat I set out for Thak, intending, if the tigress called again and I could locate her position, to try to stalk her; and if she did not call again, to sit up over the buffalo. I found her tracks on the path and saw where she had entered the ravine, and though I stopped repeatedly on my way up to Thak and listened I did not hear her again. So a little before sunset I ate the biscuits and drank the bottle of tea I had brought with me, and then climbed into the almond tree and took my seat on the few strands of rope that had to serve me as a machan. On this occasion the magpies were absent, so I was unable to get the hour or two's sleep the birds had enabled me to get the previous evening.

If a tiger fails to return to its kill the first night it does not necessarily mean that the kill has been abandoned. I have on occasions seen a tiger return on the tenth night and eat what could no longer be described as flesh. On the present occasion, however, I was not sitting over a kill, but over an animal that the tigress had found dead and off which she had made a small meal, and had she not been a man-eater I would not have considered the chance of her re-turning the second night good enough to justify spending a whole night in a tree when she had not taken sufficient interest in the dead buffalo to return to it the first night. It was therefore with very little hope of getting a shot that I sat on the tree from sunset to sunrise, and though the time I spent was not as long as it had been the previous night, my discomfort was very much greater, for the ropes I was sitting on cut into me, and a cold wind that started blowing shortly after moonrise and continued throughout the night chilled me to the bone. On this second night I heard no jungle or other sounds, nor did the sam-bur and her young one come out to feed on the fields. As daylight was suc-ceeding moonlight I thought I heard a tiger call in the distance, but could not be sure of the sound or of its direction.

When I got back to camp my servant had a cup of tea and a hot bath ready for me, but before I could indulge in the latter—my forty-pound tent was not big enough for me to bathe in—I had to get rid of the excited throng of people who were clamoring to tell me their experiences of the night before. It appeared that shortly after moonrise the tigress had started calling close to Chuka, and after calling at intervals for a couple of hours had gone off in the direction of the labor camps at Kumaya Chak. The men in these camps hearing her coming started shouting to try to drive her away, but so far from having this effect the shouting only infuriated her the more and she demonstrated in front of the camps until she had cowed the men into silence. Having accom-plished this she spent the rest of the night between the labor camps and Chuka, daring all and sundry to shout at her. Towards morning she had gone away in the direction of Thak, and my informants were surprised and very dis-appointed that I had not met her.

This was my last day of man-eater hunting, and though I was badly in need of rest and sleep, I decided to spend what was left of it in one last attempt to get in touch with the tigress.

The people not only of Chuka and Sem but of all the surrounding vil-lages, and especially the men from Talla Des where some years previously I had shot three man-eaters, were very anxious that I should try sitting up over a live goat, for, said they, 'All hill tigers eat goats, and as you have had no luck with buffaloes, why not try a goat?' More to humor them than with any hope of getting a shot, I consented to spend this last day in sitting up over the two goats I had already purchased for this purpose.

I was convinced that no matter where the tigress wandered to at night her headquarters were at Thak, so at midday, taking the two goats, and accom-panied by four of my men, I set out for Thak.

The path from Chuka to Thak, as I have already mentioned, runs up a very steep ridge. A quarter of a mile on this side of Thak the path leaves the ridge, and crosses a more or less flat bit of ground which extends right up to the mango tree. For its whole length across this flat ground the path passes through dense brushwood, and is crossed by two narrow ravines which run east and join the main ravine. Midway between these two ravines, and a hundred yards from the tree I had sat in the previous two nights, there is a giant almond tree; this tree had been my objective when I left camp. The path passes right under the tree and I thought that if I climbed half-way up not only should I be able to see the two goats, one of which I intended tying at the edge of the main ravine and the other at the foot of the hill to the right, but I should also be able to see the dead buffalo. As all three of these points were at some distance from the tree, I armed myself with an accurate .275 rifle, in addition to the 450/400 rifle which I took for an emergency.

I found the climb up from Chuka on this last day very trying, and I had just reached the spot where the path leaves the ridge for the flat ground, when the tigress called about a hundred and fifty yards to my left. The ground here was covered with dense undergrowth and trees interlaced with creepers, and was cut up by narrow and deep ravines, and strewn over with enormous boulders—a very unsuitable place in which to stalk a man-eater. However, before deciding on what action I should take, it was necessary to know whether the tigress was lying down, as she very well might be, for it was then 1 p.m., or whether she was on the move and if so in what direction. So making the men sit down behind me I listened, and presently the call was repeated; she had moved some fifty yards, and appeared to be going up the main ravine in the direction of Thak.

This was very encouraging, for the tree I had selected to sit in was only fifty yards from the ravine. After enjoining silence on the men and telling them to keep close behind me, we hurried along the path. We had about two hundred yards to go to reach the tree and had covered half the distance when, as we approached a spot where the path was bordered on both sides by dense brushwood, a covey of kaleege pheasants rose out of the brushwood and went screaming away. I knelt down and covered the path for a few minutes, but as nothing happened we went cautiously forward and reached the tree without further incident. As quickly and as silently as possible one goat was tied at the edge of the ravine, while the other was tied at the foot of the hill to the right; then I took the men to the edge of the cultivated land and told them to stay in the upper verandah of the Headman's house until I fetched them, and ran back to the tree. I climbed to a height of forty feet, and pulled the rifle up after me with a cord I had brought for the purpose. Not only were the two goats visible from my seat, one at a range of seventy and the other at a range of sixty yards, but I could also see part of the buffalo, and as the .275 rifle was very accurate I felt sure I could kill the tigress if she showed up anywhere on the ground I was overlooking.

The two goats had lived together ever since I had purchased them on my previous visit, and, being separate now, were calling lustily to each other. Under normal conditions a goat can be heard at a distance of four hundred yards, but here the conditions were not normal, for the goats were tied on the side of a hill down which a strong wind was blowing, and even if the tigress had moved after I had heard her, it was impossible for her not to hear them. If she was hungry, as I had every reason to believe she was, there was a very good chance of my getting a shot.

After I had been on the tree for ten minutes a kakar barked near the spot the pheasants had risen from. For a minute or two my hopes rose sky-high and then dropped back to earth, for the kakar barked only three times and ended on a note of inquiry; evidently there was a snake in the scrub which neither he nor the pheasants liked the look of.

My seat was not uncomfortable and the sun was pleasingly warm, so for the next three hours I remained in the tree without any discomfort. At 4 p.m. the sun went down behind the high hill above Thak and thereafter the wind became unbearably cold. For an hour I stood the discomfort, and then decided to give up, for the cold had brought on an attack of ague, and if the tigress came now it would not be possible for me to hit her. I retied the cord to the rifle and let it down, climbed down myself and walked to the edge of the cultivated land to call up my men.

V.

There are few people, I imagine, who have not experienced that feeling of depression that follows failure to accomplish anything they have set out to do. The road back to camp after a strenuous day when the *chukor** bag is full is only a step compared with the same road which one plods over, mile after weary mile, when the bag is empty, and if this feeling of depression has ever assailed you at the end of a single day, and when the quarry has only been *chukor*, you will have some idea of the depth of my depression that evening when, after calling up my men and untying the goats, I set off on my two-mile walk to camp, for my effort had been not of a single day or my quarry a few birds, nor did my failure concern only myself.

---

*Hill partridge

Excluding the time spent on the journeys from and to home, I had been on the heels of the man-eater from 23 October to 7 November, and again from 14 to 30 November, and it is only those of you who have walked in fear of having the teeth of a tiger meet in your throat who will have any idea of the effect on one's nerves of days and weeks of such anticipation.

Then again my quarry was a man-eater, and my failure to shoot it would very gravely affect everyone who was working in, or whose homes were in, that area. Already work in the forests had been stopped, and the entire population of the largest village in the district had abandoned their homes. Bad as the conditions were they would undoubtedly get worse if the man-eater was not killed, for the entire labor force could not afford to stop work indefinitely, nor could the population of the surrounding villages afford to abandon their homes and their cultivation as the more prosperous people of Thak had been able to do.

The tigress had long since lost her natural fear of human beings, as was abundantly evident from her having carried away a girl picking up mangoes in a field close to where several men were working, killing a woman near the door of her house, dragging a man off a tree in the heart of a village, and, the previous night, cowing a few thousand men into silence. And here was I, who knew full well what the presence of a man-eater meant to the permanent and to the temporary inhabitants and to all the people who passed through the district on their way to the markets at the foothills or the temples at Punagiri, plodding down to camp on what I had promised others would be my last day of man-eater hunting; reason enough for a depression of soul which I felt would remain with me for the rest of my days. Gladly at that moment would I have bartered the success that had attended thirty-two years of man-eater hunting for one unhurried shot at the tigress.

I have told you of some of the attempts I made during this period of seven days and seven nights to get a shot at the tigress, but these were by no means the only attempts I made. I knew that I was being watched and followed, and every time I went through the two miles of jungle between my camp and Thak I tried every trick I have learnt in a lifetime spent in the jungles to outwit the tigress. Bitter though my disappointment was, I felt that my failure was not in any way due to anything I had done or left undone.

VI.

My men when they rejoined me said that, an hour after the kakar had barked, they had heard the tigress calling a long way off but were not sure of the direction. Quite evidently the tigress had as little interest in goats as she had in buffaloes, but even so it was unusual for her to have moved at that time of day from a locality in which she was thoroughly at home, unless she had been attracted away by some sound which neither I nor my men had heard; however that may have been, it was quite evident that she had gone, and as there was nothing further that I could do I set off on my weary tramp to camp.

The path, as I have already mentioned, joins the ridge that runs down to Chuka a quarter of a mile from Thak, and when I now got to this spot where the ridge is only a few feet wide and from where a view is obtained of the two great ravines that run down to the Ladhya River, I heard the tigress call once and again across the valley on my left. She was a little above and to the left of Kumaya Chak, and a few hundred yards below the Kot Kindri ridge on which the men working in that area had built themselves grass shelters.

Here was an opportunity, admittedly forlorn and unquestionably desperate, of getting a shot; still it was an opportunity and the last I should ever have, and the question was, whether or not I was justified in taking it.

When I got down from the tree I had one hour in which to get back to camp before dark. Calling up the men, hearing what they had to say, collecting the goats, and walking to the ridge had taken about thirty minutes, and judging from the position of the sun which was now casting a red glow on the peaks of the Nepal hills, I calculated I had roughly half an hour's daylight in hand. This time factor, or perhaps it would be more correct to say light factor, was all-important, for if I took the opportunity that offered, on it would depend the lives of five men.

The tigress was a mile way and the intervening ground was densely wooded, strewn over with great rocks and cut up by a number of deep nullahs, but she could cover the distance well within the half-hour—if she wanted to. The question I had to decide was, whether or not I should try to call her up. If I called and she heard me, and came while it was still daylight and gave me a shot, all would be well; on the other hand, if she came and did not give me a shot some of us would not reach camp, for we had nearly two miles to go and the path the whole way ran through heavy jungle, and was bordered in some places by big rocks, and in others by dense brushwood. It was useless to consult the men, for none of them had ever been in a jungle before coming on this trip, so the decision would have to be mine. I decided to try to call up the tigress.

Handing my rifle over to one of the men I waited until the tigress called again and, cupping my hands round my mouth and filling my lungs to their utmost limit, sent an answering call over the valley. Back came her call and thereafter, for several minutes, call answered call. She would come, had in fact already started, and if she arrived while there was light to shoot by, all the advantages would be on my side, for I had the selecting of the ground on which it would best suit me to meet her. November is the mating season for tigers and it was evident that for the past forty-eight hours she had been rampaging through the jungles in search of a mate, and that now, on hearing what she thought was a tiger answering her mating call, she would lose no time in joining him.

Four hundred yards down the ridge the path runs for fifty yards across a flat bit of ground. At the far right-hand side of this flat ground the path skirts a big rock and then drops steeply, and continues in a series of hairpin bends, down to the next bench. It was at this rock I decided to meet the tigress, and on my way down to it I called several times to let her know I was changing my position, and also to keep in touch with her.

I want you now to have a clear picture of the ground in your mind, to enable you to follow the subsequent events. Imagine then a rectangular piece of ground forty yards wide and eighty yards long, ending in a more or less perpendicular rock face. The path coming down from Thak runs on to this ground at its short or south end, and after continuing down the center for twenty-five yards bends to the right and leaves the rectangle on its long or east side. At the point where the path leaves the flat ground there is a rock about four feet high. From a little beyond where the path bends to the right, a ridge of rock, three or four feet high, rises and extends to the north side of the rectangle, where the ground falls away in a perpendicular rock face. On the near or path side of this low ridge there is a dense line of bushes approaching to within ten feet of the four-foot-high rock I have mentioned. The rest of the rectangle is grown over with trees, scattered bushes, and short grass.

It was my intention to lie on the path by the side of the rock and shoot the tigress as she approached me, but when I tried this position I found it would not be possible for me to see her until she was within two or three yards, and further, that she could get at me either round the rock or through the scattered bushes on my left without my seeing her at all. Projecting out of the rock, from the side opposite to that from which I expected the tigress to approach, there was a narrow ledge. By sitting sideways I found I could get a little of my bottom on the ledge, and by putting my left hand flat on the top of the rounded rock and stretching out my right leg to its full extent and touching the ground with my toes, retain my position on it. The men and goats I placed immediately behind, and ten to twelve feet below me.

The stage was now set for the reception of the tigress, who while these preparations were being made had approached to within three hundred yards.

Sending out one final call to give her direction, I looked round to see if my men were all right.

The spectacle these men presented would under other circumstances have been ludicrous, but was here tragic. Sitting in a tight little circle with their knees drawn up and their heads together, with the goats burrowing in under them, they had that look of intense expectancy on their screwed-up features that one sees on the faces of spectators waiting to hear a big gun go off. From the time we had first heard the tigress from the ridge, neither the men nor the goats had made a sound, beyond one suppressed cough. They were probably by now frozen with fear—as well they might be—and even if they were, I take my hat off to those four men who had the courage to do what I, had I been in their shoes, would not have dreamt of doing. For seven days they had been hearing the most exaggerated and blood-curdling tales of this fearsome beast that had kept them awake the past two nights, and now, while darkness was coming on, and sitting unarmed in a position where they could see nothing, they were listening to the man-eater drawing nearer and nearer; greater courage, and greater faith, it is not possible to conceive.

The fact that I could not hold my rifle, a D.B. 450/400, with my left hand (which I was using to retain my precarious seat on the ledge) was causing me some uneasiness, for apart from the fear of the rifle's slipping on the rounded top of the rock—I had folded my handkerchief and placed the rifle on it to try to prevent this—I did not know what would be the effect of the recoil of a high velocity rifle fired in this position. The rifle was pointing along the path, in which there was a hump, and it was my intention to fire into the tigress's face immediately it appeared over this hump, which was twenty feet from the rock.

The tigress however did not keep to the contour of the hill, which would have brought her out on the path a little beyond the hump, but crossed a deep ravine and came straight towards where she had heard my last call, at an angle which I can best describe as one o'clock. This manoeuver put the low ridge of rock, over which I could not see, between us. She had located the direction of my last call with great accuracy, but had misjudged the distance, and not finding her prospective mate at the spot where she had expected him to be, she was now working herself up into a perfect fury, and you will have some idea of what the fury of a tigress in her condition can be when I tell you that not many miles from my home a tigress on one occasion closed a public road for a whole week, attacking everything that attempted to go along it, including a string of camels, until she was finally joined by a mate.

I know of no sound more liable to fret one's nerves than the calling of an unseen tiger at close range. What effect this appalling sound was having on my men I was frightened to think, and if they had gone screaming down the hill I should not have been at all surprised, for even though I had the heel of a good rifle to my shoulder and the stock against my cheek I felt like screaming myself.

But even more frightening than this continuous calling was the fading out of the light. Another few seconds, ten or fifteen at the most, and it would be too dark to see my sights, and we should then be at the mercy of a man-eater, plus a tigress wanting a mate. Something would have to be done, and done in a hurry, if we were not to be massacred, and the only thing I could think of was to call.

The tigress was now so close that I could hear the intake of her breath each time before she called, and as she again filled her lungs, I did the same with mine, and we called simultaneously. The effect was startlingly instantaneous. Without a second's hesitation she came tramping with quick steps through the dead leaves, over the low ridge and into the bushes a little to my right front, and just as I was expecting her to walk right on top of me she stopped, and the next moment the full blast of her deep-throated call struck me in the face and would have carried the hat off my head had I been wearing one. A second's pause, then again quick steps; a glimpse of her as she passed between two bushes, and then she stepped right out into the open, and, looking into my face, stopped dead.

By great and unexpected good luck the half-dozen steps the tigress took to her right front carried her almost to the exact spot at which my rifle was pointing. Had she continued in the direction in which she was coming before her last call, my story—if written—would have had a different ending, for it would have been as impossible to slew the rifle on the rounded top of the rock as it would have been to lift and fire it with one hand.

Owing to the nearness of the tigress, and the fading light, all that I could see of her was her head. My first bullet caught her under the right eye and the second, fired more by accident than with intent, took her in the throat and she came to rest with her nose against the rock and knocked me off the ledge, and the recoil from the left barrel, fired while I was in the air, brought the rifle up in violent contact with my jaw and sent me heels over head right on top of the men and goats. Once again I take my hat off to those four men for, not knowing but what the tigress was going to land on them next, they caught me as I fell and saved me from injury and my rifle from being broken.

When I had freed myself from the tangle of human and goat legs I took the .275 rifle from the man who was holding it, rammed a clip of cartridges into the magazine and sent a stream of five bullets singing over the valley and across the Sarda into Nepal. Two shots, to the thousands of men in the valley and in the surrounding villages who were anxiously listening for the sound of my rifle, might mean anything, but two shots followed by five more, spaced at regular intervals of five seconds, could only be interpreted as conveying one message, and that was, that the man-eater was dead.

I had not spoken to my men from the time we had first heard the tigress from the ridge. On my telling them now that she was dead and that there was no longer any reason for us to be afraid, they did not appear to be able to take in what I was saying, so I told them to go up and have a look while I found and lit a cigarette. Very cautiously they climbed up to the rock, but went no further for, as I have told you, the tigress was touching the other side of it. Late in camp that night, while sitting round a camp-fire and relating their experiences to relays of eager listeners, their narrative invariably ended up with, 'and then the tiger whose roaring had turned our livers into water hit the sahib on the head and knocked him down on top of us and if you don't believe us, go and look at his face.' A mirror is superfluous in camp and even if I had had one it could not have made the swelling on my jaw, which put me on milk diet for several days, look as large and as painful as it felt.

By the time a sapling had been felled and the tigress lashed to it, lights were beginning to show in the Ladhya valley and in all the surrounding camps and villages. The four men were very anxious to have the honor of carrying the tigress to camp, but the task was beyond them; so I left them and set off for help.

In my three visits to Chuka during the past eight months I had been along this path many times by day and always with a loaded rifle in my hands, and now I was stumbling down in the dark, unarmed, my only anxiety being to avoid a fall. If the greatest happiness one can experience is the sudden cessation of great pain, then the second greatest happiness is undoubtedly the sudden cessation of great fear. One short hour previously it would have taken wild elephants to have dragged from their homes and camps the men who now, singing and shouting, were converging from every direction, singly and in groups, on the path leading to Thak. Some of the men of this rapidly growing crowd went up the path to help carry in the tigress, while others accompanied me on my way to camp, and would have carried me had I permitted them. Progress was slow, for frequent halts had to be made to allow each group of new arrivals to express their gratitude in their own particular way. This gave the party carrying the tigress time to catch us up, and we entered the village together. I will not attempt to describe the welcome my men and I received, or the scenes I witnessed at Chuka that night, for having lived the greater part of my life in the jungles I have not the ability to paint word-pictures.

A hayrick was dismantled and the tigress laid on it, and an enormous bonfire made from driftwood close at hand to light up the scene and for warmth, for the night was dark and cold with a north wind blowing. Round about midnight my servant, assisted by the Headman of Thak and Kunwar Singh, near whose house I was camped, persuaded the crowd to return to their respective villages and labor camps, telling them they would have ample opportunity of feasting their eyes on the tigress the following day. Before leaving himself, the Headman of Thak told me he would send word in the morning to the people of Thak to return to their village. This he did, and two days later the entire population returned to their homes, and have lived in peace ever since.

After my midnight dinner I sent for Kunwar Singh and told him that in order to reach home on the promised date I should have to start in a few hours, and that he would have to explain to the people in the morning why I had gone. This he promised to do, and I then started to skin the tigress. Skinning a tiger with a pocket-knife is a long job, but it gives one an opportunity of examining the animal that one would otherwise not get, and in the case of man-eaters enables one to ascertain, more or less accurately, the reason for the animal's having become a man-eater.

The tigress was a comparatively young animal and in the perfect condition one would expect her to be at the beginning of the mating season. Her dark winter coat was without a blemish, and in spite of her having so persistently refused the meals I had provided for her she was encased in fat. She had two old gunshot wounds, neither of which showed on her skin. The one in her left shoulder, caused by several pellets of homemade buckshot, had become septic, and when healing the skin, over quite a large surface, had adhered permanently to the flesh. To what extent this wound had incapacitated her it would have been difficult to say, but it had evidently taken a very long time to heal, and could quite reasonably have been the cause of her having become a man-eater. The second wound, which was in her right shoulder, had also been caused by a charge of buckshot, but had healed without becoming septic. These two wounds received over kills in the days before she had become a man-eater were quite sufficient reason for her not having returned to the human and other kills I had sat over.

After having skinned the tigress I bathed and dressed, and though my face was swollen and painful and I had twenty miles of rough going before me,

I left Chuka walking on air, while the thousands of men in and around the valley were peacefully sleeping.

I have come to the end of the jungle stories I set out to tell you and I have also come near the end of my man-eater hunting career.

I have had a long spell and count myself fortunate in having walked out on my own feet and not been carried out on a cradle in the manner and condition of the man of Thak.

There have been occasions when life has hung by a thread and others when a light purse and disease resulting from exposure and strain have made the going difficult, but for all these occasions I am amply rewarded if my hunting has resulted in saving one human life.

A Mixed Bag of Zern

BY ED ZERN

B EFORE ED ZERN passed away in the early 1990s, his "Exit Laughing" column on the last page of *Field & Stream* every month was the outdoor field's towering institution of wit and good-natured humor. Search wherever you wish, you will never find a humorist with Zern's flair and originality. I doubt that there will ever be another to equal him.

One of the sources of Zern's creative genius was the fact that he genuinely loved hunters and anglers and the things they said and did. Zern was so passionate about field sports himself that he was constantly involved in some activity of shooting and fishing. When he wasn't on a trip, he was busy planning one.

Many of Ed Zern's best magazine columns, feature articles, and the old humorous Nash car ads have been collected in the book *Hunting and Fishing from A to Zern,* published by Lyons & Burford in 1985.

How to Shoot Crows

Over the years a number of readers have written, asking me to provide them with my crow-shooting system as it appeared here a decade or so ago. As both of them are regular subscribers I can hardly afford to ignore their request, and hasten to comply.

The system is based on a study of crow behavior conducted by research biologists at Phelps University which showed that crows have a relatively high level of intelligence and are actually able to count, but only in multiples of three or less, so that the conventional procedure for fooling crows—by sending several men into a blind, then having all but one of them leave—is not likely to work except with very young birds, if at all. Thus, even if six crow hunters go into a cornstalk blind and only five come out, the crows probably won't be fooled, as they will have counted off the hunters in trios and will realize that one of the groups is short a man; as a result they will stay the hell away from there until the frustrated gunner gives up and emerges.

My system for successful crow hunting is childishly simple, and consists of the following steps:

1. Build a blind overlooking a cornfield frequented by crows.

2. Assemble a group of twenty-five hunters, all dressed more or less alike and of nearly equal height, build, and facial characteristics. All the hunters should be clean-shaven, but *twelve of them should be wearing false mustaches.* The group should assemble in a barn or some sort of building not less than 350 yards from the field. (It would be prudent to have a few spare hunters on hand, to substitute in cases of pulled muscles, heart attacks or other contingencies.)

3. All of the hunters should be equipped with 12-gauge shotguns, but it is advisable that these be fairly light in weight, as it is important that *all hunters going to and from the blind must travel at a dead run,* so that the crows will not have sufficient time for their calculations.

4. As soon as a flock of crows comes into the area, eleven of the hunters are dispatched from the old barn to the blind, running at top speed. The instant they arrive, seven of them turn around and rush back to the barn.

5. When the seven hunters get back to the barn, they are joined by six other hunters and the thirteen of them sprint back to the blind as fast as possible; on arrival there, ten of them immediately turn around and dash back to the barn.

6. Before the ten arrive, eight more hunters are sent from the barn to the blind. When they meet the ten returning from the blind all of them switch hats and false mustaches while milling around in a tight huddle, then break it up and resume running to their respective destinations.

7. As soon as the eight hunters arrive at the blind, five of them turn around and rush back toward the barn; on the way they meet nine hunters running from the barn toward the blind, whereupon the hunters divide themselves into two groups of seven, one of which runs back to the barn while the other rushes to the blind, changes hats and mustaches, leaves two of its members there and dashes back to the barn.

8. Of the twelve hunters now in the blind, nine rush across the fields to the barn while twelve of the thirteen hunters in the barn charge en masse from the barn to the blind; on arrival they immediately turn and sashay back to the barn taking two of the three hunters still in the blind with them, *leaving a single hunter.*

9. It is, of course, essential that all this be done at the highest possible speed, so that the crows will fall hopelessly behind in their arithmetic and in the consequent corvine confusion fail to realize that a hunter is concealed in the blind.

10. Eventually the crows will learn to count faster, so that the system must be modified occasionally to keep ahead of them. In addition to having the hunters run faster, it may be necessary to introduce false beards and quick-change toupees as well as false mustaches, and to build a second blind on another side of the field so that the traffic will be triangular instead of simply linear, requiring the crows to start working on trigonometric permutations and geometric progressions in order to cope. In severe cases the hunters may be equipped with numbered jerseys from 1 to 25 but with the number 17 omitted and two number 21s. (This can also be done with roman numerals, when birds are very wary.)

Watch this space next month for an equally simple, foolproof system for outwitting that wily old woodchuck in the back pasture, requiring no special equipment other than a stuffed Guernsey cow and a milkmaid's costume.

How to Find True North

One of the pleasures to which I look forward each month is the arrival of *Winchester Proof*, a publication having to do with matters of interest to outdoor writers. Representing the combined talents of Winchester-Western's research biologists, ballistics experts, and public-relations geniuses, this lively bulletin is almost always worth careful perusal and sometimes—as I am about to reveal—it contains nuggets of information that are, quite literally, life-savers.

Thus, in one of last winter's issues I came across the following: "It can get mighty cold in the woods this time of year. . . . If you lose your compass and can't find the North Star, don't despair. You can still find true north, which should be a great help. Prop a stick into the ground at a 45-degree angle and hang a rock from the end of the stick. Just before noon, mark the spot where the rock's shadow falls (*a*), and again about six hours later (*b*). Starting directly under the suspended rock, draw a line to a point midway between the morning (*a*) and the afternoon (*b*) marks. This line points to within three degrees of true north."

Shortly after reading this I chanced to be hunting partridge in New York's Sullivan County and became hopelessly lost in a heavily forested area. Recalling the instructions in *Winchester Proof*, I stuck a stick into the ground at a 45-degree angle and hung a rock from it, using the lace from one of my boots as a cord. Unfortunately it was considerably after noon when I realized I was lost, so I was obliged to build a crude lean-to and spend the night huddled in it, to be on hand for the following noontime.

At five minutes before twelve the next day I marked the shadow of the stone (*a*), and as I had nothing to do until 6 o'clock I decided to take a short nap. (I first tried going for a walk, but kept stumbling over my unlaced boot and gave it up.) Unfortunately I fell into a sound sleep, and by the time I awoke the sun had gone down and it was again necessary to spend the night in the lean-to.

The next day at noon I once more marked the spot (*a*) and carefully refrained from falling asleep lest I repeat the previous day's fiasco. Unfortunately, at about 4:30 P.M. a heavy rain began to fall and softened the ground to such an extent that the stick fell down.

The following day I again arranged the stick at a 45-degree angle, being careful to prop it with stones so that it couldn't collapse, and just before noon I marked the stone's shadow (*a*). At 5:45 a large cloud came up and obscured the sun so thoroughly that the stone cast no shadow (*b*), and I again spent the night in the lean-to.

The next afternoon the cord, no doubt weakened by prolonged exposure to the elements and the weight of the stone, broke in two shortly before 6 o'clock, and by the time I could remove my other bootlace and hang the rock from it, being considerably weakened by hunger and cold, it was 6:15. Realizing that Rome wasn't built in a day, I shrugged philosophically and crawled back into the lean-to.

Unfortunately during this period the days had been getting shorter, and on the sixth day, although everything else went swimmingly, the sun set at 5:52.

By this time I was growing desperate as well as hungry, and might have panicked or gone off my rocker and stumbled about in the woods babbling incoherently and tearing holes in my good Burberry shooting jacket, if a party of Girl Scouts had not come by on a Nature Hike and, after reviving me with cookies, led me back to civilization.

Amazing Deer-Hunting Adventure

While hurrying down Madison Avenue last week, I ran into Mike Lonergan, whom I hadn't seen for some time. "How's with you, Mike?" I said, and he said, "Ed, you're just the man I've wanted to see. I had a most remarkable experience while deer-hunting last winter, and I want to tell you about it. Buy me a drink and I'll fill you in!"

When we had found ourselves a booth in a side-street saloon and ordered a brace of bourbons, Mike said, "Remember that little dirt road we discovered that time we hunted woodcock in the Bald Eagle Valley while you were at Penn State? The one that ran back into a hollow, and you said it looked like there had to be at least one moonshine still not too far up it?"

I said I remembered it was somewhere near Hannah Furnace, and Mike said, "Well, I drove up that road the first day of the Pennsylvania deer season, in that old olive-drab jeep of mine, the one I always have trouble starting in cold weather. Had to get out and haul some tree trunks off the road a few times but I got about a mile back from the highway before the road petered out in brush.

"I didn't see any stills," Mike said, "but I did see a lot of deer sign, so I parked the vehicle back in under a clump of rhododendron and threw a brown blanket over the hood. Jerry Parks had told me a blanket over the hood might make it easier to start, although I couldn't see how it would hold enough heat to make a difference, but I'd grabbed an old brown blanket on the way out of the house and I put it over the hood.

"Well, sir," Mike said, "there were deer trails every hundred yards or so, and when I saw one that looked like it got a lot of traffic I hunted downwind from it to where it ran into a couple of other trails below a limestone ledge.

"So I walked around and got on top of the ledge, where I could spot anything coming up or down, and sat there for over an hour. Saw seven or eight does and a spike buck, but the buck got wind of me too soon for a shot even if I had wanted to take it, which I didn't. There was a good bit of shooting going on up and down the valley, and I figured the deer would be moving pretty well, but after an hour I got too cold to sit still and started hunting my way back toward where I had left the car.

"Finally, when I figured I was just about back to where I'd started I caught a glimpse of what looked like a deer in a clump of rhododendron. I stood real still and watched that spot of brown for a long time, but couldn't even tell which end was head and which was tail, much less if it was a legal buck. Finally my eyes could just barely make out the outline of the animal, and then I was pretty sure I could see antlers. In fact, I was positive!"

Mike took a long pull at his bourbon and water, and I said, "Yes, yes. What then?" (I have this flair for repartee.)

"Well," Mike said, "when I was positive—absolutely *positive,* mind you—that it was a buck with legal antlers, I slowly raised Old Betsy—I was shooting my old reliable thutty-thutty, and that 180-grain slug sort of elbows its way through shrubbery, so I wasn't much concerned about the brush—held where I figured that buck's boiler-room ought to be, and pulled the trigger. Kaboom!"

"Keep talking, for heaven's sake!" I said. "What happened?"

"Well," said Mike, "I was sort of surprised that that deer didn't come swarming out of the rhododendrons, because of course a lung shot doesn't nail 'em down right away. So I walked on down there, and what do you think I found in that clump of rhododendron?"

"Tell me!" I said. "For Pete's sake, what did you find?"

"A dandy little four-point buck," Mike said proudly, "as dead as Rutherford B. Hayes. That bullet had caught him in the neck, and I doubt he had even twitched. I dressed him out, hauled him over to the jeep—it was less than a hundred yards away—and was back home that same evening with a hundred pounds of prime venison!"

"Very nice," I said. "But tell me, exactly what was so remarkable about this experience?"

"Oh, yes!" Mike said. "Almost forgot! That blanket trick really works. Engine started right off—barely touched the starter! Thanks for the drink, Ed—see you around."

"Not if I see you first," I said.

Or would have if I had thought of it.